VIETNAM

A WAR LOST AND WON

VIETNAM

A WAR LOST AND WON

NIGEL CAWTHORNE

CHARTWELL
BOOKS, INC.

This edition printed in 2008 by

CHARTWELL BOOKS, INC.
A Division of **BOOK SALES, INC.**
114 Northfield Avenue
Edison, New Jersey 08837

Copyright © 2003 Arcturus Publishing Limited
26/27 Bickels Yard, 151–153 Bermondsey Street,
London SE1 3HA

ISBN-13: 978-0-7858-2445-9
ISBN-10: 0-7858-2445-6

Book design: Alex Ingr

Printed in China

CONTENTS

INTRODUCTION

In early 1968, the hill fort at Khe Sanh came under siege for seventy-seven days. Two months after it was relieved, it was abandoned.

THE WAR in Vietnam was the longest war in American history. US ground troops were in Vietnam for eight long years. In all the American commitment in Southeast Asia lasted fifteen years. During that time over 50,000 US servicemen died and around 300,000 were wounded, figures which pale beside Vietnamese losses. South Vietnam, America's ally, lost over 200,000 soldiers; Communist North Vietnam lost a further 900,000. It has been estimated that over a million civilians lost their lives and much of Southeast Asia was devastated; even now Vietnamese children are being born with horrifying physical disabilities as a direct result of the US use of chemical defoliants during the war. While America in comparison was physically unscathed, the psychological damage inflicted was incalculable. Vietnam was the first war that America failed to win outright, and it left the country bitterly divided. Many of the 2.7 million Americans who served in Vietnam suffered psychologically for decades to come and America discovered that, for all its might and technological superiority, it could not defeat a small and fiercely determined enemy. It is too early to say whether the country has taken that lesson to heart. Now, however, thirty years after US forces pulled out of Vietnam, from a geopolitical perspective, it can perhaps be argued that America did, in fact, win...

1

INTO THE 'NAM

ON THE morning of 8 March, 1965, the Leathernecks of Ninth Marine Expeditionary Brigade stormed Nam O Beach – military designation Red Two – outside the port of Da Nang in South Vietnam, America's ally in Southeast Asia. This was a classic World War II amphibious assault, like that on Guadalcanal, Okinawa, or the beaches of Normandy. Indeed, Nam O had been used by the US Marines as a training beach before the outbreak of the Pacific War.

Six weeks before, Amphibious Task Force 76 had set sail from Japan. Their arrival in the Bay of Da Nang was supposed to coincide with the end of the monsoon, but the officer commanding, General Frederick J. Karch, himself a veteran of the landings on the Japanese-held islands of Saipan, Tinian and Iwo Jima during World War II, said that during the last days the Marine assault force spent bobbing up and down in heavy seas off the coast of Vietnam he experienced the worst weather he had ever encountered in the South China Sea.

Some 3,500 Marines on board the USS *Vancouver*, *Union*, *Mount McKinley* and *Henrico* anxiously awaited the order to make a frontal assault on the undefended beach of a friendly nation. The Leathernecks – as the Marines called themselves – had been drilled from boot camp that while there was no such thing as a friendly beach, the only thing here that was unfriendly was the weather. As they prepared to disembark, a light drizzle gave way to a strong on-shore wind, creating a heavy swell which snapped mooring lines and made it almost impossible for the Marines to clamber down the nets into the landing craft. H-hour had to be postponed from 0730 to 0900hrs.

At 0903, Marine frogmen reached the beach, pulled themselves out of the surf and made a dash to the line of palms and fir trees that ran along the top of the beach. Hard behind the frogmen were eleven Marine amphibious tractors – LVTPS – carrying 34 men each. They thrust their 45-ton steel hulls through the white foam. With the ten-foot swell, this was a 'high surf' landing and smaller LCVPs had to be abandoned in favour of heavier landing craft. The LVTPS were followed by 61-ton LCM-8s, whose steel jaws disgorged 200 men at a time. Within fifteen minutes, four waves of heavily armed Marines were digging in on the sand just as their fathers' generation had on the beaches of Pacific atolls barely twenty years before.

Fifty minutes later, 1,400 men were ashore, carrying rifles, machine-guns, and grenade and rocket launchers. They were ready for any eventuality – except what actually happened.

A party of pretty Vietnamese schoolgirls came down the beach to greet them and coyly hung garlands of gladioli and dahlias around the necks of the towering Marines. The scene was recorded by the mayor of Da Nang with his new Polaroid camera and the waiting press corps. Banners were unfurled that read 'Vietnam welcomes the US Marine Corp' and 'Happy to welcome the Marines in defence of this free world outpost.' Throughout it all the straight-backed Annapolis-trained General

*Opposite:
An M48 tank comes ashore at Da Nang in March 1965 in an amphibious assault designed to remind the world of the seaborne landings of World War II – only this time American forces were unopposed.*

Regimental landing Team 4 comes ashore on beaches defended only by the world's press corps, the mayor of Da Nang with his new instant camera, and a welcoming committee of Vietnamese schoolgirls.

Karch remained unsmiling. His picture, festooned with flowers, was distributed worldwide by the wire services.

'That picture was the source of a lot of trouble for me [he later told an interviewer]. People said: "Couldn't you have been smiling?" But, you know, if I had to do it over, that picture would have been the same. When you have a son in Vietnam and he gets killed, you don't want a smiling general with flowers around his neck as leader at that point.'

The beach landings were supposed to send a message to the Communist North Vietnamese and their Russian and Chinese allies that the US was not prepared to stand by and watch South Vietnam fall to the Communists. Indeed, although Da Nang had a deep-water port and the 3,000 yard runway which was

medium tanks, 105mm howitzers and the latest Ontos antitank weapons (tracked vehicles carrying batteries of recoilless rifles). However, the winsome welcoming committee and the prearranged photo-opportunity turned the landing into a farce.

Although the landing had been announced in a Pentagon press release two days before, no one had thought to inform the South Vietnamese government, or even asked their advice – even though the Marines were going in at the 'request' of the South Vietnamese, the press release said. The first the South Vietnamese Prime Minister Phan Huy Quat knew of it was when he was visited by a US Army officer on the morning of 8 March and asked to draft a joint communiqué in English and Vietnamese announcing the Marine landings, which were underway at the time.

The head of the American Military Assistance Command in Vietnam, General William Westmoreland, the US commander in South Vietnam who had requested two Marine battalions to protect the airbase at Da Nang, was also appalled. He had expected the Marines to maintain a low profile. The very public landings were the idea of US President Lyndon B. Johnson. He overruled his ambassador in Saigon, Maxwell Taylor, who had been chairman of the Joint Chiefs of Staff under President John F. Kennedy. Taylor warned that a Marine landing would be the first step in a growing American commitment. Not only would the South Vietnamese expect the US to do their fighting against their Communist neighbour for them, it would look as if the Americans had inherited 'the old

destined to become one of the three busiest airports in the world, an amphibious assault on the beaches was the quickest way to get the maximum amount of men and machines ashore in the shortest possible time. The port had no cranes, heavy-duty fork-lift trucks, cargo nets, lighterage or even a marked channel, and the airstrip was not equipped to handle a large body of men, let alone M-48

French role of alien colonizer and conqueror'. And Taylor doubted whether 'white-faced' Americans could do any better in the forests and jungles of Asia than French troops had.

Despite these dire warnings, there were no objections from Congress or in the American press. Although the Marine landings – America's first commitment to fight on the ground in Vietnam – was the single most significant event of the war, Johnson presented it at home as a short-term expedient. Indeed, the Joint Chiefs of Staff's order directing the landing was modestly entitled 'Improved Security Measures in the Republic of South Vietnam'. But the military strategists in Hanoi, the capital of Communist North Vietnam, were not fooled. In their eyes the landings on the beaches were viewed as a troop build-up which would cause them new difficulties. They doubted that Johnson would have authorized such an enormous expenditure on men and matériel unless he felt certain of victory.

The Marine landings on 8 March were not altogether unopposed. When more Marines from bases on Okinawa began landing at the airstrip in Da Nang that afternoon, a sniper put a bullet through the wing of one of their C-130 Hercules transports. There were no casualties.

Nevertheless, the surreal atmosphere persisted. Although the ARVN (Army of the Republic of Vietnam, the South Vietnamese non-Communist forces) were fighting not two miles from the perimeter of the airbase on the night of 8 March, they did not ask for American assistance.

The Marines found themselves penned up in an enclave of just eight square miles around the airbase, where they were more in danger from friendly fire than from the enemy as an ARVN training range nearby often sent rounds whistling overhead. Otherwise Marine helicopters were used to ferry live chickens and cows up-country to beleaguered ARVN bases.

A few days after the landing, officers of the 9th MEB were invited to a garden party 'replete with several orchestras and accompanying niceties' by Major General Nguyen Chanh Thi, the South Vietnamese I Corps Commander and the virtual warlord of South Vietnam's five northern provinces. Lieutenant-Colonel Herbert J. Bain, commanding officer of the 1st Battalion, 3rd Marines and a veteran of World War II, recalled that the festivities were followed by a 'return to my foxhole and C rations'.

When the US ground troops, or grunts as they were known, were allowed out on patrol they found that the ARVN detachments they were sent to relieve either refused to budge or ran away when they approached. But soon, the Marines took their first casualties on a patrol out in the hills to the west of Da Nang. It was night, the tropical air was full of exotic noises and it was easy to imagine strange shapes moving through the jungle all around. A three-man patrol ventured out. Two of its members lost their way and came up behind their comrade in the dark. He turned and fired, wounding the other two mortally. The war in Vietnam had, officially, claimed its first American casualties.

The servicemen sent to fight the Vietnam war were young and fresh-faced. Their average age was nineteen, three years younger than the US soldiers who fought in World War II and Korea. The impact the war had on their young lives would be devastating.

15

2

THE ORIGINS
OF THE WAR

Under France, the colonial power, Vietnam, Laos and Cambodia formed French Indochina. After the defeat of the French at Dien Bien Phu in 1954, Laos and Cambodia became independent countries, while Vietnam was split along the 17th parallel for administrative reasons until the country could be reunited by an election. That election never took place, and as the American war in Vietnam unfolded, neutral Laos and Cambodia became embroiled with tragic consequences.

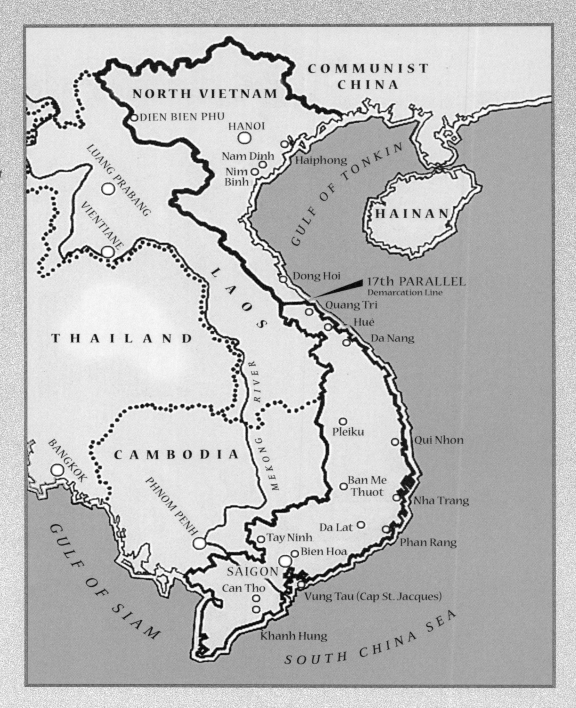

COMMUNIST CHINA

NORTH VIETNAM

DIEN BIEN PHU

HANOI

Nam Dinh

Haiphong

Nim Binh

GULF OF TONKIN

HAINAN

LUANG PRABANG

VIENTIANE

L A O S

Dong Hoi

17th PARALLEL
Demarcation Line

Quang Tri

Hué

THAILAND

Da Nang

MEKONG RIVER

Pleiku

Qui Nhon

CAMBODIA

Ban Me Thuot

Nha Trang

BANGKOK

PHNOM PENH

Da Lat

Phan Rang

Tay Ninh

Bien Hoa

SAIGON

Can Tho

Vung Tau (Cap St. Jacques)

GULF OF SIAM

Khanh Hung

SOUTH CHINA SEA

FOR THE Vietnamese, the war had begun many centuries before the Marines landed. In their minds, it started in AD 40 when the Trung sisters, Trung Trac and Trung Nhi, led the first Vietnamese insurrection against Chinese rule. One woman who fought with them, Phung Thi Chinh, supposedly gave birth during the battle, but continued fighting with the infant strapped to her back. The Trungs' newly independent realm extended from southern China to the ancient city of Hué. The Chinese crushed it two years later and the Trung sisters committed suicide by drowning themselves in a river. They have been revered by the Vietnamese ever since and are venerated in temples in Hanoi and Son Tay, both of which lay in North Vietnam in 1965. But in 1962, Madame Ngo Dinh Nhu, sister-in-law of South Vietnam's President Ngo Dinh Diem, erected a statue of the Trung sisters in downtown Saigon, capital of what was then South Vietnam, to commemorate their patriotism and promote herself as their reincarnation.

In AD 248 another woman, Trieu Au, Vietnam's equivalent of Joan of Arc, led another revolt. Wearing golden armour, she rode into battle on an elephant at the head of a thousand men. She was just twenty-three when she was soundly defeated and committed suicide. Like the Trung sisters she was commemorated in a temple and is remembered for her words of defiance: 'I want to rail against the wind and the tide and the whales in the sea, sweep the whole country to save the people from slavery, and I refuse to be abused.'

China referred to Vietnam as Annam, the 'pacified south'. But it was far from pacified. There were regular rebellions, often led by Chinese colonists who, like English settlers in North America, sought independence from the mother country. In 938, the Chinese sent a flotilla to put down a rebellion by the provincial mandarin Ngo Quyen. As the junks approached, Ngo Quyen ordered his men to drive iron-tipped spikes into the river bed in the estuary of the Bach Dang river so their points remained hidden just under the surface of the water. He then withdrew his own ships as the tide ebbed. When the Chinese fleet gave chase and impaled themselves on the spikes, Ngo Quyen's boats turned back and destroyed them. The Vietnamese, it seems, had already learnt how to use guerrilla tactics to defeat a superior force.

The Mongol emperor Kublai Khan invaded Vietnam three times to take control of the spice routes of the Indonesian archipelago to the south. Each time the Vietnamese general Tran Hung Dao defeated the superior Chinese forces. Like many Vietnamese commanders since, he abandoned the cities, avoided frontal attacks, and used mobile forces to harass the enemy until they were confused and exhausted and ripe for a great defeat. In a last great battle in 1287, the Vietnamese routed 3,000 Mongol troops. Tran celebrated his victory with a poem in which he declared that 'this ancient land shall live forever'. General Vo Nguyen Giap, the North Vietnamese military strategist responsible for beating the Americans, evoked Tran's memory when he attacked the French in the same area.

In 1287, Vietnam – Annam – occupied only the northern part of the country, roughly the area that became North Vietnam. After defeating the Mongols, the Vietnamese turned their attention to Champa, the kingdom occupied by the Cham people which lay to the south. The war against Champa raged on for nearly 200 years. Then in 1471, the Vietnamese captured and razed the capital Indra-Champa, leaving only its magnificent stone sculptures which can still be seen today. Even after the Vietnam War was over, the people of Laos and Cambodia, which lay to the west, feared the Vietnamese hunger for expansion – with good reason.

HIS 1919 APPEAL TO THE VERSAILLES PEACE CONFERENCE FELL ON DEAF EARS

The conquest of Champa left Vietnam exhausted and vulnerable to invasion by China once more, the Chinese this time imposing a brutal slavery on the country. The peasants were forced to mine for gold and other ores, while the country was looted of spices, pearls, precious stones, elephant tusks and rhinoceros horns. The Vietnamese were forced to adopt Chinese forms of dress and hair styles, issued with identity cards and forced to pay punitive taxes. The worship of Vietnamese gods was outlawed, and Vietnamese literature was suppressed and only Chinese was taught in the country's schools.

Vietnam's own King Arthur rose up against this oppression. According to legend, he was a young fisherman named Le Loi who cast his net into a lake one day and brought up a magic sword. In fact, Le Loi was a wealthy landowner from Thanh Hoa province in the north who served the Chinese before turning against them.

'Every man on earth ought to accomplish some great enterprise', he said, 'so that he leaves the sweet scent of his name to later generations. How, then, could he willingly be the slave of foreigners?'

In 1418, Le Loi declared himself the 'Prince of Pacification', withdrew to the hills, and began a guerrilla war against the Chinese. As the insurrection spread, the Chinese held on to the cities, but their columns had to stick to the roads which were defended by fortified towers. Le Loi's adviser, the poet Nguyen Trai, set down their strategy in an essay that could be a handbook of modern-day insurgency. 'Better to conquer hearts than citadels,' he wrote.

In 1426, on a muddy battlefield west of Hanoi, in a rainstorm, Le Loi defeated the Chinese. A magnanimous victor, he gave them thousands of horses and five hundred junks to carry them home. Two years later Vietnam was recognized as an independent state, though Le's descendants, known as the Le dynasty, continued to pay tribute to the Chinese emperor, just in case.

Nguyen Trai wrote a poem celebrating the country's independence after nearly fourteen centuries of struggle:

Henceforth our country is safe.
Our mountains and rivers began life afresh.
Peace follows war as day follows night.
We have purged our shame for a thousand
centuries,
We have regained tranquillity for ten
thousand generations.

He was a little over-optimistic. There was another abortive attempt by the Chinese to take back Vietnam in 1788.

Since the sixteenth century, the country had been divided between the Trinh family and the Nguyen family, roughly along the lines of the later division of the country into North and South Vietnam. In 1630, the rivalry became so acute that the southerners built two walls across the plain at Dong Hai, along the 18th parallel to the jungle, sealing off the north until the late eighteenth century. Meanwhile the Nguyens actively courted Chinese help in their conflict with the Trinh.

The battle to free Vietnam from Chinese domination was not entirely won until 1802, when the country was reunited under a Nguyen emperor, Gia Long, with the help of the French. Once in power, Gia Long turned against the French, expelling his French advisers and executing French missionaries. In 1858, Napoleon III sent an army to Vietnam which established a colony in the south called Cochinchina. Central Vietnam – Annam – and the north – Tonkin – were taken over as protectorates in 1883. Along with Laos and Cambodia, Vietnam was incorporated into French Indochina and the Vietnamese struggle for independence had to begin again.

At the Versailles Peace Conference in France in 1919 that concluded World War I, a young Vietnamese calling himself Nguyen Ai Quoc, 'Nguyen the Patriot', stood up and demanded his country's freedom. Born Nguyen That Thanh in Vietnam in 1890, he used several names during his life. He called himself Ba when he visited New York and Boston as a ship's cook in 1911. After living in London from 1915 to 1917, he moved to France, where he worked as a gardener, sweeper, waiter, photograph retoucher, and oven stoker. His 1919 appeal to the Versailles Peace Conference fell on deaf ears, but it made him a hero to many politically conscious Vietnamese. The following year, inspired by the success of the Communist revolution in Russia and Lenin's anti-imperialist doctrine, he joined the French Communists when they split from the Socialist Party. In 1923, he went to Moscow and, in January 1924, on the death of Lenin, he published a eulogy to the founder of the Soviet Union in the Communist Party newspaper *Pravda*. Six months later, at the fifth Congress of the Communist International, he criticized the French Communist Party for not opposing colonialism more vigorously and, in his statement to the congress, first formulated the revolutionary role of oppressed peasants, as opposed to industrial workers mentioned by the founder of Communism, Karl Marx. In 1924, he travelled to Canton, a Chinese Communist stronghold, under the name Ly Thuy, where he began recruiting fellow Vietnamese for his nationalist movement and, in 1930, he founded the Vietnamese Communist Party

THE ORIGINS OF THE WAR

Like many generations before him, Ho Chi Minh — 'he who enlightens'– dedicated his life to freeing Vietnam from foreign occupation. After his death in 1969, he continued to inspire his people in their struggle against US forces.

with former school friend Vo Nguyen Giap.

Vo Nguyen Giap was born in 1912 at An Xa, Vietnam, just north of the 17th parallel which later became the border between North and South Vietnam. While a law student at Hanoi University, he met Ngo Dinh Diem, who went on to become president of South Vietnam and Giap's bitter enemy. Giap's anti-colonist views forced him to flee to China in 1939, but his young wife was arrested and died with their child in a French jail three years later, while his sister-in-law was guillotined.

In 1940 Ly Thuy changed his name to Ho Chi Minh, which means 'he who enlightens'. It was under this name that he became the father of Communist Vietnam and, despite his authoritarian rule, the seemingly kindly 'Uncle Ho' became a symbol of resistance to his people. In 1941, again with Giap, he founded the League for the Independence of Vietnam, or Vietminh. Ho Chi Minh was the political leader of the Vietminh, while Giap became its military leader. Returning to Vietnam, Giap formed 'armed propaganda

teams' – guerrilla bands which would later form the nucleus of the North Vietnamese Army – while Ho found himself languishing in the jail of an anti-Communist warlord for over a year. With the backing of the US, the Vietminh fought the Japanese who occupied Vietnam during World War II. When the Japanese were defeated in 1945, Giap entered Hanoi at the head of his troops. Soon after, in a speech in Hanoi where he quoted the US Declaration of Independence, Ho Chi Minh proclaimed the Democratic Republic of Vietnam, which he led as president until his death in 1969.

However, while the Vietminh held Hanoi in the North of the country, the British had liberated Saigon in the South. To legitimize the reoccupation of its own colonies in Asia,

Britain returned control of the South to the French, rearming the Japanese to keep order until French troops arrived. Under the Potsdam Agreement of August 1945 which settled territorial disputes that arose at the end of World War II, the Nationalist Chinese (China only became Communist in 1949) were to disarm the Japanese in the north. A Chinese army under General Lu Han arrived in Hanoi, and began looting the city and killing all political opposition. Giap barely escaped with his life. Meanwhile the Chinese Nationalist leader Chiang Kai-shek agreed to hand North Vietnam – Tonkin – back to the French in return for relinquishing its old concessions in Shanghai and other Chinese ports.

For five months, Ho Chi Minh tried to get other countries to recognize his government

The Vietnamese Commander-in-Chief Vo Nguyen Giap reviews his anti-colonial troops in 1952. A high-school history teacher, he turned himself into a master strategist and tactician, defeating both the French and the Americans on the ground.

in Hanoi. The US now backed the French. The Soviet Union would not even send an observer to Hanoi. Ho's old friends in the French Communist Party also deserted him. The party boss, Maurice Thorez, was then deputy premier in General de Gaulle's post-war government and later said that he 'did not intend to liquidate the French position in Indochina'.

Ho Chi Minh was quick to appreciate the political reality of the situation. If he resisted the return of the French to Tonkin, they showed every intention of reestablishing their old colony of Cochinchina in the south, while leaving the north in the hands of the Chinese who seemed to be in no hurry to leave. Ho Chi Minh was committed to national unity. He agreed to permit 25,000 French troops to garrison the north for five years, provided the French recognized Vietnam as an independent state within the French Union, the new name for the old French Empire. The question of uniting Tonkin and Cochinchina would be decided later by a referendum. Ho Chi Minh came in for severe criticism from colleagues for allowing the French back in without even setting a date for the plebiscite. At a meeting in Hanoi, he rounded on his critics.

You fools. Don't you realize what it means if the Chinese remain? Don't you remember your history? The last time the Chinese came, they stayed for a thousand years. The French are foreigners. They are weak. Colonialism is dying. The white man is finished in Asia. But if the Chinese stay now,

they will never go. As for me, I prefer to sniff French shit for five years than eat Chinese shit for the rest of my life.

In 1946 Ho went to France to try to negotiate the unification of Vietnam. Again he got no help from the French Communists, whose help he sought, and the political lobby for the establishment of a separate 'Republic of Cochinchina' was so strong that he was forced to initial an interim agreement to that effect. As he left the room, he said to his bodyguard, 'I've just signed my death warrant.'

Indeed, when Ho returned to Hanoi, Giap and other militant members of the Vietminh were preparing to depose him when fighting broke out between the Vietminh and French troops in the port of Haiphong over who had the right to collect customs duty. On the morning of 20 November 1946 a French patrol boat had seized some Chinese smugglers. The Vietminh intercepted the French boat and arrested its crew. This sparked an incident, and by the afternoon there were barricades in the streets. When these were flattened by French tanks, the Vietminh opened up with mortars, while a troop of Vietnamese actors in the Opera House held off the French with antique muskets. A ceasefire was agreed, but the French decided to use the incident as an excuse to drive the Vietminh out of the city. This resulted in hand-to-hand fighting with Vietminh positions being bombed and strafed by the French air force and shelled by the French navy. When it was all over, the Vietminh claimed there were 20,000 dead. The French say it was no more than 6,000.

No one denies that there were several thousand civilian casualties.

The French then ordered Ho Chi Minh to disarm the Vietminh. This was easier said than done: Giap deployed some 30,000 armed men in the suburbs, and on the evening of 19 December, fighting broke out again. Ho fled the city before he could be arrested while Giap issued what was virtually a declaration of war.

'I order all soldiers and militia', he declared, 'to stand together, go into battle, destroy the invaders, and save the nation… The resistance will be long and arduous, but our cause is just and we will surely triumph.'

Thus began the First Indochina War.

The French were confident of victory to start with by dint of force of arms. But they ignored the real cause of the war, which was

French and Vietnamese colonial prisoners of war march from the battlefields of Dien Bien Phu under the guard of Vietminh troops on 28 July 1954. It was the ultimate humiliation for the French, and a spectre that would haunt the Americans.

the desire of the Vietnamese people, Communist and anti-Communist alike, to achieve independence for their country. However, the French could offer unity. In 1949, they reunited Cochinchina with the rest of Vietnam, proclaiming the Associated State of Vietnam with the former emperor Bao Dai as head of state. However, Bao Dai was seen as a schemer. Succeeding his father in 1925 at the age of twelve, he did not ascend to the throne until 1932, after completing his education in France. He cooperated first with the French colonial government then with the Japanese in World War II. In 1945 he abdicated and briefly joined the Vietminh, before fleeing to Hong Kong in 1946 where he led a playboy lifestyle. In nationalists' eyes the 'Playboy Emperor' was nothing more than a French puppet when he returned in 1949. Meanwhile, the Vietminh waged an increasingly successful guerrilla war, aided after 1949 by the new Communist government in China. Fearful of the spread of Communism in Asia, the US began sending large amounts of aid to the French. But Giap had learned the lessons of Ngo Quyen, Tran Hung Dao and Le Loi well and, after harassing the enemy for five long years, he surprised French military strategists by moving his artillery 400 miles over rough terrain and supplying his troops over that huge distance to besiege the remote garrison at Dien Bien Phu, which fell in May 1954.

Britain, France, the US and the Soviet Union had already called a peace conference in Geneva to negotiate a ceasefire. To separate the warring factions, it was decided that the Vietminh should stay north of the 17th parallel, while the French remained to the south. Between them would be a five-mile wide DMZ – a Demilitarized Zone. Bao Dai rejected the peace plan. However, he was defeated in a referendum by his Prime Minister Ngo Dinh Diem, who proclaimed himself president of a newly created Republic of Vietnam, that is, non-Communist South Vietnam. With an area of 66,200 square miles and a population of some twenty million, it was a country bigger than England and Wales put together with less than a third of the population. On the other hand, imagine the population of Texas crammed into area less than a quarter of that state's size.

Meanwhile the Communist-controlled area north of the 17th parallel became known as North Vietnam, though it was still officially the Democratic Republic of Vietnam, with Ho Chi Minh as head of state and General Giap as Commander-in-Chief and Secretary of Defence. Both were committed to reunifying the country – by peaceful means at first. Under the Peace Accords worked out at Geneva, an election was to be held in 1956 with the aim of unifying the country under one government. The Communists, who had built up a powerful political organization in both halves of the country, were confident of victory. But Diem refused to hold the elections. He was backed by the US, who feared a Communist takeover. The Communists saw Diem as an American puppet and, in 1960, the government in Hanoi decided that the only way to reunify the country was by force. For Ho and Giap, the Vietnam War was part of their centuries-old war of national liberation to free themselves from the influence of foreign powers: this time the enemy was the US. While the avuncular Ho Chi Minh spent his time portraying the war as the defensive action of a backward nation bullied by a superpower, Giap took charge of the war. In 1961, Giap spelt out exactly how he intended to reunify the country. He published a manual of guerrilla warfare called *People's War, People's Army*. It told the US military exactly what they were up against, if anyone had bothered to read it.

For America, the war in Vietnam had entirely different origins. Since the establishment of the Soviet Union in 1917 the US had feared the spread of Communism, a fear which grew after World War II, following the Soviet seizure of Eastern Europe, and the beginning of the Cold War. In 1949, China fell to the Communists. The following year, Communist North Korea invaded South Korea, starting the Korean War. There had been Communist revolts in Malaya and the Philippines and the US feared that the rest of Asia might fall.

The US response to this was a policy of 'containment' first proposed by US diplomat George Kennan in July 1947 in an article that appeared in the magazine *Foreign Affairs* signed simply 'X'. He had analysed in detail the structure and psychology of Soviet diplomacy and concluded that the Russians were bent on worldwide extension of the Soviet system. However, he realized that, while they were fundamentally opposed to coexistence with the West, they were sensitive to military force and would hold back or even retreat in the face of determined Western opposition. Consequently, Kennan proposed that the US apply counterpressure wherever the Soviets threatened to expand. The result, he predicted, would be that either the Soviets would have to cooperate with the US or that this concerted counterpressure would lead to the internal collapse of the Soviet Union. This view became the core of US policy toward the Soviet Union for the next forty-five years.

Kennan's containment policy found a corollary in the 'domino theory' or 'domino

PEOPLE'S WAR, PEOPLE'S ARMY TOLD THE US MILITARY WHAT THEY WERE UP AGAINST, IF ANYONE HAD BOTHERED TO READ IT.

effect' that was uppermost in much of US military and foreign policy thinking after World War II. The theory states that the fall of a non-Communist state to Communism would precipitate the fall of non-Communist governments in neighbouring states. It was first proposed by President Harry S. Truman to justify sending military aid to Greece and Turkey in the 1940s, but it became popular in the 1950s when President Dwight D. Eisenhower applied it to Southeast Asia, and especially South Vietnam. On 7 April, 1954, in a speech about the situation in Indochina, he said, 'You have a row of dominos set up, you knock over the first one, and what will happen to the last one is the certainty that it will go over very quickly.'

A US representative at the UN points out Russian ship missiles. Following the Cuban missiles crisis of 1962, the US had every reason to fear Communist expansionism.

The argument here was that if South Vietnam went Communist, so would Laos and Cambodia, then the rest of the Malay peninsula. Communist revolution would then island-hop across Indonesia, Borneo and New Guinea and, before you knew it, Communism would be knocking on the gates of Australia. The domino theory was one of the main arguments used by the Kennedy and, later, the Johnson administrations to justify their growing military involvement in Vietnam. As vice-president, Johnson remarked that if South Vietnam was lost, America would find itself fighting 'on the beaches of Waikiki'.

'The battle against Communism must be joined in Southeast Asia with strength and determination', he said, 'or the United States, inevitably, must surrender the Pacific and take up our defences on our own shores.'

The idea that it was better to confront Communism in Asia than 'in our own backyard' continued throughout the war. In 1967 labour leader George Meany said, 'I would rather fight the Communists in South Vietnam than fight them down here in the Chesapeake Bay.'

The Joint Chiefs of Staff regularly prefaced their war plans with an inflated version of the domino theory. South Vietnam, they said, was 'pivotal' in America's world-wide confrontation with Communism. Defeat there would not only surrender Asia to Communism, it would also erode America's anti-Communist stance in Africa and Latin America.

When Fidel Castro, who had seized power in Cuba in 1959, declared his allegiance to Communism in 1961, it seemed to many people in Washington that the spread of Communism was coming a little too close for comfort. It also vindicated the Joint Chiefs of Staff, as Castro's charismatic sidekick Che Guevara did indeed attempt to export revolution to Africa and Latin America. The takeover led to an abortive CIA-backed invasion of the island at the Bay of Pigs. Hard on its heels came the Cuban missile crisis. In 1962, the Soviet Union deployed nuclear missiles on the island. President Kennedy demanded that they be removed. For ten days, the world seemed to teeter on the brink of nuclear war until a peace deal was worked out. The Soviets would remove their missiles, provided Kennedy promised never to invade Cuba and, secretly, to remove US missiles from Turkey.

Although Kennedy claimed victory in the Cuban missile crisis, he knew that this eyeball-to-eyeball confrontation had brought humankind close to nuclear annihilation. He knew that it must not happen again. He also knew that confrontation between the Communist world and the free world was inevitable.

President John F. Kennedy makes the 1962 State of the Union address. Concerning Vietnam, he says, 'The systematic aggression now bleeding that country is not a "war of liberation" for Vietnam is already free. it is a war of attempted subjugation — and it will be resisted.'

What the world needed was a safety valve, a theatre war where the battle between the super-powers could be played out. Vietnam would be it. The Soviet Union and China backed Communist North Vietnam and President Eisenhower had already given military aid to the Diem government in South Vietnam. Kennedy increased it. He also sent a new elite corps of frontline troops who would wage the war against Communism: the Green Berets.

A designated Special Forces unit had been set up at Fort Bragg, North Carolina as early as 1952. From 1953, Special Forces troops wore the distinctive green beret – borrowed from the British Royal Marine commandos – when they went into the field, although the army refused to authorize its official use. However, when President Kennedy visited Fort Bragg on 12 October 1961 he sent word to the Special Warfare Center commander, Brigadier General William P. Yarborough, that all Special Forces soldiers should wear their green berets during his inspection. Afterwards the president told the Pentagon that he considered the green beret to be 'symbolic of one of the highest levels of courage and achievement of the United States military'. Soon, the green beret became synonymous with Special Forces and the two terms became interchangeable.

There were already three Special Forces groups, one based at Bad Tolz in West Germany, one in Fort Bragg, and one in the Far East. A then unofficial Green Beret, Captain Harry G. Cramer Jr of the 14th Special Forces Detachment, had become the first American soldier to die in Vietnam on 21 October, 1956.

Throughout the late 1950s and early 1960s, the number of Special Forces military advisers in Vietnam increased steadily. Their job was to train South Vietnamese soldiers in the art of counter-insurgency and to mould minority tribes into anti-Communist forces. In September 1964, the Green Berets' 5th Group set up its headquarters in Nha Trang, where it remained until it returned to Fort Bragg in 1971, although some Special Forces teams stayed in Thailand from where they launched secret missions into Vietnam. By the time the Fifth left Southeast Asia, its soldiers had won 16 Medals of Honor, 1 Distinguished Service Medal, 90 Distinguished Service Crosses, 814 Silver Stars, 13,234 Bronze Stars, 235 Legions of Merit, 46 Distinguished Flying Crosses, 232 Soldier's Medals, 4,891 Air Medals, 6,908 Army Commendation Medals, and 2,658 Purple Hearts.

During the 1960s, other Special Forces training teams were operating in Bolivia, Venezuela, Guatemala, Columbia and the Dominican Republic. Counter-insurgency groups in Latin America carried out some 450 clandestine operations against guerrilla forces between 1965 and 1968. In 1968, the Green Berets were involved in tracking down and capturing the notorious Cuban revolutionary Che Guevara in the wilds of south-central Bolivia. They took their place in American mythology when Barry Sadler's 'The Ballad of the Green Beret' went to number one in the US in 1966 and John Wayne starred in the movie *The Green Berets* in 1968. The Green Berets' A-teams – twelve-man teams comprising two officers, two operations and

Lyndon B. Johnson takes the oath of office on board Air Force One, 22 November 1963, after the assassination of John F. Kennedy. Within eighteen months he would commit US ground troops to the war in Vietnam. Despite the advances he made in civil rights and social programmes at home, the war would wreck his presidency. Military failure would prevent him standing for a second term and he would die just five days before the Paris Peace Accords were signed, ending the US involvement in the war.

intelligence sergeants, two weapons sergeants, two communications sergeants, two medics, and two engineers, all trained in unconventional warfare, cross-trained in each other's specialties, and speaking at least one foreign language – were later celebrated in a long-running TV series.

Whether President Kennedy would have continued with his strategy of employing the Green Berets 'theatre wars' against Communism if he had lived has been widely debated. But after he was assassinated in November 1963 his successor, Lyndon B. Johnson announced that he would not let South Vietnam go the way of China and the stage was set. For America, Vietnam was the place the Cold War finally became hot.

The North Vietnamese had already begun their struggle to reunify the country in December 1960 with the establishment of the National Liberation Front, the NLF, in the South, a front organization that aimed to collect together all the political opponents of the increasingly dictatorial regime of President Diem in Saigon. These comprised the remnants of various cultural, religious, youth, and peasant organizations founded by the Vietminh during the war against the French: the Cao Dai, a religious and political sect founded in the 1920s by Vietnamese intellectuals; the Hoa Hoa, a Buddhist sect founded in the Mekong Delta in the 1930s; and the

General Nguyen Chi Thanh, Vietcong commander of the Communist force in South Vietnam and four-star general in the North Vietnamese Army, pictured in March 1967. Note the plain dress and 'Ho Chi Minh sandals', traditionally made from old tyres. Architect of the 1968 Tet Offensive, he died of a heart attack shortly before it was put into effect.

Binh Xuyen, a crime syndicate that had controlled much of the underworld and the police in Saigon until Diem seized power in 1955, when it retreated to strongholds in the Mekong Delta.

The chairman of the NLF was Nguyen Huu Tho, a French-educated lawyer from Saigon, who had demonstrated against the French in the early 1950s but had subsequently been jailed by Diem, who considered him left-wing. He was well known and respected and attracted a large moderate following.

However, the NLF was a Trojan horse. Ostensibly a purely Southern movement, it did not violate the 1954 Geneva Accords that prohibited Hanoi sending forces into the South, but at every level of its organization the NLF was twinned with the People's Revolutionary Party, which was the southern arm of the Lao Dong or Communist Party of North Vietnam; indeed, some of the leaders of the PRP sat on the Lao Dong Central Committee in Hanoi.

The NLF and PRP jointly formed a guerrilla army and its headquarters command structure was known as the Central Office for South Vietnam, but it was the PRP who called the shots because of its backing from Hanoi and consequent control over the arms and matériel coming down the Ho Chi Minh trail. This was the supply route from North Vietnam that ran down through neighbouring Laos (and later Cambodia), skirting the DMZ. Begun in 1959, it was a network of trails rather than a single route. It was hacked through the jungle by Special Youth Shock Brigades, crossing ravines and rushing mountain streams on flimsy bamboo bridges. At first men and women had to carry everything on their backs, resting at camouflaged huts and feeding themselves from vegetable patches planted along the way. Later, when cuttings had been blasted through mountains and ridges, supplies were carried on over-laden bicycles. Eventually, it became a highway.

The NLF had no external allies and no

access to arms. However, it remained important as its anti-Communist credentials allowed the Hanoi government to portray the war as a patriotic struggle, rather than a Communist takeover. The Buddhist monk and scholar Thich Nhat Hanh wrote:

The more American troops are sent to Vietnam, the more the anti-American campaign directed by the NLF becomes successful… Pictures showing NLF soldiers with arms tied, followed by American soldiers holding guns with bayonets, make people think of the Indochina war between the French and the Vietminh and cause pain even to anti-Communist Vietnamese. The peasants do not see the victims of the American military effort as dead Communists but as dead patriots.

The NLF/PRP's guerrilla army was dismissively dubbed the 'Vietcong' by the Diem regime. The name stuck. At its core were some 10,000 Vietminh veterans – after the partition of Vietnam in 1954, many of its seasoned soldiers who had defeated the French at Dien Bien Phu had returned home to the South. The Vietcong's campaign began with a propaganda offensive. Agitation and propaganda teams visited South Vietnamese villages at dusk, holding meetings and denouncing the Diem regime as an American puppet. Diem's repressive tactics, his corrupt tax gatherers, and the wealthy landowners who supported him had already made his regime unpopular with the peasantry. The agitprop teams would also dispose of government officials. Their

heads would be left stuck on stakes to greet government troops the next morning.

One eyewitness recalled being on a bus in Long Kanh province to the northeast of Saigon when the bus was halted by six VC. They went through the bus collecting government-issue identity passes. Two men – plain-clothed policemen, apparently – were taken off the bus.

'We have been waiting for you,' said the leader of the VC cadre. 'We have warned you many times to leave your jobs, but you have not obeyed. So now we must carry

TWO MEN WERE FORCED TO KNEEL AT THE ROADSIDE AND WERE DECAPITATED … 'VERDICTS' WERE PINNED TO THE BODIES

out sentence.'

The two men were then forced to kneel at the roadside and were decapitated with machetes. Ready-printed 'verdicts' were pinned to the bodies. The VC then got back on the bus and handed back the passengers' identity cards.

'You'll get into trouble without these,' they said, 'and we don't want that to happen.'

Reprisals by the government forces for such atrocities helped recruit for the Vietcong, although some peasants had to be drafted at gunpoint. Added to that, some 28,000 trained men were infiltrated from the North and by the end of 1964 the Vietcong was 300,000 strong.

The Vietcong was divided into two main sections. There was the main force – some 50,000 to 80,000 men in 1965 – who operated in large formations. This was supported by irregulars, who stayed in their villages raising crops but acted as intelligence gatherers and undertook reconnaissance and occasionally sabotage missions. Younger men were sometimes organized into suicide squads.

Vietcong soldiers were small by American standards, averaging 5ft 3in and 120 pounds. Their uniform was a pair of black pyjamas. They kept a spare pair in a rucksack, along with a sheet of nylon which was used as a tent or a raincoat, a homemade oil lamp, a hammock and a mosquito net. They also carried a digging tool, a water flask, and a long tube, known as an elephant's intestine, filled with rice. On their feet they wore the famous 'Ho Chi Minh sandals' – flip-flops made from old tyres. Their pay was $2 a month, enough to buy a toothbrush, soap, or some cigarettes from the unit's supply officer who visited a Cambodian market town once a month.

At the beginning of the war, the Vietcong were very badly equipped. Up to 1963 they made their own weapons. Shotguns and single-shot pistols were fashioned out of pipes, nails, and doorbolts, and were often more dangerous to the firer than the intended victim. However, they gave recruits access to more effective weapons. Government soldiers who had fallen into Vietcong pits filled with sharpened bamboo spears, or punji stakes, were dispatched with a single shot and their weapons would then be taken. After 1963, the Vietcong were supplied with Soviet- or Chinese-made Kalashnikov AK-47 assault rifles, though they continued to sweep battlefields for enemy weapons. As the war hotted up, they were supplied with mines, grenade launchers and rocket launchers to use against tanks, usually of Soviet origin.

Local Vietcong guerrillas were augmented by more seasoned Vietminh troops infiltrated down the Ho Chi Minh trail. At the same time, in the North, General Giap was building his North Vietnamese Army. He was a follower of the military theories developed in China in the 1930s by the Communist leader Mao Zedong who said, famously, that all political power came out of the barrel of a gun. First, political cadres would be infiltrated into remote rural areas and convince the population to support them. Next, guerrilla groups would make hit-and-run attacks on government forces. When the government troops hit back, they would find themselves overextended – they would then be vulnerable to attack by conventional forces. By 1962, the hit-and-run guerrilla phase was well underway. Meanwhile, a large new conventional army, the North Vietnamese Army – the NVA – was being trained in the North, some of whom soon began to infiltrate into the South.

The NVA was organized along political lines. The officers had to understand the politics of the war and they were watched over by political commissars. The conscripts were also given indoctrination, although it was not really necessary: Marxist theory was taught in school, Ho Chi Minh was universally revered, and the idea of a war of national liberation

US Air Force C-123 aircraft drop Vietnamese paratroopers over Tay Ninh in June 1963. Despite their American 'advisors', in full-scale battle the ARVN were no match for the highly motivated Vietcong and the well-trained North Vietnamese Army.

was deeply embedded in Vietnamese culture. Vietnamese art and literature celebrated the centuries-old struggle against the Chinese and recruits had grown up with the story of the war against the French.

Although President Kennedy had increased assistance to South Vietnam in 1961 and 1962, the Vietcong defeated the ARVN at the battle of Ap Bac in January 1963. The war was unpopular and protests began in South Vietnam, where South Vietnamese troops and police opened fire on demonstrators in the old imperial capital, Hué. In June 1963, a Buddhist monk burnt himself to death in protest. He was the first of many.

The American Ambassador in Saigon, Henry Cabot Lodge, discovered that South Vietnamese army officers were planning a coup against Diem, who had already survived the bombing of his palace by the South Vietnamese Air Force. On 2 September 1963, President Kennedy went on TV and criticized Diem, effectively giving Washington's endorsement to the coup. A month later Diem was

A woman weeps over the body of her husband, one of the Vietnamese casualties of the war with the Vietcong in South Vietnam in 1965. The indiscriminate use of US firepower and Communist reprisals created ever-mounting civilian casualties. There were atrocities on both sides.

deposed and murdered. Three weeks after that, Kennedy himself was assassinated in Dallas.

When President Johnson came to office in 1963, the Pentagon already had well-developed plans for the bombing and amphibious invasion of North Vietnam. Johnson was enthusiastic and upped US support. By the end of 1963, there were 15,000 US military advisers in South Vietnam.

Colonel Bui Tin, the NVA officer who would accept the South Vietnamese surrender in Saigon in 1975, travelled down the Ho Chi Minh trail in late 1963 to assess the military situation in the South. Already a hardened soldier of eighteen years standing,

he described the journey as 'extremely arduous'. His party travelled by foot through steamy forests, fording icy mountain streams. They were plagued by leeches, mosquitoes and other insects they could not identify. Some came down with malaria. But the jungle canopy was still intact, so they could travel undetected by the helicopters that patrolled the region from the early 1960s. They carried socks filled with rice around their waists and a knapsack on their backs, containing thirty or forty pounds of food, medicine, clothes, a waterproof sheet and a hammock. They slept in jungle clearings. There were few villages on the route and they were resupplied from lonely outposts, guarded by North Vietnamese or Vietcong soldiers, or their Communist Laotian allies, the Pathet Lao.

Bui Tin travelled back up the Ho Chi Minh trail in the spring of 1964 to report that the guerrilla war against the South Vietnamese government was failing. North Vietnamese troops had to be committed, or the war was lost. In order to conduct a conventional war in South Vietnam, the Ho Chi Minh trail had to be turned into a modern logistical system that could handle the hundreds of thousands of tons of weapons, ammunition, food and other matériel required to fight major battles.

Colonel Dong Si Nguyen, who became minister of construction in Hanoi after the war, was brought in. Furnished with the latest Chinese and Soviet equipment, engineer battalions built roads and bridges that could handle heavy trucks and military vehicles. Do Si Nguyen anticipated the relentless American bombing of the trail and built a sophisticated system of anti-aircraft defences. Barracks, workshops, hospitals, warehouses and fuel depots were all built underground. By the time the US committed ground troops to the war in March 1965, the Communists were ready. Motorized transport was already running down the trail using Soviet and Chinese trucks, and platoons of doctors, nurses, ordnance experts, traffic managers, radio operators, drivers, mechanics and other support personnel were already in position. When the trail was begun in 1959, transit time was six months. By the mid-1960s, the never-ending flow of traffic took just twelve weeks to complete the journey.

The Vietcong and the NVA were now ready for all-out war. Johnson was also eager to get on with it, but felt he needed a mandate from the American people.

'Just let me get elected,' Johnson told the Joint Chiefs of Staff at a White House reception on Christmas Eve 1963, 'then you can have your war.'

The presidential election was to be in November 1964, but by then things had already got ahead of themselves. On 4 August 1964, President Johnson went on television to tell the American people that Communist gunboats had that morning made an unprovoked attack on two American warships, the USS *Maddox* and the *C. Turner Joy*, off the coast of North Vietnam in the Gulf of Tonkin. This was the so-called Gulf of Tonkin incident. As Johnson spoke, American planes were making reprisal strikes against targets in North Vietnam. Three days later, both houses of Congress showed their approval of this retaliation by passing the Gulf of Tonkin Resolution, which gave the President a free hand to wage war in Southeast Asia and begin the war in Vietnam in earnest.

The Gulf of Tonkin incident was one of the key events of the history of the decade. However, subsequent investigations have revealed that it probably never took place. A veteran of the Pacific war and a staunch anti-Communist, Johnson's finger was already itching on the trigger. The Communist North Vietnamese were making significant gains in US-backed South Vietnam, while nearly all of the more than eighty CIA teams sent into North Vietnam had been killed or captured.

The US destroyer C. Turner Joy – one of the two American warships said to have been attacked off the coast of North Vietnam on 4 August 1964. It has now been shown that the 'Gulf of Tonkin Incident', which provided the excuse for President Johnson to send ground troops into South Vietnam, never really happened.

To expand the US role in Vietnam, Johnson needed the approval of Congress. However, he considered that asking Congress to declare war on North Vietnam would provoke opposition. The administration particularly feared Senator Wayne Morse of Oregon, a Democrat who already opposed the administration's actions in Southeast Asia. Rather than risk a congressional row, Johnson had a resolution drawn up that stopped short of a declaration of war, but would give him a free hand. It was based on a 1955 resolution which gave President Dwight D. Eisenhower the power to deploy US forces 'as he deemed necessary' to protect Taiwan from a Communist invasion.

The resolution was ready by the beginning of June 1964, but on 15 June Johnson changed his mind. With the presidential election coming up in November, he did not want to appear to be a warmonger. However, offensive actions were being taken against North Vietnam regardless. To probe the North's coastal defences, the US had bought a fleet of foreign-made high-speed patrol boats. Manned by South Vietnamese commandos who had been trained by the CIA, these were used to harass Communist radar installation and naval bases. US warships were on hand in the Gulf of Tonkin to collect electronic intelligence from the coastal radar installations as the patrol boats went in.

In July, these operations were stepped up. The US aircraft carrier *Ticonderoga* was sent in, and on 10 July, the destroyer *Maddox* sailed from Japan. On 30 July, a major attack began. The destroyer was ordered to sail up to eight miles from the coast of North Vietnam, just four miles from its islands, on the pretext that the North Vietnamese maintained the three-mile limit set by the former colonial power, the French. However, Naval Intelligence knew that the North Vietnamese had extended their territorial waters to twelve miles, like the Chinese and other Communist countries.

On the morning of 2 August, the *Maddox* encountered a fleet of Vietnamese junks. Captain John Herrick sounded general quarters and radioed the Seventh Fleet that he expected 'possible hostile action'. A North Vietnamese message was intercepted, saying the Communists were preparing for 'military operations'. At 11.00 a.m, the *Maddox* was within ten miles of the Red River delta when three Communist patrol boats emerged from the estuary. The *Maddox* turned out to sea and the high-speed patrol boats gave chase. At 10,000 yards, Herrick opened fire. At 5,000 yards, two of the gunboats fired a torpedo. Both missed. A torpedo fired by the third gunboat turned out to be a dud.

The *Maddox* hit one gunboat and sank it. The other two were crippled by strafing from US warplanes from the *Ticonderoga*. Herrick wanted to go in and finished them off, but was ordered back. There had been no US casualties. The *Maddox* had been hit by only one bullet. That one bullet was enough to start a war.

The Republican presidential candidate, Senator Barry Goldwater of Arizona, was a rabid right-winger and urged tougher action against the North Vietnamese. Using the 'hot line' to Moscow for the first time, Johnson warned of dire consequences for the North Vietnamese if US vessels were attacked again in what he maintained were 'international waters'. A second aircraft carrier, the USS *Constellation*, and a second destroyer, the *C. Turner Joy*, were dispatched to the Gulf of Tonkin.

About 8 a.m. on 4 August, the *Maddox* intercepted a message that gave Captain Herrick the 'impression' that the North Vietnamese were preparing to attack. Sonar operators reported twenty-two incoming enemy torpedoes, none of which hit the ship. The *Maddox* opened fire. Gunnery officers reported sinking two or perhaps three Communist craft. But US warplanes circling overhead saw nothing. When the shooting had stopped, Herrick questioned his men. None of them had actually seen an enemy vessel. The sea was rough and Herrick concluded that the blips his inexperienced sonar operators had interpreted as torpedoes were, in fact, waves. Even Johnson, a navy veteran, did not believe that the *Maddox* was under attack.

'Hell, those dumb stupid sailors were just shooting at flying fish,' he said.

It hardly mattered. In the White House, Johnson's advisers decided he was being put to the test. If he wanted to defend himself against Goldwater and the Republican right wing, he could not be seen to be a vacillating or indecisive leader. Congressional leaders and ambassadors of allies, such as Britain, were briefed. Air strikes were ordered and Johnson went on television to explain the

JOHNSON DID NOT BELIEVE THE MADDOX WAS UNDER ATTACK. 'THOSE DUMB SAILORS WERE JUST SHOOTING AT FLYING FISH'

situation to the American people.

Sixty-four sorties were flown against four North Vietnamese patrol boat bases and a major oil storage depot. An estimated twenty-five enemy vessels were put out of action. Two US planes were downed and one pilot, Lieutenant Everett Alvarez Jr, became the first US prisoner of the war to be captured by the North Vietnamese. It would be eight years before he returned home.

On 7 August, the resolution Johnson had

prepared was put before Congress. Now called the Gulf of Tonkin Resolution, it was passed by the House 416–0 and by the Senate 88–2, with only Senators Morse and Ernest Gruening of Alaska voting against it. This is what it said:

THE GULF OF TONKIN RESOLUTION

SECTION 1:

Whereas naval units of the Communist regime in Vietnam, in violation of the principles of the Charter of the United Nations and of international law, have deliberately and repeatedly attacked United States naval vessels lawfully present in international waters, and have thereby created a serious threat to international peace.

Whereas these attacks are part of a deliberate and systematic campaign of aggression that the Communist regime in North Vietnam has been waging against its neighbors and the nations joined with them in the collective defence of their freedom.

Whereas the United States is assisting the peoples of southeast Asia to protect their freedom and has no territorial, military or political ambitions in that area, but desires only that these peoples should be left in peace to work out their own destinies in their own way. Now, therefore, be it resolved by the Senate and House of Representatives of the United States of America in Congress assembled, That the Congress approves and supports the determination of the President, as Commander-in-Chief, to take all necessary measures to repel any armed attack against the forces of the United States and to prevent further aggression.

SECTION 2:

The United States regards as vital to its national interest and to world peace the maintenance of international peace and security in southeast Asia. Consonant with the Constitution of the United States and the Charter of the United Nations and in accordance with its obligations under the Southeast Asia Collective Defense Treaty, the United States is, therefore, prepared, as the President determines, to take all necessary steps, including the use of armed force, to assist any member or protocol state of the Southeast Asia Collective Defense Treaty requesting assistance in defence of its freedoms.

SECTION 3:

This resolution shall expire when the President shall determine that the peace world security of the area is reasonably assured by international conditions created by action of the United Nations or otherwise except that it may be terminated earlier by resolution of the Congress.

Johnson was delighted. Authorizing him to 'take all necessary measures' to repel attacks on US forces and to 'prevent further aggression', the Resolution meant that he could take any action he wanted, without further reference to Congress.

'Like grandma's nightshirt,' Johnson said, 'it covered everything.'

Long before the war was over, it was discovered that the Gulf of Tonkin incident as portrayed by the administration was a fraud. Senate Foreign Relations Committee hearings in 1968 established that any North Vietnamese action in the Gulf of Tonkin was far from 'unprovoked'. The *Maddox* had been involved in covert action against North Vietnam. It was also established that plans to bomb North Vietnam had been drawn up before the Gulf of Tonkin incident. The architect of the Resolution, National Security Adviser Walt W. Rostow, said of the incident, 'We don't know what happened, but it had the desired result.'

Senator Morse had also known that the Gulf of Tonkin incident was a cynical ploy from the beginning. A lean and humourless teetotaller, he had been a progressive Republican when he arrived in Washington in 1945, but he fell out with the GOP over education and labour relations and switched to the Democrats. Known to oppose his party's policy in Vietnam, he received a phone call on the morning of 6 August 1964 from an officer in the Pentagon – whose name he would never divulge – telling him that the *Maddox*, rather than being an innocent party, had been involved in raids on North Vietnam. He had little influence in the Senate but, with Senator Gruening, voted against the Gulf of Tonkin Resolution, while doubters such as George McGovern of South Dakota and John Sherman Cooper of Kentucky were talked around by Senator William Fulbright, who later became a robust opponent of the war.

In February 1966, Morse introduced an amendment to repeal the Gulf of Tonkin Resolution. This time, other senators expressed their doubts about the powers the resolution gave the President. Morse managed to prolong the debate for two weeks but, when it came to a vote, only five senators backed him. By then others judged that America was in too deep to back out. With Gruening, Morse backed a bill barring draftees being sent to Vietnam without congressional approval. Only the two of them voted for it.

Flight deck crewmen work feverishly beneath an A-4C Skyhawk, positioning it for launch from the attack carrier USS Enterprise in the Tonkin Gulf off North Vietnam. American air power ringed North Vietnam. Planes attacked from aircraft carriers in the South China Sea and airbases in South Vietnam and Thailand, while B-52s flew in on bombing raids from Guam and Okinawa. The North Vietnamese could only defend themselves with anti-aircraft batteries and Soviet-made MiG fighters.

The Gulf of Tonkin Resolution was only repealed in 1970 on the initiative of Senator Robert Dole of Kansas (a supporter of Nixon and, later, a Republican presidential candidate) after President Nixon had been censured for extending the war into Cambodia. Dole figured that, by 1970, the resolution had become obsolete. Nixon did not oppose its repeal, asserting that his authority to conduct the war in Vietnam did not depend on the Resolution but rather on his power as commander-in-chief. The bill was passed on 24 June by eighty-one votes to ten.

Even though the Gulf of Tonkin Resolution gave Johnson all the powers he wanted to prosecute the war, the Communist leadership in Hanoi decided to step up the struggle in the South, even though it realized that the US was likely to intervene. The Vietcong went on the offensive. They attacked an isolated government forces camp near Binh Dinh, hurling themselves against the perimeter for six hours. An estimated 500 died. One hundred bodies were picked off the wire by the defenders when the assault force withdrew. On 31 October 1964, the Vietcong attacked Bien Hoa airbase, northeast of Saigon, floating past on sampans disguised as farmers, before opening up with mortars. Four Americans were killed, five bombers were destroyed and eight more damaged. But with the election just a few days away, Johnson rejected proposals for retaliatory raids against the North.

Johnson was re-elected president on 3 November, and did not have to wait long for a fresh excuse to attack the North Vietnamese.

On 24 December the Vietcong blew up the Brinks Hotel in Saigon, where US officers were billeted. On Christmas Eve, the hotel was packed with US soldiers waiting for Bob Hope, a regular performer for the troops in Vietnam, when a VC driver parked a truck packed with explosives outside. The explosion ripped through the hotel, killing two Americans and injuring fifty-eight others. Again Johnson stayed his hand.

The event more than any other that brought the Marines to the beaches of Da Nang occurred on the night of 7 February 1965. At Camp Holloway, an airbase near the provincial capital of Pleiku, some 400 Americans of the 52nd Combat Aviation Battalion were asleep when 300 Vietcong crept up on them. For the previous week, there had been a ceasefire for the Vietnamese festival for the lunar new year, Tet. The Vietcong had used that time to stockpile captured American mortars and ammunition. At 0200hrs, they began bombarding the airbase, turning it into a conflagration of exploding ammunition and burning aircraft which left seven American dead and 100 wounded.

'They are killing our men while they are asleep at night,' said President Johnson. 'I can't ask American soldiers to continue to fight with one hand behind their back.'

On 2 March 1965, 100 US jet bombers took off from Da Nang airbase to strike at targets in the North. As it was Vietcong who had attacked Camp Holloway, this was the first air strike against North Vietnam that could not be justified as retaliation and it began a sustained campaign of graduated

bombing known as Operation Rolling Thunder that continued, on and off, for the next three years. Its aim was to slow the infiltration of men and supplies from the North and bomb the Communists to the negotiating table. It succeeded in neither, but America was now committed to a course of action and President Johnson had raised the political price of failure. That same day, the four ships of Amphibious Task Force 76 sailed from Japan. The Second Indochina War – the American war in Vietnam – was now underway.

The aftermath of the Vietcong's bombing of the Metropole Hotel in Saigon on 12 April 1965.

3

THE WAR ON THE GROUND

ALTHOUGH US ground troops had now been committed to a land war on the Asian mainland, President Johnson still hoped to make peace. On 7 April, in a speech at Johns Hopkins University in Baltimore, he offered Ho Chi Minh a chance to join a $1 billion Southeast Asian development programme in exchange for peace. Hanoi rejected the offer.

Johnson publicly denied that the Marine landings at Da Nang were part of a 'far-reaching strategy' to escalate the war, but the war soon developed a momentum of its own. The year of 1965 began with 23,000 Americans in Vietnam and ended with 184,300. The Da Nang landings were followed by a steady commitment of Marines to I Corps Tactical Zone in the northern provinces of South Vietnam. By mid-April, General William Westmoreland announced a more aggressive patrolling policy and the first clashes between American ground troops and the Vietcong took place. This was part of Westmoreland's belligerent 'search and destroy' strategy. He believed that by hunting down the enemy he could use superior American firepower to kill off Communist soldiers faster than they could be replaced. It would be a war of attrition. But to succeed in such a strategy, more men would be needed.

Soon US troops were pouring into Vietnam. At home in the US, young men of draft age realized that they risked being sent to a

Helicopters bring in troops of 173rd during a search-and-destroy mission, 40 miles south of Saigon on August 1965. For the next seven years, US troops would hunt an enemy that would constantly elude them.

Opposite: Soldiers of the US 101st Airborne drag the body of a Vietcong fighter to the rear after fierce fighting around An Khe in September 1966. They seldom showed much respect for their enemy.

A sit-down peace demonstration temporarily halts the Armed Forces Day Parade on New York's Fifth Avenue on 15 May 1965. From the very beginning of the war, there was opposition from young people already radicalized by the Civil Rights Movement.

war in a far-flung part of the world where no vital American interest seemed to be at stake. On 17 April 1965, 15,000 students staged an anti-war rally in Washington, DC – to no avail. At a conference in Honolulu on 19–20 April, Westmoreland asked Secretary of Defense Robert McNamara for the US presence to be raised from 40,200 to 82,000 and, on 5 May 1965, the 173rd Airborne Brigade, 'the Herd', which was the US Army's rapid-response unit for the western Pacific, was flown from Okinawa to Bien Hoa to provide temporary assistance to MACV – Military Assistance Command Vietnam. The first US Army combat unit to join the conflict, they should have been relieved by the First Brigade of the 101st Airborne Division in late July. But when the 'Screaming Eagles' arrived, the Herd stayed on.

The North Vietnamese high command was not surprised by the commitment of American ground troops. Plans had already been laid for a long war. By June 1965, small contingents of

North Vietnamese troops were fighting alongside the Vietcong to test American strength and observe US tactics.

On 21 September, the 1st Cavalry Division (Airmobile) was moved from Fort Benning, Georgia, to An Khe in II Corps Tactical Zone to the south. In October, the whole of the First Infantry Division, 'the Big Red One', was sent to III Corps Tactical Zone, which covered the area around Saigon. And the Americans were not the only ones involved. The government in Canberra was also an advocate of the domino theory and in 1962 the Australians had sent thirty military advisers to South Vietnam. On 4 April 1965, Australian Prime Minister Robert Menzies praised the US for accepting the challenge to 'human freedom' in Vietnam and, on 26 May, 800 more Aussies turned up in-country, while New Zealand announced it would send a battalion. By the end of the year, there were 1400 Australians in Vietnam. Their commitment peaked at 7,672; New Zealand's at 552. The British managed to stay out of the

Australian Army Minister Phillip Lynch (centre) visits Saigon, accompanied by General Robert Hay (left), commander of Australian forces in South Vietnam. Having been attacked by the Japanese in World War II, Australia naturally feared an Asian nation hostile to the Western way of life to the north. Australian and New Zealand troops fought bravely throughout the war, despite vociferous opposition at home.

war, officially, but there have been persistent rumours that British SAS men served in Vietnam as 'instructors' in Australian and New Zealand SAS units and as part of an exchange programme with the US Special Forces. British citizens who were permanent residents in the US – green card holders – were also eligible for the draft. Americans were also trained in British jungle training schools and

the British sent printing presses for the Saigon government to produce propaganda.

South Korean troops – the ROKs – had arrived in Vietnam in February 1965. They first came under fire on 3 April, by which time there were 200 in country. At the peak of their commitment, 44,829 ROKs controlled a coastal strip of II CTZ. Thailand sent 11,568 troops and allowed American bombers, fighters, and reconnaissance planes to use their airbases. They also allowed an Infiltration Surveillance Center and other US intelligence outfits to operate from their territory. President Ferdinand Marcos of the Philippines sent 2,000 men. The Republic of China (Taiwan) sent thirty-one and Fascist Spain sent a thirteen-man medical team. More bizarrely, Morocco sent 10,000 cans of sardines, while the Swiss sent microscopes for Saigon University.

Alongside these foreign troops were South Vietnam's forces, the ARVN, who numbered around 620,000 men. But they were not

WARNINGS . . . THAT THE USSR WOULD START A NUCLEAR WAR IF US AGGRESSION CONTINUED WERE IGNORED

terribly effective. While 90 per cent of American largest-scale operations managed to make contact with the enemy, less than half of ARVN operations did. Officers sold drugs and prostitutes and the desertion rate ran at over twenty per cent. Under Westmoreland's new search-and destroy strategy, the ARVN were relegated to searching for guerrillas in areas cleared by US forces in major operations. But their performance did not improve and their assignment was quickly nicknamed 'search and avoid'. However, the ARVN did have some successes. On 4 April, they destroyed a Vietcong enclave in the U Minh forest, a Communist stronghold in the Mekong Delta

to the south of Saigon, killing 238 VC. On 29 April they killed another eighty-four and took thirty-one prisoner, while US air support claimed a further seventy VC dead. And the ARVN claimed another 250 VC dead in the Mekong Delta on 13 August.

On 21 April, the restrictions limiting the Marines to the eight square miles around the Da Nang airbase were lifted, so that they could support the ARVN. The following day another Buddhist monk burnt himself to death publicly in Saigon in protest at the war. The picture was carried in the press around the world. It did nothing to halt the escalation.

On 24 April, Johnson stepped up the bombing campaign and declared the whole of Vietnam a combat zone, meaning that all US servicemen serving there would receive combat pay and get tax advantages. Already the war was costing America $15 billion a year, McNamara announced. Congress quickly approved a further $700 million for the war but on 1 June Johnson asked for another $89 million in economic aid.

Warnings by Cyrus Eaton, a millionaire industrialist newly returned from a peace mission to Moscow, that the USSR would start a nuclear war if US aggression continued were ignored, and a British MP who went to Hanoi in an attempt to open peace negotiations was rebuffed.

The Vietcong stepped up its attacks, scoring major victories. In mid-June, the Vietcong attacked a Special Forces camp and the district headquarters of the ARVN at Dong Xoai, besieging it for four days. In the heaviest fighting so far, the ARVN suffered 900

Members of the 1st Battalion, Royal Australian Regiment, during an 81mm mortar fire mission from within the Australian perimeter at the Bien Hoa Airfield in June 1965. Australian soldiers won four Victoria Crosses during the Vietnam war. First arriving as trainers in 1962, some 50,000 Australians — including ground troops and air force and navy personnel — served in Vietnam; 520 died and almost 2,400 were wounded.

casualties. The vc were eventually driven off by heavy US air strikes, losing 350 in the fighting on the ground and maybe twice that number in the bombing.

The Roman Catholic opposition forced Prime Minister Quat from office. He was replaced by the flamboyant South Vietnamese air force chief General Nguyen Cao Ky, who was installed as the head of a military regime in Saigon on 18 June. Known for his mirrored shades and his good-looking wife, he was later reported saying that Adolf Hitler was one of his 'heroes'. Ky urged the US to stage an all-out invasion of the North. Politically, this was

THE WAR ON THE GROUND

out of the question. Nevertheless Johnson upped the draft from 17,000 a month to 35,000. The US ground forces also abandoned their defensive posture, and at the end of June launched a major offensive on a Vietcong enclave twenty miles northeast of Saigon, which failed to make contact with the enemy. The VC could fade away at will.

By this time the Marines in Da Nang were getting itchy trigger fingers. They had been trained for aggressive action, not for defence, and had spent five frustrating months filling sandbags and patrolling the perimeter of the airbase. Plagued by mosquitoes, their fitful sleep in the hot oppressive air was disturbed by monkeys setting off trip flares or rattling the rock-filled beer cans that were hung in the wire to warn them of Vietcong infiltrating the base. Patrolling the hills to the west of the base provided little diversion. Loaded with heavy equipment, the Marines dropped like flies from heat exhaustion. Occasionally, they would catch a fleeting glimpse of a VC dressed in the traditional black pyjamas disappearing into the trees and, seemingly, vanishing into thin air. Morale was at rock bottom.

'The Marine mission was to kill Vietcong,' said the Marine Corps General Wallace M. Greene. 'They can't do that by sitting on their ditty boxes.'

Even inside the airbase they were taunted by the Vietcong. At 0130hrs on the morning of 1 July, a sentry was alerted by a noise down by the perimeter wire. He threw an illumination

Major Harry Honner of the New Zealand 161st Field Battery receives a gift from South Vietnamese premier Nguyen Cao Ky at Nui Dat in January 1967.

grenade, which brought down mortar fire from the VC. In the midst of the barrage, Vietcong sappers cut through the wire and tossed explosives, destroying three planes and damaging three others. Only one American was killed, but the action attracted worldwide attention. In response, the Marines stepped up their patrolling, to little avail. Trying to find Vietcong among the Vietnamese population, it was said, was like trying to find tears in a bucket of water. Soon the frustration was too much for them. Marines were filmed setting fire to the village of Cam Ne, six miles west of

MORTARS RAINED DOWN AND THE VC RAKED THE AREA WITH MURDEROUS MACHINE-GUN FIRE

Da Nang, with their Zippo lighters, even though the Vietcong had long since left the area. CBS aired TV footage of the incident on 3 August, sparking international condemnation. It was the first of many such incidents. Two days later, the VC struck again, attacking the Esso terminal near Da Nang and destroying two million gallons of gasoline, nearly 40 per cent of the US fuel supply.

Westmoreland received permission to use his troops as he saw fit in more aggressive action. The American 'tactical area of responsibility' was increased to 600 square miles and US forces prepared themselves to launch new search-and-destroy operations. On 15 August, a VC defector told his interrogators that 1,500 men of the 1st Vietcong Regiment were massing in the villages around Van Tuong, around 80 miles down the coast from Da Nang, ready to attack the new Marine enclave at Chu Lai. For the Marines this was too good an opportunity to miss. But they had to move fast. They decided to attack the VC from three directions simultaneously, surrounding them and pushing them back into the Van Tuong peninsula. They would advance overland from Chu Lai, blocking any breakout to the north. A Marine battalion would make an amphibious landing to the south, while helicopters would land more Marines to the west. The VC would then find themselves trapped with their backs to the sea. This time the elusive enemy would find no escape.

Operation Starlite began on the morning of 18 August, when the giant forty-ton amtracs of the 3rd Battalion of the 3rd Marines clawed their way up the soft sand of the beach at An Cuong. As the Marines rushed the thatched huts of a nearby hamlet, they found themselves halted by a wall of fire. Mortars rained down and the VC raked the area with murderous machine-gun fire. The Marines called in support from the guns of the light cruiser USS *Galveston*. Six-inch shells bombarded the hillside where the VC were dug in. When the smoke cleared, the Marines advanced through the shattered trees, only to be pinned down once more by withering VC fire. A pitched battle developed until the Marines pushed forward into the VC complex of trenches and bunkers. After hours of savage, hand-to-hand fighting, the hillside was secured.

To the west, HH-34 helicopters landed H

Company of the 4th Marines at LZ Blue almost on top of the 60th Vietcong Battalion, who were dug in on a low hill. The VC held their fire until the Marines landed, then poured machine-gun fire and rocket-propelled grenades into the landing zone. UH-1B helicopter gunships – Hueys – tried to suppress enemy fire. A Marine platoon tried to make it up the slope, but were beaten back; only with the help of tanks and massive air strikes did they manage to take the hill.

At LZ White, the incoming HH-34s carrying E Company were hit by rifle and machine-gun fire from a ridge overlooking the landing zone to the east. The Marines that landed took heavy casualties as they tried to make their way up the slope. Again, navy firepower had to be brought to bear and the battlefield was littered with dead and wounded before the Marines reached the crest.

As they closed in on the enemy's main force, the Marines faced heavy fighting around the villages of An Cuong and Nam Yen. An armoured column on its way to resupply I Company got lost and was knocked out in an enemy ambush. When I Company sent a detachment to relieve it, they found themselves under furious attack from hidden fortifications, but managed to hold out. The following day, the Marines began clearing out the complex of tunnels, bunkers, and trenches in the area. Often they literally had to dig the enemy out and came under regular harassment from snipers. But by nightfall, the Marines were claiming victory. The body count was 614 VC with 45 Americans dead. As a consequence Westmoreland's strategy of search and destroy won out over the counter-insurgency techniques that had been used in Vietnam up to that time.

The proponents of counter-insurgency urged the close coordination of political, military and social programmes to isolate the guerrillas from the general population. Once the allegiance of the local people was won, it was argued, the guerrillas could then be defeated. The British had employed counter-insurgency effectively during the Malayan Emergency, from 1948 to 1960, establishing 'New Villages' where the local population could be protected from intimidation by Communist insurgents. Sir Robert Thompson, who headed the British Advisory Mission to South Vietnam, had persuaded President Diem to establish 'strategic hamlets'. Diem established over 3,000 of them but used them to intimidate the populace himself. Nor were they adequately defended. The government's showpiece strategic hamlet at Ben Truong was burnt down by the VC in August 1963. This destroyed the people's confidence in the whole concept. The Marines had their own counter-insurgency strategy called the Combined Action Program with specially trained teams providing protection, along with medical and civic aid, a strategy used successfully in the Caribbean and Central America. Westmoreland, however, was eager to fight a conventional war against large concentrations of enemy troops. The success of Starlite silenced those pushing counter-insurgency. The US would now put all its eggs in one basket and depend exclusively on search-and-destroy operations, supported by the massive destructive power of American

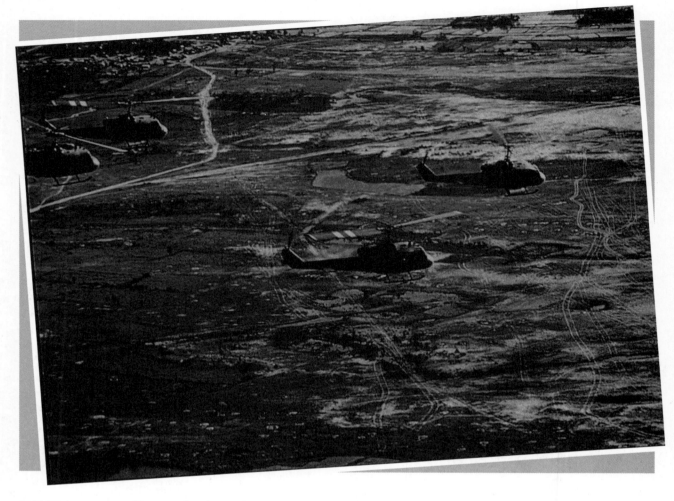

US UH 1B helicopters, known as 'Hueys', fly a reconaissance patrol. Hueys became a symbol of the war, working as scout helicopters, gunships and troop carriers and medevacking out the injured.

military technology. The Vietcong had learnt a lesson from Starlite too. They went back to a strategy of small guerrilla actions in the jungles, villages and paddy fields, using ambushes and booby traps.

In October 1965 the first draft-card burning took place during an anti-war demonstration in New York, though President Johnson had already signed into law a bill making it a crime to mutilate or destroy a draft card with a penalty of up to five years in prison and a $1,000 fine. This was to become a symbol of resistance to the war.

October also brought the first serious clash between the North Vietnamese and US Armies. Two regiments of the NVA came across the border from Cambodia and attacked the Special Forces camp at Plei Me, inland in the central highlands. Their aim was to drive to the coast, cutting South Vietnam in two. Plei Me held out, but found itself surrounded. Westmoreland sent the newly arrived First Cavalry Division (Airmobile) to relieve the base. As the Air Cav's helicopters swooped in to break the siege, the NVA pulled back towards Cambodia, but Westmoreland did not want them to get away and ordered the Air Cav to go on the offensive. The NVA had regrouped in the Ia Drang valley, a dense jungle area near Pleiku, fifteen miles west of Plei Me. On 14 November a battalion of the First Air Cavalry landed at LZ X-Ray in the valley and began searching for the enemy. They quickly came under heavy fire and a close-quarters battle developed. They were heavily outnumbered, but they held on with support from artillery, gunships, and massive B-52 Stratofortresses, until then used for strategic bombing, not tactical support of ground forces.

The ground troops were reinforced by another battalion the next day. Heavy fighting continued until, several days later, the NVA fled back into Cambodia or melted into the jungle. When the First Air Cavalry returned to their base at An Khe they had lost 300 men, but claimed 1,200 NVA dead. Again Westmoreland seemed to have demonstrated that, by throwing large units into full-scale engagements and exploiting the superior mobility of helicopter-borne troops and massive air support, the US forces could win the day. However, the Communists did not seem to get the message. The Vietcong continued their attacks on American outposts and airfields, and the American forces began to realize that they did not know who to trust. On 13 October, 56 Vietcong had been killed by Marines in an assault ten miles from Da Nang. Among the dead they found a thirteen-year-old boy who had been selling them drinks the previous day. On his body was a sketch map showing their positions. The Vietnamese did not know who to trust either. That same day, the Americans

bombed a friendly Vietnamese village, killing 48 non-combatants and wounding 55 others. The following month the Vietcong attacked an ARVN regimental headquarters in the old Michelin rubber factory, inflicting heavy casualties. And, on 4 December, the Vietcong blew up a hotel in Saigon used by US soldiers, killing eight servicemen and civilians and wounding 137.

Once again the Pentagon asked for an increase in men, from 120,000 to 400,000, but Secretary of Defense Robert McNamara was growing pessimistic. He warned that there was no guarantee of victory and that casualties would mount.

'US killed in action can be expected to reach one thousand a month,' he cautioned, 'and the odds are that we will be faced in early 1967 with a "no-decision" at an even higher level.'

He warned President Johnson that the NVA and Vietcong had settled into a war of attrition. 'They continue to believe that the war will be a long one,' he said, 'that time is their ally and that their staying power is superior to ours.'

Indeed, the Vietcong were waging what they called the 'war of the flea'. Like dripping water, they believed that they would wear away stone. They attacked at night, appeared from nowhere, killed, and vanished. They would try to achieve overwhelming superiority in numbers, typically five to one. If necessary they would use 'human wave' tactics to overwhelm defences before the enemy could call in artillery or air support. Their orders were to kill as many Americans as possible. The war was unpopular in America, they were told, and if the US death toll continued mounting the American people would rise up and overthrow their government. However, they had to avoid large-scale engagements which risked the superior American firepower. The Vietcong had no defence against artillery and air strikes, but in a firefight at close quarters their legendary Kalashnikov AK-47 assault rifle – made in the Soviet Union, Eastern Europe or China – was more than a match for the US standard issue M14, later replaced by the lighter but chronically unreliable M16 Armalite rifle.

It was easy for the US military to dismiss the Vietcong as a ragtag peasant army. They found it laughable when, in November 1965, the VC – Victor Charlie, or just Charlie to the grunts – attacked the air base at Qui Nhon with bows and arrows dipped in rancid fat. It is easy to laugh at people who fire arrows at helicopter gunships, but on the other hand it is not so easy to defeat people who are willing to fire arrows at helicopter gunships.

The Vietcong were highly organized. Their strategy was summed up as 'one slow, four quick'. The one slow was meticulous preparation. Local Vietcong irregulars would make repeated reconnaissance of the target. Back at base camp, they would build a scale model of the objective, so every soldier could recognize every feature of it. Detailed plans would be drawn up and the action rehearsed repeatedly so that every man knew exactly what was expected of him. Then the four quicks began. The main force would be infiltrated into the area in small groups, guided by local irregu-

lars. They could pick up arms and food supplies from caches hidden along the way. The strike force would only reassemble shortly before the attack. The attack itself came swiftly, without any warning. Only rarely did the Vietcong bombard enemy positions with mortars before attacking. Usually they depended on their superiority in numbers and the element of surprise. As soon as the objective had been achieved, they would withdraw before there was time for the enemy to call in a counter attack. As they retreated they would pick up weapons from the battlefield. The Vietnamese considered it important to be buried with their ancestors, so the dead were hauled off the battlefield with a wire tied around the ankle or looped through the special leather thong Vietcong soldiers wore around their wrist. The fourth 'quick' was the retreat to their reassembly point which was usually about twelve hours march from the scene of the attack. From there they would either return to their base in the central highlands, the Mekong Delta, or across the border in Laos or Cambodia, or they would be sent back into action in support of some other unit.

What made the Vietcong such a formidable fighting force was that once they had been inducted, willingly or not, they had no choice but to see the fighting through to the bitter end. Unlike US troops, they were not rotated home after a year. They had total confidence in their commanders, particularly Ho Chi Minh and General Vo Nguyen Giap, who had led previous generations to victory against the Japanese and the French. Many Vietcong

soldiers were highly motivated, fighting against a corrupt regime which oppressed them, then against Americans who had sprayed defoliant Agent Orange on their crops and burnt their villages. Another powerful motive for men to join the Vietcong was 'shrinking bird disease'. South Vietnam was being overrun with huge American soldiers whose free-spending ways turned many traditionally moral Vietnamese women into prostitutes. Vietnamese men came to believe that their penises would slowly shrivel up after sexual contact with a woman who had slept with an American. The VC used this belief to their own ends, spreading rumours that US troops were abducting Vietnamese women and forcing them to become concubines. American chaplains warned their men to refrain from sleeping with Vietnamese women, believing that it gave the VC a strong incentive to fight. 'It is one thing to fight for political principles,' said one padre, 'another to fight to vindicate your manhood'.

Large numbers of women also joined the Vietcong and the NVA. In the North, they were conscripted at eighteen like the men. Women ran most of the supply convoys down the Ho Chi Minh trail.

A female Vietcong patrol is briefed in 1967. Many women fought as front line troops for the Vietcong throughout the war. In the North, they manned anti-aircraft batteries and helped carry matériel down the Ho Chi Minh trails.

The diary of one of these women, Duong Thi Xuan Quy, records her three-month journey to the South with a heavy rucksack on her back:

The boils on my back hurt me the whole of the last night. Could neither sleep nor think clearly. Impossible to lie on my back and it was torture to lie on my side. Had to rock the hammock frequently to ease the pain. Haven't had a bath since Post 1. Will stay here till tomorrow morning and will cross the river at four... Have lost my appetite for several days now. Never thought it could take so much effort to eat... I must not break down, not even with colic. I'd be left behind. Up at two in the morning. The moon is hidden by clouds. We crossed the pontoon bridges across the Sepon River. These pontoons will be dismantled before daybreak.

Pontoon bridges were used to cross rivers so they could be dismantled quickly to prevent them being targets for American air strikes. In other places, her party had to build makeshift bamboo bridges across razor-backed ridges and where the trail had been washed out by the monsoon rains. They would see young NVA men heavily laden with weapons and ammunition passing them at night. After three months, Quy had to make the dangerous crossing of Highway 9 which ran from Laos into Quang Tri province. After snatching a brief nap in the early morning chill and eating a little of the cooked rice balls they carried, she set off to cross it:

It's a scorcher and there are no trees along the road. My skin is peeling and I'm tired out... I limped along and it was not even six o'clock when I crossed Highway 9... The road was not wide, but we had to sprint across it to evade the attention of enemy aircraft... It appeared before me suddenly, a curve blanched by summer sun and strewn with boulders. It looked harmless enough though. Thus I set foot on Highway 9, a road which would long be remembered in the history of our heroic people.

Towards the end of 1965, General Giap began to test the Americans by putting large NVA units into the field. The US brass relished the idea that they would now be facing a conventional army, rather than guerrilla bands, believing that no regular army could resist American might. The NVA suffered huge losses, but still managed to kill Americans. However, the fact that the NVA could take the losses and continue fighting gave them a huge psychological advantage. They, too, were fighting a war of attrition.

In November 1965 the British tried to make peace once again. Foreign Secretary Michael Stewart flew to Moscow in an effort to persuade the Soviets to reopen the Geneva conference. The Soviet foreign minister Andrei Gromyko said that the talks could not begin again until the US had pulled all its troops out of South Vietnam and stopped bombing the North. Meanwhile, on a flying visit to Saigon, Senator Richard Nixon pledged Republican support for the administration's policy, saying, 'There is only one basis for negotiations... a Communist withdrawal'.

The Vietcong seemed more amenable, though. In December, they proposed a Christmas truce. The US and South Vietnamese forces accepted and suspended the bombing of the North in the hope that the ceasefire might lead to talks. They proposed extending it, but Vietcong attacks forced the US and ARVN back into action and the bombing of the North resumed on 31 January after a thirty-seven-day bombing pause. By then, Senator Strom Thurmond was calling for the use of nuclear weapons.

Westmoreland also considered using tactical nuclear weapons until he was banned from doing so by the administration. Westmoreland later condemned the ban, arguing that two atomic bombs had 'spoken convincingly' to the Japanese during World War II. As it was, he had 200,000 US troops in Vietnam by the end of 1965, but he had already sent a memo asking for 443,000 by the end of 1966, upping his demand to 460,000 in January 1966. Despite his pessimistic view, McNamara backed Westmoreland's demands, though warning that this would not ensure success. The Senate took a similarly gloomy view, with majority leader Mike Mansfield warning that the whole of Southeast Asia was a potential battlefield.

On the ground, things were going from bad to worse. A Special Forces camp at Khe Sanh, near the DMZ, came under fire from 120mm mortars, the first time that the Vietcong had deployed such an awesome weapon. Meanwhile, the VC managed to kid-

nap US diplomat Douglas Ramsey. However, the Australians achieved some success in a full-scale search-and-destroy sweep called Operation Crimp through the 'Iron Triangle', a Vietcong stronghold northwest of Saigon. The troops came up empty-handed for the first few days until Sergeant Stewart Green saw what he thought at first was a scorpion on the jungle floor. It turned out to be a nail in a trapdoor. Under it was the mouth of a narrow shaft that led down to a tunnel. Green explored part of the tunnel, but the darkness and claustrophobia soon drove him back. The

EXTENSIVE TUNNEL SYSTEMS HAD BEEN USED DURING THE FRENCH INDOCHINA WAR... THESE WERE EXTENDED RAPIDLY

troops tried pumping coloured smoke down the shaft and found that it came up out of hidden openings all over the surrounding jungle. At last, they had discovered how the Vietcong could vanish so easily. They were standing on top of a huge complex of tunnels, much of which they destroyed, though they could not confirm a high body count.

The Vietnamese people had a special affinity with the soil of their country and their guerrilla armies had been making use of tunnels for centuries. Extensive tunnel systems had been used during the French Indochina War, but when the Americans arrived these were extended rapidly. Underground the Vietcong had dormitories and workshops, hospitals, kitchens, headquarters facilities and supply depots. Some tunnel systems ran for hundreds of miles, from the Cambodian border to the gates of Saigon itself. They were dug by villagers in the laterite clay which set as hard as concrete and, where the water table permitted, were several storeys deep. Levels were separated by airtight doors and U-bends in tunnel floors were filled with water to stop the spread of gases and impede the shock waves from explosions. Short tunnels often looked as if they were dead ends when in fact a concealed trap door connected to a vast network. The tunnels were narrow, which suited the small Vietnamese soldiers, but not the larger Americans or Australians. And they were filled with booby traps: rigged grenades, tethered poisonous snakes and punji sticks, sharpened bamboo stakes. Pits of these stakes were concealed along jungle trails, deadly to anyone who stumbled into them.

Other types of punji traps sprang up, impaling the luckless grunt. Wooden or metal spikes would often be smeared with human excrement to cause blood poisoning in anyone not killed directly. Trails also concealed mines and grenades rigged to tripwires. These were often hidden under water in places where patrols had to wade through swamps. The VC also littered areas with 'toe-poppers,' upright bullets half-buried with the primer resting on a nail or firing pin. When a GI stood on one it would blow his foot off. Some 10,000 US servicemen lost at least one limb in Vietnam – more than in World War II and Korea put together. Grenades were attached to bamboo arches over the trails so that their shrapnel

caused messy head and face wounds. The idea was to sap the morale of the grunts. It also had an added political bonus. An eighteen-year-old GI who had just seen a buddy mutilated by a booby trap was more likely to commit atrocities. Even experienced jungle fighters used local peasants as human booby-trap detectors, causing the Vietnamese people to hate and mistrust the Americans.

The entrances to tunnel complexes were usually surrounded by mines – GIs tended to avoid places where their buddies had been killed or wounded. The entrance shafts were often booby-trapped with a slit at about the level of the eyes of anyone hanging by his fingertips from the lip before dropping down. A spear would be thrust through the slit. Items GIs liked to take as souvenirs were booby-trapped. Even coconuts were filled with explosives. Nowhere in Vietnam was safe. It was even rumoured that prostitutes in Saigon would booby trap their sexual parts with broken glass. Among the Australians there was talk of a young squaddie whose penis was sliced in two by a razor blade mounted on a cork inside a prostitute's vagina – though no one ever met the man or woman concerned. But bad things did happen. One young GI was bought a prostitute by his buddies for his birthday so that he could lose his virginity. After she had relieved him of it, she left a bomb under his bed which blew his arms and legs off. Marine fliers were not allowed downtown in Da Nang in 1965 after a booby-trapped cigarette lighter bought from the street vendor blew a Marine's head off. In another case, a toddler was booby-trapped with explosives so when a kindly GI picked him up, the two of them were blown to smithereens. The GIs got their own back, salting enemy ammunition dumps with doctored rifle bullets and mortar rounds that would blow up in the weapon. The idea was to wound the enemy, not kill him. The VC and NVA had limited medical facilities and an injured man put a lot of strain on their resources. It also bred in the enemy soldiers a mistrust of their own weapons.

Even without the booby traps, life for the grunts in the jungles was bad enough. It was full of blood-sucking insects and leeches that had to be burnt off with a cigarette. There are also 133 species of snake in the jungles of Vietnam – 131 of them poisonous. Some had venom that killed within hours. The damp rotted everything. Monsoon rains turned jungle tracks to mudslides, chilled GIs who had acclimatized to the stifling heat, gave them trench foot, rotted their kit, and turned c-rations into a greasy, cold soup. And twenty-four hours a day they had to be ready for ambush by an unseen enemy.

Conditions for the VC were even worse. Vietnamese peasants were used to life in the paddy fields and were no more at home in the jungle than Americans were, and they were less well prepared. Wearing sandals made

A member of the 9th Interrogation Translation Team questions two NVA prisoners after their capture by B Company, 1st Battalion, 7th Marines during an operation 17 miles southwest of Da Nang in 1968. Vietcong and NVA prisoners were treated very badly and were not returned when the Americans withdrew. Instead they were left in the hands of their sworn enemies, the South Vietnamese.

Operation Oregon – an infantryman is lowered into a tunnel during a search and destroy mission west of Duc Pho. These 'tunnel rats' were formed into a special volunteer force under Captain Herbert Thornton. They risked all in close-quarters combat in the tunnel complexes, also braving booby traps, not to mention the snakes and scorpions that inhabited the tunnels.

them very vulnerable to snake bites. Thousands would have been saved if they had had solid army boots. Antivenom tablets were issued, one to be swallowed, a second to be chewed and placed on the bite. However, the Vietcong had no defence against mosquitoes. More Vietcong died of malaria than of any other cause. Even those who survived were permanently weakened. With few medical supplies available, Vietcong soldiers did their best with traditional remedies, but any wound almost inevitably resulted in a painful and lingering death.

Vietcong troops were constantly hungry. Twice a day they ate a small ball of cold rice made palatable with a few small chillies and occasionally a little dried meat, fish or salt. One

chicken would feed up to thirty men. Most suffered from vitamin deficiencies. Bomb craters filled with water were stocked with fish and ducks. Otherwise they would eat monkey, rat, dog, and even tiger and elephant, which is, apparently, tough and tasteless. Some ate moths attracted by the flame of their lamps. The Vietcong would also scavenge c-rations discarded by the ARVN and their American allies, until the GIs started booby-trapping them. Vietcong soldiers were in constant danger of discovery. Where a cooking fire was lit, an elaborate chimney had to be constructed to carry the smoke away into the earth. They also lived in constant fear of artillery and air raids. If they stopped for more than half a day, they would dig in.

In base areas, they lived below ground in tunnels. This was no picnic. The air was bad and what food they had rotted quickly. The tunnels were full of mosquitoes, ants, spiders, and parasites called chiggers that burrowed under the skin, causing intensive irritation. Often dead bodies were dragged below ground to foil the Americans' body counts, but their rotting flesh filled the tunnels with a sickening stench. The wounded operated on without anaesthetic in the underground hospitals often begged to be taken above ground to die. Nevertheless an underground lifestyle flourished. There were morale-boosting lectures and other entertainments. Weddings were held and babies born.

Initially, the Americans knew nothing about the tunnels. Indeed, the US Army's biggest base in South Vietnam was built right on top of a Vietcong tunnel system at Chu Chi. When the 25th Infantry Division arrived in 1966, an enterprising VC called Huynh Van Co and two comrades hid underground for a week while the GIS settled in. Then they began to emerge at night to steal food, sabotage equipment, and set off explosives: the newly arrived 25th thought they were being mortared from outside the perimeter. After seriously undermining the morale of the 25th, Huynh Van Co and his comrades withdrew undetected and their tunnels were never discovered.

After Operation Crimp, the American forces tried destroying the tunnel systems with explosives or pumping burning acetylene gas down them. This was ineffective due to the hardness of the tunnel walls and the doors and seals the VC had installed. Dogs were sent down, but they were easily killed by the Vietcong or their booby traps. There was no alternative but to send men down. Special teams of volunteers called 'tunnel rats' were formed under a southerner named Captain Herbert Thornton, the Chemical Officer of the 1st Infantry Division. He narrowly escaped death when crawling behind a rookie tunnel rat who detonated a booby trap. The explosion in such a confined space deafened Thornton in one ear, though the rookie's body protected him from much of the blast.

While a high-tech war raged above ground, the tunnel rats took on the enemy on their own territory underground with nothing more than a flashlight, a handgun and a knife. Facing all manner of booby traps along with armed men hidden in the dark recesses of their own tunnel systems, the tunnel rats earned enormous respect from their above-ground colleagues. Smaller men, often Hispanics, were used, often accompanied by 'Kit Carson Scouts': Vietcong who had defected to the Americans. They were used to negotiate with cornered VC and persuade them to surrender. Valuable intelligence was gained this way. Careful searches were made as the Vietcong's battle plans, along with other vital documents, were stored underground. The tunnel rats developed their own procedures. They never fired more than three shots without reloading, otherwise the enemy would know they were out of ammunition. They also whistled 'Dixie' when they emerged, as a mud-covered figure clambering out of a tunnel shaft might be mistaken for a VC. The tunnel rats had their own code of honour too. No dead tunnel rat was ever left underground and rats would often disobey direct orders to return underground and kill whoever had killed one of theirs. And they were not without a sense of irony: their unofficial motto was cod Latin for 'not worth a rat's ass'.

The year of 1966 saw the big build up in Vietnam, with 385,500 men in country by the end of the year. However, only 14 per cent of US servicemen deployed were front-line troops. The rest were concerned with administration, construction and logistics, much

'WE ARE DETERMINED TO WIN NOT ONLY MILITARY VICTORY OVER HUNGER, DISEASE AND DESPAIR"

of it dedicated to providing the men with everything from colour TVs to Napoleon brandy. By 1968, there were forty ice-cream plants in Vietnam and over 760,000 tons of supplies were being delivered every month. With American goods on sale in the PXs, American movies and stage shows, American music on the radio station Armed Forces Vietnam, American TV and chilled American beer, it was possible for rear-echelon troops who never left the base to imagine that they were still back home. This, General Westmoreland remarked, was 'one of the more remarkable accomplishments of American troops in Vietnam'.

President Johnson wanted to go further in the Americanization of Vietnam. A liberal

Democrat, Johnson had already begun his 'Great Society' reforms at home, an enormous programme of social welfare legislation that included his 'war against poverty', federal support for education, medical care for the aged through an expanded social security programme, and an extension of African-American civil rights which were still being restricted by state voter registration laws in the South. In February 1966, Johnson met Premier Ky in Hawaii and offered to extend his 'Great Society' to Vietnam, saying, 'We are determined to win not only military victory over hunger, disease and despair.'

But Ky was no liberal Democrat and he was losing support at home. When the mayor of Da Nang rebelled against the Saigon government, Ky sent in troops, and America was forced to look the other way while its ally Ky, a military dictator, butchered elected representatives who were exercising the right of free speech.

If that was not irony enough, the cost of the Vietnam War, both in monetary and political terms, killed Johnson's Great Society. After he left office, Johnson told his biographer Doris Kearns:

I knew from the start that I was bound to be crucified either way I moved. If I left the woman I really loved – the Great Society – in order to get involved with that bitch of a war on the other side of the world, then I would lose everything at home. All my programs. All my hopes to feed the hungry and shelter the homeless. All my dreams to provide education and medical care to the

President Johnson wrecked his political career over the war in Vietnam. A man of liberal convictions, he will always be remembered for dragging his country into the Vietnam debacle. Renowned as a master political wheeler-dealer, he could not understand how he could not cut a deal with the government in Hanoi.

A Republic of Vietnam officer interrogates a suspected Vietcong guerrilla in the presence of US Marines. He could expect little quarter.

browns and the blacks and the lame and the poor. But if I left that war and let the Communists take over South Vietnam, then I would be seen as a coward and my nation would be seen as an appeaser, and we would both find it impossible to accomplish anything for anybody anywhere on the entire globe.

With South Vietnam virtually in a state of civil war, Johnson realized that his ally could not be relied upon and the prosecution of the

68

war would have to be done by the Americans. All he could do was escalate the war. But even though B-52 strategic bombers dropped hundreds of tons of bombs on the Ho Chi Minh trail, Secretary of Defense Robert McNamara estimated that 4,500 men a month were being infiltrated into South Vietnam. B-52s bombed Hanoi and North Vietnam's principal port Haiphong, destroying up to 90 per cent of North Vietnam's oil reserves. But this only served to harden the Communist world's support for Hanoi, while turning allies, such as Britain and France, against US involvement. Civilian casualties mounted. After a visit to South Vietnam, US Representative Clement Zablocki claimed that five civilians died for every one Vietcong killed. The war also began to spill over into neighboring Laos and Cambodia. Westmoreland asked for more men. By the end of 1966, there were 400,000 US troops in Vietnam, but the Vietcong still seemed to be able to attack American bases, seemingly at will.

The American response grew more extreme. Armour was deployed, particularly the M113 Armored Personnel Carrier. These heavily armed 'battlefield taxis' which carried eleven troops, plus the driver, into battle at up to 40 miles an hour achieved some success in a series of battles along the Minh Thanh road in June and July 1966, when the 1st Infantry Division opened Route 13 from Loc Ninh to Saigon and blocked the VC's attempt to withdraw into Cambodia. On 9 July, ACAVS (Armored Cavalry Assault Vehicles) broke through the enemy's flanks and decimated elements of the 9th Vietcong Division, killing over 240 VC.

However, the M113 were vulnerable to anti-tank mines and the men would pack the floor with sandbags, flak jackets, empty ammunition boxes and even C-ration tins full of sand for protection. The VC and NVA were also armed with 57mm and 75mm recoilless rifles and RPG-2 rocket-propelled grenades, which turned the inside of the M113 into a blizzard of lacerating metal fragments. Grunts often found it safer to ride on the roof. The tactic devised by the 1st Squadron of the 4th Cavalry Regiment to avoid enemy fire was the 'herringbone defence'. The ACAVS would move forward in a criss-cross pattern, ending with guns pointing in all directions and giving overlapping fields of fire. Then they would unleash a 'mad minute', sixty seconds of fire from the M113's 0.5-inch machine-gun and two M60 general purpose machine-guns or M163 20mm Gatling guns whose armour-piercing ball and tracer was designed to flatten everything in sight.

Despite the 1st Air Cav's victory in the Ia Drang valley, fighting continued in the Central Highlands. Huge operations were mounted by US, ROK and ARVN troops, now under close US supervision, but no matter how many victories they won and no matter how high the body count – 2,389 enemy casualties claimed in Operation Masher/White Wing in Binh Dinh province alone – the moment the troops moved on the area was reoccupied by the Vietcong and the NVA, who were turning up in the South in increasing numbers.

4

THE GROWING COMMITMENT

IN THE highlands, the Green Berets still worked with Khmer, Mnong, Montagnard and other tribesmen who were ethnically different from the Vietnamese and persecuted by both Communist and anti-Communist Vietnamese alike. They were organized into Civilian Irregular Defense Groups (CIDGS). The cidgees often brought their families into Special Forces camps for such protection as these afforded them. However, these remote camps strung along the border with Cambodia and Laos came under increasing pressure from the Communist forces. Once more the US forces adopted a sledgehammer approach to defending their forward bases in the shape of 'Puff the Magic Dragon'. These were AC-47s – armed C-47 Dakota transport planes – named for the song by the folk trio Peter, Paul and Mary, to the singers' great annoyance. They carried three six-barrelled Gatling guns, each capable of delivering 6,000 rounds a minute, along the port side. The Magic Dragons would drop a flare to illuminate the target, then circle, sometimes in pairs, raining down bullets on the enemy and forcing even the toughest NVA formations to withdraw. 'Spooky', the 4th Air Commando Squadron who flew them, sometimes also worked with PSYWAR C-47s of the 5th Air Commando Squadron. These 'Bullshit Bombers' carried huge speakers that blasted the jungles with appeals from the South Vietnamese government urging the VC to defect. This was not ineffective: by 1967,

US Secretary of Defense Robert McNamara is briefed by General Westmoreland in Vietnam on 10 October 1966.

75,000 guerrillas had come over to the government side on the promise of money, better food and conditions, and a chance to see their family and friends.

Even so, the US forces were amazed at how much punishment VC units could take without cracking, the more so as many were drafted at gunpoint. This did not necessarily make them any worse fighters than other conscript armies. After all, most of the Americans and Australians fighting in Vietnam were draftees. But the Vietcong had unique methods of dealing with the problems handling the hardships of their plight and homesickness among recruits, many of whom had not been outside their village before. Each recruit joined a three-man cell, which included at least one veteran. They would stick together through thick and thin as long as they survived, so they formed the strongest of ties. In turn, these three-man cells were attached to three-cell squads, which made up three-squad platoons. Few were Communists or had any knowledge of Marxism. Nothing was done to remedy this. Propaganda lectures concentrated on Vietnam's historic struggle to oust foreign invaders – first the Chinese, then the Japanese, then the French. The war against the South Vietnamese government and the US was portrayed as a continuation of the French anti-colonial war with the US in the role of a neocolonial power. Occasionally, when morale was low or a unit was doing particularly badly, a political officer would organize a session of self-criticism. But these attempts to shame men into greater effort were far more humane than the hard physical

punishments other armies use. The factor most on the side of the Vietcong was that they were peasant farmers, used to backbreaking toil, deprivation, and hardship. Few saw their families again, and for most a terrible death awaited. They were gassed like vermin in their tunnels, buried alive by artillery strikes, incinerated by napalm, or blown into unidentifiable hamburger by bombs. But what the Vietcong and NVA feared most was the B-52 strikes. They called them the 'whispering death' because the first they knew of the presence of the bombers high above the jungle

FEW WERE COMMUNISTS OR HAD ANY KNOWLEDGE OF MARXISM. NOTHING WAS DONE TO REMEDY THIS

canopy and the clouds was the whistling of their bomb. Aerial bombardments could go on for days or weeks at a time. Even the most battle-hardened veterans lost control of their bodily functions, soiling their pants and shaking uncontrollably. Some went mad and no one who survived could ever be cured of the abject terror a B-52 strike inspired. A B-52 mission could drop up to 54,000 pounds of bombs on a single target.

By 1966, B-52s began to strike against the Ho Chi Minh trail. The North Vietnamese had instituted a series of control points every three miles, where trucks could be hidden from US reconnaissance planes. As the Ho Chi Minh trail ran for most of its length outside

Vietnam and US rules of engagement required that American planes only attack vehicles actually moving down the trail, bringing them in low and making them easy targets for the Communists' anti-aircraft defences, high-level carpet bombing was thought to be the answer. Tran Thi Truyen, a sixteen-year-old nurse who served in a field hospital in southern Laos, recalled how intense American bombing denuded the jungle and there was no place to hide. During her month-long march down the trail, she carried a rifle, a sixty-pound knapsack and a shovel. When American planes came overhead, her group would disperse and dig foxholes. After the bombing had stopped, she said she could not focus her eyes and her head ached for hours. Wounded Vietnamese soldiers were brought up the trail for her to treat in her underground hospital. Most were so badly wounded, nothing could be done for them. Eventually Tran contracted malaria and was sent back to the North.

The bombing did little to halt the Communist war effort. While a B-52 could unleash over a hundred 750-pound bombs in thirty seconds, cutting a huge swathe through the jungle, it was estimated that this huge firepower only killed one infiltrator for every 300 bombs dropped, while the casualty rate due to disease was 10 per cent. With nearly six million tons of aid arriving in North Vietnam from the Soviet Union and China every day, only a tiny fraction had to find its way down the trail to maintain the war effort. The annual North Vietnamese infiltration soared from 10,000 in 1964, to 35,000 in 1965, to 90,000 in 1966, to 150,000 in 1967. Most of the North Vietnamese who died on the journey were killed by malaria, dysentery and other diseases, rather than US bombing. However, in 1966, the B-52 strikes along the Ho Chi Minh trail persuaded the North Vietnamese that it was safer to infiltrate their men across the DMZ. They took advantage of the rebellion in Da Nang, Hué, and other northern cities that lasted from March to June 1966 to attempt an invasion of Quang Tri, the northernmost province of South Vietnam. Civil disorder in the area hampered the Marine operations and the Green Berets were forced to abandon several Special Forces camps along the Lao border and in the A Shau Valley. Nightly reconnaissance flights had been keeping an eye on the DMZ with infra-red cameras since the Marines landed in Da Nang in 1965. At first, when each night's film was developed at Dong Ha air base, it came out completely black, showing empty jungle. Then in early May 1966, a number of white specks showed up. These were camp fires. Within days, the film was a mass of white dots and the jungles below were swarming with NVA. The Marines had already established a firebase on the 'Rockpile', a 750-foot jagged fang of granite that stood at the intersection of three river valleys and two infiltration trails. But to hold it they would also have to take nearby Hills 400 and 484, two other granite outcrops infested with NVA bunkers. K Company of the 3rd Battalion of the 4th Marine Regiment were tasked to take the first objective, Hill 400. They headed out at 0930hrs on 27 September 1966.

When one of K Company's veterans saw

Opposite: The craters made by bombs dropped from Royal Laotian Air Force planes along the Ho Chi Minh trail in south-eastern Laos. The bombing was an attempt to reduce the infiltration of North Vietnamese soldiers and guns through Laos into South Vietnam. It failed. What began the war as a jungle track that forded rivers ended it as a paved highway.

Operation Prairie –
Fire team members
of F Company, 2nd
Battalion, 5th
Regiment, wade
through a stream
roofed over by dense
jungle about 430 yards
south of the DM in
October 1966.

the objective, he complained, 'Mountains like Korea, jungles like Guadalcanal. The only thing missing is snow.'

As they made their way along the ridgeline, they came across a human skull placed on the side of the trail. Under it was a note in flawed English which read, 'We come back kill Marines.'

Soon afterwards, the man on point – the advance guard of the group – tripped over a bamboo pole that triggered a claymore mine and several hand grenades. In the confusion, the Marines were raked with machine-gun fire and hit with mortars.

'I got a feeling they don't like us,' said one Marine during a lull.

'Personality conflict,' was his buddy's laconic reply. Captain James 'Jay Jay' Carroll

76

called in an air strike. Soon after, two Phantom fighter-bombers came roaring over at tree-top level, dropping 500-pound high-explosive bombs and napalm 200 yards ahead of the Marines' position. A second strike came in at 90 yards. But the NVA were already familiar with the American tactics. Knowing that US ground forces always directed artillery and air strikes on enemy positions, they moved in close, into what was known as the 'safety zone,' as soon as the planes turned up. Although the Phantoms pounded the area for

30 minutes, as soon as the Marines tried to move out they were cut down by the crossfire from automatic weapons.

After two hours, the NVA broke off contact, though they left a couple of snipers to keep the Marines busy. A quick head count told Carroll that he had seven dead and twenty-five wounded. The problem was that, at their altitude, the air was too thin for medevac choppers to hover as they winched up the wounded. K Company had to retreat down the trail towards their battalion head-

Ronald W. Johnson of C Company, 2nd Battalion, 1st Cavalry Division, Airmobile, stays on guard as troops take a short rest during Operation Masher near Bong Son in January 1966. The name was changed to Operation White Wing at the insistence of the President. Some 2,389 Vietcong casualties were reported.

quarters, where an LZ was being blasted out of the rock. On the way, they were ambushed from positions that the NVA had dug in the hillside. Pinned down 400 yards from their headquarters without food or water, Carroll and his men dug in for the night.

In the morning, the NVA began lobbing mortars at the Marines from fortified bunkers. Artillery fire and air strikes appeared to pulverize the NVA positions, but did not shift them. A frontal assault by K Company faltered until they were reinforced by I and M Companies. While satchel bombs were being used to clear the bunkers, the NVA regrouped and launched a savage counter-attack in the rear, cutting off their supply of ammunition. But further air strikes coming in every thirty seconds and helicopter gunships won the day. The Marines claimed an NVA body count of fifty for the loss of a further six American dead and nine wounded.

When the wounded had been medevacked out, the skies opened and the hillsides turned into a sea of mud. In these conditions, on 4 October, M Company led an assault on Hill 484, 500 yards to the north. They struggled up the waterlogged slope, being fired on by the NVA who were concealed in well-hidden bunkers, and finally had to pull back. Throughout the night, Hill 484 was bombed and shelled. But when the advance on Hill 484 began again the following day, it took two hours to reach the crest and still the NVA would not retreat. Only at 1330 did they turn and flee into the jungle, leaving just ten dead, though trails of blood indicated they had many wounded. During the engagement,

Captain Carroll had been killed when a salvo of shells from Marine tanks mistakenly hit Hill 400. The artillery platform there was named Camp Carroll in his honour. He had been in country less than a month. The hills became known as 'Mutter's Ridge' after the 3rd Battalion's call sign, in honour of the men who had died there. The Marines had won another costly victory, but with all their fire-power, the enemy had still got away.

But the DMZ and the Ho Chi Minh trail were not the only infiltration routes. Although the ARVN always denied that supplies were reaching the Vietcong by sea, the Americans discovered that sampans and larger fishing vessels were bringing arms and ammunition from North Vietnam to the VC stronghold in the Mekong Delta, south of Saigon. This was not entirely the ARVN's fault. From November to February South Vietnam's thousand-mile South China Sea coast was buffeted by the northeast monsoon, and from May through to October, the 200 miles of coast along the Gulf of Thailand was hit by the southwest monsoon, so it was hard to intercept shipping. However, the ARVN did not relish the firefights that ensued when they stopped the gun runners and did not dare venture into Vung Ro Bay where the guns were landed as it was Charlie country. If patrol boats did come across a fisherman smuggling a few guns or mortars under the fish in their hold, it was easier to take a bribe.

When the Pacific Fleet arrived in the South China Sea it did not have the right ships to stage a naval blockade, but by 1966, they had deployed nearly 100 fast patrol boats and some 500 armed junks, backed by thirty US Coast Guard cutters. Directed by reconnaissance planes flying from Tan Son Nhut air base in Saigon or the Philippines, these boats were equipped with metal detectors to make searching under the heaps of stinking fish in the hold more palatable, though it was still a job that was best carried out on an empty stomach. It was not without its dangers. On the night of 14 February 1966, a cutter made a high-speed interception of a sampan that was within a hundred yards of a VC stronghold when a huge explosion suddenly tore through its aluminum hull, sinking the boat and killing four of its crew.

The US Mobile Riverine Force, or Brown Water Navy, carried soldiers, helicopters, artillery, defoliants and flame-throwers up the Mekong Delta, though they did little more than clear the banks of VC. However, on 25 October 1966, anti-shipping operations off the coast of North Vietnam intensified and US destroyers started a gunnery duel with shore batteries. Over the next four weeks, 230 Communist vessels were sunk and 35 junks were sunk in the Mekong Delta. Even a Chinese fishing fleet was hit in international waters by mistake, sinking five boats and killing fourteen sailors. Later the USS *Ingersoll* was damaged by fire from a shore battery. Eventually the Navy closed down large-scale sea-borne infiltration which simply meant that the VC extended the Ho Chi Minh trail down through Cambodia so that supplies

Members of the Army-Navy Mobile Riverine Force prepare a 105mm howitzer from the 2nd Brigade, 9th Infantry Division for a fire mission along the Mekong River in 1968. Even though the 'Brown Water Navy' operated there throughout the war, the Mekong Delta remained a Communist stronghold.

could be brought directly into their stronghold from the north.

In late August 1966 the 196th Light Infantry Brigade arrived in Vietnam and set up camp near Tay Ninh City, north of Saigon. In October, they began operations in this crucial area between the South Vietnamese capital city and the Communist sanctuaries over the Cambodian border just 30 miles away. American troops had not been in action in this area before, though it was known to be home to the formidable VC 9th Division. A single untried boot battalion headed out into the boondocks. Soon their rifle companies hit pay dirt. Between 29 and 31 October, they unearthed supply depots containing more than 25 tons of salt and 1,000 tons of rice. They also found a VC field hospital, ammunition caches, tunnel complexes, and, more importantly, documents that showed that other VC and NVA formations were in the area. Operation Attleboro, named after Attleboro, Massachusetts near Fort Devens, birthplace of the 196th, was immediately instigated to search out the enemy. Brigadier General E. H. deSaussure was ordered to commit all three

battalions to the operation. He also sent for an infantry division from the 25th Division and more reinforcements from the 27th. This was to be the first multi-battalioned operation of the war.

When C Company of the 1st Battalion of the 27th Infantry ventured deep into the jungle, they were attacked by the VC. A battalion of the 196th went in on 3 November to help them. B Company hit the LZ at 0922 and reported it cold – no enemy contact – and began to spread out. The helicopters went back to pick up C Company, but when they hit the LZ again at 1029 all hell broke loose. Heavy automatic fire from the tree line wounded six and C Company found themselves trapped under the hot sun in open ground. Within half an hour six more were dead and still more wounded. Twenty minutes later the count was up to ten KIA (killed in action) and fourteen WIA (wounded in action). C Company's commander was wasted and the battalion commander Major Guy S. Meloy flew in to take charge. He was followed by A Company, whose PFC Thomas Conners managed to keep the VC back with his M60

A US Strike Patrol Boat (STAB) on high-speed river patrol near the Cambodian border, Mekong River, in June 1970. When such operations were successful, they simply forced the Vietnamese guerrillas to retreat into Cambodia, destabilizing that country.

machine-gun, known to those in Vietnam as the 'pig'. The remains of the battalion fell back into a tight perimeter for the night and it was only the occasional burst from Conners' M60 that kept them alive.

Two klicks (kilometres, or 1¼ miles) to the south, Lieutenant-Colonel Charles E. Weddle's battalion received orders to speed up their push northwards to relieve Meloy. To make better time, instead of hacking their way through the virgin jungle, Lieutenant Perkin's platoon took to the jungle trails. This was a bad move. They were bunched up when a Chinese claymore mine went off. Thousands of steel shards cut through Perkins and twenty-four of his men. Soon the entire battalion was pinned down in the searing afternoon heat and rapidly dehydrating. The following day a battalion of the 25th tried to get through to Meloy, but found themselves cut off by the VC who were well dug in.

Weddle's C Company under Captain James P. Thompson made another attempt to break through that night but, in the darkness, ran into elements of the 273rd NVA in the darkness. They too found themselves pinned down by murderous fire and surrounded, just 150 yards from Meloy's men. The following morning, Meloy's main force resisted three mass attacks on their position by the NVA in as many hours. Meanwhile the remaining battalions of the 196th fought their way towards the stranded men. The lead platoon ran up against a VC machine-gun bunker, while six VC poured semi-automatic fire against its flanks. Their M60 gunner got caught up in vines and was unable to help. Platoon leader Sergeant Lester

SOON THE ENTIRE BATTALION WAS PINNED DOWN IN THE SEARING AFTERNOON HEAT AND RAPIDLY DEHYDRATING

Armstrong seized the M60 and killed the six VC, while PFC Conners managed to hold off repeated VC attacks with his M60, though he was injured in the shoulder and the spine.

Eventually, air strikes and artillery drove the VC and NVA away and the supply and medevac helicopters swooped in. On 6 November, conduct of the battle was handed over to the 1st Infantry Division under Major-General William E. DePuy and the 196th were withdrawn. DeSaussure was relieved of duty, but the next time the men of the 196th went into action they would no longer be cherries. Over the next two weeks, more than 22,000 US and ARVN troops joined in the battle in Tay Ninh province. US forces lost 155 dead and over 800 wounded, but claimed a VC body count of 1,106. However, the enemy melted away again, with the VC 9th Division escaping over the Cambodian border.

'We hit more dry holes than I thought we were going to hit,' said General DePuy. 'They were more elusive. They controlled the battle better. They were the ones who decided whether there would be a fight.'

Once again, the VC lived to fight again another day. Nevertheless the body count pleased Westmoreland.

'We'll just go on bleeding them until Hanoi wakes up to the fact that they have bled their

country to the point of national disaster for generations,' he said.

Unfortunately, the body counts were wrong. As the Communist forces dragged their dead from the battlefield when they could, the body counts were estimates – inflated estimates, often bumped up by the inclusion of civilian dead. But in 1967, the idea that US forces were taking on and killing large formations of the enemy persuaded Westmoreland to change strategy. Until then, US troops had concentrated on searching out and destroying the enemy while the ARVN policed the pacified areas. The problem was that the South Vietnamese forces were not much good at their job. When the Americans had cleared an area, the VC rapidly reoccupied it. Even though there were 380,000 Americans in Vietnam by the end of 1967, they still had too few troops to conduct both offensive operations and holding operations simultaneously. So they took more drastic action. They would clear vast tracts of the countryside to make 'free-fire zones'.

In January 1967, US forces went into the Iron Triangle, the Communist stronghold just forty miles from Saigon. Their first objective was the village of Ben Suc which, like other villages in outlying districts, supplied and paid taxes to the Vietcong. Loud hailers mounted on helicopters announced in Vietnamese, 'Attention people of Ben Suc. You are surrounded by the Republic of Vietnam and

Operation Billings – Infantry from B Company, 1st Battalion, 16th Infantry, 1st Infantry Division disembark from a helicopter during an air assault at Rufe in June 1967. The bodycount claimed was 347 VC.

Allied forces. Do not run away or you will be shot as VC. Stay in your homes and wait for further instructions.'

Within two hours the 6,000 inhabitants of Ben Suc and neighbouring hamlets were rounded up, while the surrounding jungle was bombed and napalmed. The people were ruthlessly interrogated in the schoolhouse and 28 VC suspects were taken away. Then all the men between 15 and 45 were separated out, and taken to police headquarters for further interrogation. Those without Communist affiliations were inducted into the South Vietnamese army. The women, children and old men were put on trucks and taken to a hastily erected camp at Phu Loi. Above its entranceway hung a sign that read, 'Welcome to the reception center for refugees fleeing Communism.' The camp had no proper toilets or water supply, or even an adequate supply of firewood. Villagers were allocated a cramped living space of just ten foot square per family. They would never see their homes again.

Once the last villagers had left Ben Suc, the buildings were doused with petrol and zippoed. The charred remains were then flattened by M48 'tankdozers'. A trench was then dug in the town's centre and filled with a thousand gallons of napalm and 10,000 tons of explosive and the whole lot was detonated with a chemical fuse. The centuries-long history of Ben Suc ended that day. Meanwhile huge bulldozers flattened the surrounding area. The idea was to rob the Vietcong of the

Members of the 503rd Airborne Infantry Division guard Vietcong prisoners during Operation Cedar Falls in January 1967.

tree cover that sheltered them from American bombers. In this free-fire zone, anything that moved could be bombed or shot. Infantry, airborne troops and armoured cavalry then swept through the area in an hammer-and-anvil operation, killing anyone who remained behind, on the grounds that, as the civilians had been removed, anyone still in the area must be VC or NVA. Although this operation – Operation Cedar Falls – was planned in such secrecy that even the commanding general of the ARVN in III CTZ did not know about it until two days beforehand, the Communists knew exactly what was happening and pulled their forces out. The American search and destroy operation found no one.

However the 242nd Chemical Detachment of the 1st Infantry, the tunnel rats, had more luck. The bulldozing of the forest exposed the entrances to the tunnels. They crawled through nearly twelve miles of tunnels during the operation, capturing over 7,500 uniforms, 60,000 rounds of small-arms ammunition, and 3,700 tons of rice – enough to feed an army of thirteen thousand VC for a year. They also came across a huge cache of documents: plans for terrorist assaults, lists of sympathizers, and detailed maps of Saigon and Tan Son Nhut air base. Once these were removed, the tunnel complex was filled with CS gas, packed with explosives and blown up.

When Operation Cedar Falls was officially terminated after three weeks, the Iron Triangle was, in the words of Lieutenant-General Jonathan Seaman, 'a military desert'. Over 2,700 acres of jungle had been cleared. Five hundred tunnels and 1,100 bunkers had

been destroyed and the 'body count' was 750 – at a cost of seventy-two American lives. In the official US Army report on Operation Cedar Falls, Lieutenant-General Bernard Rogers concluded that 'a strategic enemy enclave had been decisively destroyed'.

But even the tunnel rats had underestimated the extent of the tunnel complex. Below the burnt ruins of Ben Suc 1,700 metres of the tunnel network remained intact, as Rogers himself observed. 'It was not long before there was evidence of the enemy's return,' he said. 'Only two days after the termination of Cedar Falls, I was checking out the Iron Triangle by helicopter and saw many persons who appeared to be Vietcong riding bicycles or wandering around on foot.'

The vegetation quickly grew back. The VC restored their old bunkers and rebuilt their lifeline to Cambodia. By the following year the Iron Triangle was once again a deadly stronghold and the launch pad for the Tet Offensive in Saigon.

In February 1967, the US staged another large-scale operation – once again the largest to date – in Tay Ninh province. The object was to capture the Central Office of South Vietnam (COSVN). This was the name the US forces gave to the military leadership in the South. Strategists envisaged it as a mini-Pentagon, a slimmed-down version of the US military headquarters in Arlington, Virginia, across the Potomac from Washington, DC. In Operation Junction City, Westmoreland was determined that the Communists would not be able to escape. First B-52s went in to knock out the VC .50-calibre anti-aircraft guns. Then the 503d

Airborne made the first and only parachute assault in Vietnam. They were followed by 249 helicopters that deployed the equivalent of eight battalions to close the north end of the giant inverted horseshoe. Again, a hammer-and-anvil strategy would be employed, but this time the anvil would be armour. This resulted in ferocious counter-attacks by the VC, which even intense bombing, artillery support and gunships could not suppress. Some 3,235 tons of bombs and 366,000 artillery rounds were expended during Junction City. Even with the inflated body counts, this worked out at several tons of ordinance for each VC killed.

Junction City unearthed what was assumed to be COSVN's public affairs office, complete with 120 reels of movie footage and the printing presses of the propaganda and indoctrination sections. However, COSVN itself proved more elusive. It seemed to flit from village to village, eluding the American net and escaping into Cambodia. A subsequent incursion into Cambodia did not locate it there either. Some began to believe that COSVN did not exist at all or, if it did, it was merely some faceless coordinating office in Hanoi.

More free-fire zones were created. In June 1967, the 8,465 inhabitants of the Song Ve valley were told that they would have to leave the villages that their families had inhabited for centuries. They were moved out with their 1,149 animals while their crops were burned. That year, 12,750 were cleared in the 'Hamlet Evacuation System'. In Binh Dinh Province, the 1st Cavalry Division (Airmobile) moved 129,202 from Binh Dinh province into 85 refugee camps, though an undetermined number ended up squatting along Route 1. Again US troops swept through the area uninhibited by the possibility of that the people they were killing might be civilians. Operations Pershing and Thayer II clocked up a body count of 1,757, though this was only achieved by the expenditure of 5,105 rounds of naval gunfire, 139,769 artillery rounds, and 171 B-52 sorties. Some 3,078 bombs were dropped containing 2.5 million pounds of high explosives, 500,000 pounds of napalm and 35,000 pounds of CS gas.

This so-called 'Pacification Program' also

TO ADD INSULT TO INJURY, THE VILLAGERS WERE SUPPOSED TO BUILD THE DEFENCES OF THEIR NEW HAMLETS WITHOUT PAYMENT

aimed to move the civilians out from areas where the local population either supported or were intimidated by the guerrillas. Destroying crops was meant to deny supplies to the Vietcong. It also meant that the inhabitants that had been moved out could not return. The villagers were given food and medical attention but, to add insult to injury, the villagers were supposed to build the defences of their new 'defended' hamlets without payment. The move was particularly traumatic for the ancestor-worshipping Vietnamese who had to leave behind their graveyards and ancestral fields. The social institutions that flourished in the villages were destroyed and the villagers became resentful and uncooperative. This was

A gunner fires into the jungle from a helicopter. The killing became indiscriminate as disillusioned airmen rained down gunfire on innocent peasants and livestock.

no way to win their hearts and minds – which was the official policy. This mattered little to cynical GIS who remarked in words later attributed to Richard Nixon, 'If you've got them by the balls, their hearts and minds soon follow.'

Robert Komer, director of Civil Operations and Revolutionary Development Support, reckoned that 60 per cent of the countryside was under VC control. Indeed, an estimated 36,752 village officials and South

Vietnamese civil servants were summarily executed by the Vietcong between 1957 and 1972. To counter this, Komer recommended setting up the Phoenix Program, a joint MACV-CIA operation to identify the estimated 70,000 members of the Vietcong infrastructure. Under the programme 17,000 VC sought amnesty and 28,000 were captured. In 1971, 20,000 had been killed, but the number increased sharply after that. Former CIA operative Frank Snepp said that, once the prisons were full, suspects were simply murdered by hit squads. There have been allegations that the Saigon government used the programme to eliminate political enemies. It has also been alleged that the Phoenix Program built up a profile of those likely to join the Vietcong – students, dispossessed peasants, those with VC in the family – and they were sought out and shot. William Colby, who took over the programme from Komer and later became director of the CIA, ordered that, 'If any American sees anyone being assassinated he's to object and he is to report it to me.' But this did little to stop the abuses. The problem was that the information gleaned on suspects came from unreliable sources: paid informants, victims of torture, and those trying to ingratiate themselves in the government. In the end it became an unchecked hit list.

The indiscriminate use of US firepower drove more peasant farmers off the land. At any one time there were at least 1.2 million refugees within South Vietnam. This peaked at around 3.5 million. Refugees swelled the population of the cities where corruption was rife and broke down the social cohesion that was the best defence against Communist insurgence. Although some men were inducted into the Regional and Provincial Forces, the 'Ruff-Puffs', which formed Combined Action Platoons with the US Marines, the refugee population remained a fertile recruiting ground for the Vietcong.

Even though it took a massive expenditure of ordinance for each VC killed, the US forces kept upping their firepower. They built fire-bases on the tops of hills, which puzzled the Vietnamese who assumed they were looking for gold. These firebases could rain down shells on the surrounding area. Artillery support could be devastatingly effective when the position of the enemy was known and relayed to the gunnery officers accurately. But the VC and NVA often melted away while this was being done or corrections were being made. If the Communists found themselves in real trouble, they would move in on the US positions so it was impossible to hit them without hitting US troops too. Artillery barrages were called in at the slightest excuse and caused tremendous damage. Shells could not discriminate between insurgents and friendly locals, who suffered a lot of 'collateral

THEY BUILT FIREBASES ON THE TOPS OF HILLS, WHICH PUZZLED THE VIETNAMESE WHO ASSUMED THEY WERE LOOKING FOR GOLD

damage'. And US forces have traditionally had a problem with 'friendly fire', killing their own troops and those of their allies rather than the enemy's.

On 7 September 1967, Secretary of Defense Robert McNamara announced that a huge fortified barrier sixty miles long was to be built two miles south of the DMZ in an attempt to stop Communist infiltration. It would be called the McNamara Line. A cratered area 700 yards wide, called the Trace, had already been bombed flat in preparation.

This ran along the northern edge of 'Leatherneck Square', the area that the Marines had been told to hold against NVA infiltration from the North. Beyond it the Green Berets and the cidgees had tried to hold a line, but their camps had been overrun. These were retaken by the Marines, who began stringing barbed wire, creosoting bunker timbers and filling sandbags to fortify these forward bases.

The NVA decided to smash the McNamara Line before it even got started. They attacked at the forward base at Con Thien, which was fourteen miles inland and two miles south of the DMZ at the northwest corner of Leatherneck Square. It overlooked one of the NVA major infiltration routes. If they could take it, the NVA would overlook the major US logistics depot at Dong Ha and the way would be open for Quang Tri province to be overrun by the 35,000 NVA troops massing to the north of the DMZ.

Although the DMZ was supposed to be inviolable, neither side respected its demilitarized status. The NVA infiltrated directly across it, and in July 1966, the US Joint Chiefs of Staff authorized the bombardment of the DMZ and limited incursions, provided that no public disclosures were made. It was feared that occupying the DMZ – or indeed, any part of North Vietnam or Laos – would invite the Chinese to intervene as they had done in the Korean War. From December 1966, it was permitted to return fire across the DMZ. Pre-emptive fire, including air strikes, was allowed from February 1967. Then in May, a sweep by the Marines and ARVN through the southern part of the DMZ, up to the Ben Hai river, cleared 13,000 people from the area to permit the unrestricted bombing of NVA positions.

On 2 July two companies of Marines were sweeping around to the north of the Trace, well outside the DMZ, when A Company tripped two claymore mines, taking heavy casualties. B Company then came under heavy mortar fire, forcing them out into the open where they were hit with artillery and flame-throwers. The NVA swarmed forward to finish them off but were repelled by air attacks using napalm. The Communist artillery bombardment continued, though. Two of the tanks carrying dead Marines off the battlefield were damaged by mines. The LZ where the wounded were being mustered was hit by artillery and mortars, adding stretcher bearers and medics to the casualty list, and fifty of the wounded had to walk back to Con Thien. Meanwhile three more companies were committed to the action, only to be forced back to Con Thien at nightfall. Only twenty-seven of B Company walked out of the action.

Con Thien then found itself under siege. Enemy mortars zeroed in on the LZs and the relief companies had to go without water for thirty-six hours. Three thousand NVA troops surrounded the firebases, but air strikes and artillery kept them at bay. More NVA troops engaged the Marines to the south of Con Thien and a huge force was spotted crossing the Ben Hai river. Marine positions to the east of Con Thien were hit by 1,500 rounds of artillery fire. The NVA 90th Regiment made costly 'human wave' attacks in an attempt to overrun their positions. Communist soldiers climbed over heaps of their own dead to get close enough to hurl grenades and fused blocks of TNT. An NVA bunker to the southwest of Con Thien was cleared, which cut NVA activity to harassing fire and the planting of mines. By this time 159 Marines were dead and 345 wounded. The NVA body count stood at 1,290, though their bodies were so badly mutilated that their casualties had to be estimated from the number of water bottles that

A wounded Vietcong soldier awaits evacuation at Nam O Village.

were left on the battlefield.

The NVA then began lobbing shells over the DMZ using 152mm howitzers, which outranged any field artillery the Marines had. The tiny firebase of Con Thien perched on top of the Hill of Angels was only big enough to accommodate one reinforcement battalion. It took at least 200 rounds incoming a day during September: on 25 September alone, it took 1,200 rounds. Under this bombardment, the NVA made repeated attacks in force. On 4 September, Marines just a mile south of Con Thien had to be relieved by tanks. A similar action on 7 September left 14 Marines dead. The NVA 812th Regiment, reportedly wearing USMC helmets and flak jackets, swept around to the southwest on 10 September, knocking out a Marine flame tank and a gun tank with rocket-propelled grenades. Thirty-four Marines were killed and 192 were wounded.

The NVA moved against Con Thien itself on 13 September, but were driven back. Anticipating another attack, two more Marine battalions were moved up. For seven days, they suffered a furious pounding with mortars and artillery. When they finally went on the attack, they ran straight into the 90th NVA regiment and called in tanks, but the previous 96 hours of rain meant that the tanks could not reach them. Eventually the weather became so bad that the battle for Con Thien became an artillery battle. From 19 to 27 September, more than 3,000 mortar and artillery rounds hit the hill fort. The American response was one

of the greatest concentrations of firepower in support of a single division in the history of warfare. US field units fired 12,577 rounds at enemy positions, with the 7th Fleet contributing 6,148 more. Eventually, NVA activity eased off, but the Marines continued to find new bunkers and trench complexes around the perimeter. The enemy barrage did

A CH-47 Chinook helicopter brings in a sling-load of artillery shells to the landing zone 12 miles north of Tuy Hoa, during Operation Bolling, a search and destroy mission in Phu Yen province on 17–18 September 1967. The bodycount was 705, while 2,488 suspects were rounded up. Between them they had 237 weapons.

not cease and the Marines began to call the Hill of Angels 'the meatgrinder'.

With Con Thien more or less in American hands, the construction of the McNamara Line went ahead. Building a defensive barrier along the DMZ had been the idea of Robert Fischer at the Havard Law School. He had sent a memo outlining the concept to McNamara. General Westmoreland dismissed it. He disliked the idea of static defence on principle, as did Admiral Ulysses Grant Sharp Jr, commander of the Pacific Fleet, who did not like the plan either. But McNamara called together a group of top academic scientists known as the Jasons, after Jason and the Argonauts, who also took a mythological trip into uncharted territory, to assess its feasibility. They met in the summer of 1966 in the cloistered atmosphere of Dana Hall, a secluded prep school for girls in Wellesley, Massachusetts. The initial suggestion was a line 160 miles long and ten miles wide made of stretches of barbed wire and studded with mines, chemical weapons, and sensor devices, interspersed with huge free-fire zones that had been denuded of forest cover.

The Jasons figured that a sixty-mile long fence could be built within a year. It would be protected by 'gravel mines', three inches square, that would explode when they were stepped on or run over by a truck. Smaller 'button mines' the size of an aspirin would blow off a finger or a toe. Any explosion would be picked up by acoustic sensors, which would be monitored by patrol aircraft flying overhead that would drop cluster bombs containing baseball-sized bomblets. The

REPORTS ARE FULL OF INCIDENTS WHERE AIR STRIKES WERE CALLED DOWN ON HAPLESS WATERBUFFALO

Jasons reckoned that 240 million gravel mines, 300 million button mines, and 120,000 cluster bombs a year would be needed. The cost: $1 billion.

Unfortunately, no mines could be found that could tell the difference between a human being and a wild animal: Vietnam engagement reports are full of incidents where air strikes were called down on some hapless water-buffalo. But the boffins were not discouraged. They experimented with bed bugs which were known to be inactive until a human body came into the vicinity and they began to move excitedly at the prospect of a meal. Electrodes that would detect movement were to be glued to the backs of bed bugs. It is said that these wired-up bed bugs were actually spread over the DMZ, but either the bugs did not take to the jungle or the glue melted.

The Jasons also came up with the idea for a pigeon-borne bomb that would explode when it landed on an enemy truck, though no one had figured out how to train a pigeon to tell the difference between a Communist and a non-Communist truck. Then there was the sensor disguised as a pile of dog excrement, known as Turdsid. But this was quickly dropped after an Air Cav commander pointed out that, while a bear might shit in the woods, there was no evidence of dogs doing so in the jungles of Southeast Asia. Even Q, of James

Bond fame, would have balked and the idea was quickly dropped.

However, some ideas did work. The 'Daisy Cutter', a massive bomb that cuts a swathe of destruction across a wide area and was recently used in Afghanistan, was developed in Vietnam. Some of the acoustic monitors worked, too. In 1970, a recording from one of the devices was played for a Congressional Sub-Committee. Representatives heard a conversation in Vietnamese, followed by the sound of axes chopping down the tree on which the device had been snagged. Then there was a crash, followed by screams as the tree fell on the men below. But the McNamara Line as a whole did not work. It proved impossible to construct it properly under the mortar and artillery barrages of the NVA, and increased activity in the DMZ meant that Communist supply lines simply reverted to the Ho Chi Minh trail which ran through Laos, around the end of the McNamara Line. In 1968, when the Marine base at Khe Sanh just south of the McNamara Line came under siege, the idea was finally discredited.

At Dak To in the Central Highlands, as at Con Thien, the fighting took on many of the characteristics of World War I. Battle raged over the muddy ridge of Hill 875 near the Lao-Cambodian border. On 19 November 1967, the 2nd Battalion of the 503rd Infantry of the 173rd Airborne Brigade headed up the western slope to annihilation. Of their sixteen officers, eight were killed. The other eight were wounded. And of the battalion's thirteen medics, eleven were killed. The wounded huddled under a tree that had been blasted to the ground for more than fifty hours. Bloody ponchos kept the night chill off. Ten helicopters that attempted to medevac them out were disabled by enemy fire. Some drew comfort that at least an effort was being made to get them out. Others died when a 500-pound bomb intended for an NVA bunker hit their position. Forty-two died in that incident. More of the wounded perished from shock, dehydration or just plain giving up.

When the 4th Battalion turned up to relieve them, they found a moonscape scattered with dead bodies. The following morning, the NVA began pounding them with 82mm mortars, often hitting men who had already been wounded. All the grunts could do was scuttle for cover when they heard the plop of a mortar dropping down the tube and dig their foxholes a bit deeper. But as the day wore on, foxhole after foxhole got hit. A platoon under First Lieutenant Bryan MacDonough from Fort Lee, Virginia, started with twenty-seven men on Sunday and was down to nine by midday on Tuesday. The NVA kept on coming, whatever casualties they took. Seven-hundred-and-fifty-pound bombs and napalm did nothing to deter them.

By the afternoon of 22 November, a new LZ had been blasted in the hillside further down the slope. NVA mortars tried to hit it but, by the evening, 140 wounded had been medevacked out. At dusk, flame-throwers were brought in and they began to clear the enemy bunkers. By morning the 4th Battalion had made it to the line of the ridge only to be thrown back that afternoon. They finally secured Hill 875 the following day, Thanks-giving, while the NVA fell back into Cambodia.

Although things were hotting up on the battlefield throughout 1967, efforts were still continuing to reach peace. In January, remarks made by North Vietnamese Prime Minister Pham Van Dong led to international speculation that the Communists might be softening their position, though seven days later Ho Chi Minh said that Hanoi's former four-point plan for peace could now be reduced to one point: the United States should quit Vietnam. Nevertheless, the British put forward a fresh plan for a peace conference. This was rejected by Hanoi. Fresh international controversy was caused when UN Secretary General U Thant poured scorn on the idea that South Vietnam was vital to western security. However, in his State of the Union address, President Johnson promised that the US would 'stand firm in

1st Cavalry paratroopers take off from Dak To during Operation MacArthur on 20 November 1967. During the three-week battle, Army aviation flew more than 13,000 hours; eighteen US and Vietnamese artillery batteries fired more than 170,000 rounds; and the Air Force executed 2,100 tactical air and 300 B-52 sorties.

Vietnam' even though America would face 'more cost, more loss, and more agony'. On a goodwill tour of New Zealand, Premier Ky was described as a 'murderer' and a 'miserable little butcher' by the leader of the Labor opposition, Arthur Caldwell. Meanwhile in the US, Senator William Fulbright published the influential book *The Arrogance of Power*, criticizing American foreign policy and advocating face-to-face talks between the US and the Vietcong. Letters were exchanged between Johnson and Ho Chi Minh, but Johnson dismissed peace feelers from Hanoi, saying that there were no 'serious indications that the other side is ready to stop the war'. Soon after, North Vietnam rejected Secretary of State Dean Rusk's suggestion that they scale down their military activities in return for a halt in the bombing campaign. In February, Congress passed a bill authorizing the expenditure of another $4.5 billion on the war and $700 million in aid was given to South Vietnam, though on 12 November 1967 *The New York Times* reported that due to corruption and blackmarketeering in Saigon 40 per cent of US aid failed to reach its destination. Senator Fulbright, chairman of the influential Senate Foreign Relations Committee, attacked Johnson's broad interpretation of the Gulf of Tonkin Resolution, saying that Johnson had no mandate to wage war on the present scale. Meanwhile the US revealed that Moscow and Peking had reached an agreement to supply North Vietnam. However, China denounced the Soviet leaders as 'a pack of traitors' and 'number one accomplices to the US gangsters'. The Chinese had fallen out with the Soviets in 1963 and in 1967 were in the middle of their 'Cultural Revolution'. They repeatedly accused the USSR of colluding with the US and 'resorting to dirty tricks with the aim of compelling the Vietnamese people to lay down their arms and give up the struggle'. Dean Rusk invoked the spectre of the 'yellow peril', but it was the Soviets rather than the Chinese who continued to support the North Vietnamese, pouring hundreds of millions of roubles' worth of food, weapons and economic aid into the country.

With peace no nearer, U Thant told the United Nations in New York that they were witnessing the 'initial phases of World War III' and warned that direct confrontation between the US and China was likely. Johnson continued to urge Ho Chi Minh to help lead 'our people out of this bloody impasse' with a compromised peace. In June, two days of talks were held between President Johnson and Soviet Prime Minister Aleksei Kosygin in Glassboro, New Jersey.

Johnson was a wheeler-dealer Texan politician, an acknowledged master of the backroom deal. In foreign affairs, though, he was completely out of his depth and simply could not understand the Communists' intransigence. Despite the massive firepower that was ranged against them – on the battlefield Communist firepower was inferior by a ratio of about five to one – Hanoi was becoming increasingly confident. In the summer of 1967, General Giap published a book entitled *Big Victory, Great Task* in which he gallingly analysed the shortcomings of the US in combat. Again no one in the Pentagon took it to heart.

There were political changes in South Vietnam that summer. A democratically elected government was to replace the Ky military dictatorship. In May, Ky had announced that he would run for President, but in June the South Vietnamese Armed Forces Council persuaded him to be the running mate to General Nguyen Van Thieu, who had less of a gangster image and had been trained in the US. Thieu boasted about free speech and freedom of the press during the election campaign while cheerfully closing down opposition newspapers. Amid accusations of ballot-rigging, Thieu and Ky were elected. As they were sworn in at the Independence Palace in Saigon, three mortar shells exploded on the lawn.

A machine gunner of 173rd Airborne 2nd Battalion 503rd Infantry with an M60, in readiness for the final assault on Hill 875 in November 1967.

Since World War II it had been the accepted wisdom among the military that air power won wars. However, it was of little use against an enemy who travelled in small units at night or under the cover of jungle canopy, hid in tunnel complexes or mixed seamlessly with the local population.

T

HE AIR WAR began on 8 August 1964, when President Johnson used the Gulf of Tonkin incident as an excuse to order retaliatory air strikes against coastal targets in North Vietnam. After Americans were killed at Camp Holloway, the bombing campaign Operation Rolling Thunder began in earnest when a hundred bombers from the airbase in Da Nang hit military targets in the north on 2 March with bombs cheerfully daubed with the slogan 'Ho Chi Minh ain't gonna win'. At first they used high explosives, then cluster bombs, then, on 9 March, the use of napalm against targets in North Vietnam was authorized.

Although death came just as surely with high explosives, the lacerating shards of cluster bombs, bullets, mortar, or fragmentation grenades – and the Vietnam War came up with many unpleasant ways to die – it was the pictures of billowing red clouds of burning napalm and victims with their burnt skin hanging off in tatters that have become the enduring images of the war. Napalm is gasoline thickened by various additives. Although it was developed in World War II for use in flame-throwers, during the Vietnam War Dow Chemicals manufactured a version that was thickened into a gel. When a canister was dropped by a plane, it exploded near the ground, covering the target with a sticky petroleum jelly that burnt at 1,800 degrees Fahrenheit.

Gasoline had first been used as a weapon in flame-throwers in World War I, but jets of raw gasoline are difficult to aim and the gasoline burns off too quickly to set fire to the target. During World War II, scientists at Harvard found that by adding aluminium naphthenate and aluminium palmitate the gasoline was turned into a sticky syrup, which burned slowly. The additive was known as napalm, from naphthenate and palmitate. Only later on did the thickened mixture adopt the name.

During World War II, a six per cent mixture was used in flame-throwers and a twelve to fifteen per cent mixture in the fire-bombs dropped on German and Japanese cities. During the Korean War, napalm was used against enemy troops. The napalm of that era was difficult and dangerous to handle and a safer version was developed. This was known as NP2, super-napalm or napalm B. In fact, it did not use any of the original naphthenate and palmitate mixture. Instead the gasoline was turned into a gel by the additions of benzene and polystyrene – Styrofoam. This produced a more controllable incendiary that could be handled quite safely. You could even stub a cigarette out in it, but it could be deployed against an enemy to devastating effect.

In the bombs used in Vietnam, a canister of 110 gallons of napalm was ignited by Thermite, which itself was used in World War II incendiary bombs and burns at around 4,400 degrees Fahrenheit. The new napalm B had the added advantages that it was stickier and adhered to the target – the victim – and it burnt longer. Not only was it a very effective weapon against an enemy hidden below the jungle canopy, it also had a terrible psycholog-ical effect on all who faced it.

As early as 1962, there were press reports that napalm was being used in Vietnam. Then on 29 March 1964, after a photograph of a badly burnt small child appeared in the press, the Department of Defense admitted that napalm bombs had been supplied to South Vietnam and had been dropped from aero-planes with US instructors on board. From then on napalm was used widely in Vietnam and the angry red clouds of flame produced by pods of napalm exploding over the jungle were seen on TV screens and in newspapers and magazines around the world. It has been estimated that some 400,000 tons of napalm bombs were dropped on Vietnam – two or three times the amount of incendiaries used by US forces in World War II. It is hard to get an accurate figure as some bombs were filled during production; others were shipped empty and filled with gasoline and thickening agent in the Far East. Military procurement from 1964 to 1973 shows that US forces had the necessary ingredients to make 1.5 million napalm bombs in all.

Napalm was used in South Vietnam for the destruction of both food supplies and forest cover, as well as close air support during search-and-destroy operations. Napalm was used in preference to fragmentation or high-explosive bombs in close combat as it could be dropped more accurately from a lower level and had a more clearly prescribed area of devastation. This was useful as the Commu-nists had learnt that their best tactic was to stay as close as possible to the American troops who were engaging them, so, if the

Americans called in an air strike, they risked having their own positions hit too.

It was also used in parts of the South where it was difficult to deploy troops on the ground and against readily flammable targets such as bamboo huts. Napalm was also dropped in North Vietnam, largely on troop and matériel marshalling areas near the 17th parallel. Its use was widespread too in Laos

and Cambodia, completely illegally.

As the war progressed, the use of napalm became more indiscriminate. It regularly hit civilians, and images of women and children with their skin blackened and peeling from napalm were flashed around the world by television. Its use was condemned by the Soviet Union, though they employed it later in Afghanistan. However, Britain and other

C-123 Ranchhands spray the jungle canopy with defoliation liquid so that troop movements will be visible. Unfortunately the defoliant contained the contaminant dioxide which later caused birth defects.

sympathetic nations also condemned its use, turning world opinion against the war. Senator Morse claimed the use of napalm was a violation of international law, and although few backed his position, the use of napalm also helped turn opinion at home against the war.

By 1971, the United Nations was becoming concerned about the use of napalm and commissioned a special report. On 14 November 1972, the UN condemned the use of napalm by the Portuguese in their colonies in Africa, and on 29 November it condemned its use in other conflicts. But napalm was not banned by an international convention until 1980. The United States backed this move, recognizing that images of badly burnt women and children are counterproductive. A programme was instituted to decommission the

weapon by burning the remaining stocks of napalm, but this brought complaints from environmentalists.

The most famous victim of napalm was Phan Thi Kim Phuc. AP photographer Nguyen Kong 'Nick' Ut photographed the nine-year-old fleeing naked down a road. She had been hiding in a pagoda when her village was hit by napalm. Her clothes and much of her skin were burnt off. The photograph was printed in newspapers and magazines around the world and won Ut a Pulitzer Prize. Nine-year-old Phuc became a potent symbol of the civilian suffering in the war and the horrors of napalm. It helped turn the American people against the war.

Phuc ran down the road for about half a mile before being taken to hospital. She lay in a coma for six months, her back, neck and left

Collateral damage killed friends as well as foe. Here South Vietnamese civilians flee from the accidental bombing of their village with napalm by the US Air Force. The extensive use of airpower turned South Vietnamese civilians against their own government and their American allies.

staggering 250,000 tons of bombs.

B-52s were used for ground support in the South as well as the strategic bombing of the North. This was criticized as 'swatting flies with sledgehammers'. Indeed, one mission during Operation Arc Light, designed to destroy the VC bases to the north of Saigon, cost $20 million when two B-52s collided. In all B-52s flew 126,000 sorties in support of ground troops.

To begin with, Operation Rolling Thunder, the bombing of the North, had limited objectives. Then on 14 March 1965, military and naval targets on the North Vietnamese island of Conco were attacked. Between 3 and 5 April Rolling Thunder was extended to non-military targets. The operation was supposed to last for just eight weeks. It ran for three years, dropping on average one 500-pound bomb every 30 seconds. As well as B-52s, F-4 Phantoms and F-105D Thunderchiefs, or Thuds, flew from bases in South Vietnam or aircraft carriers in the South China Sea. In all more than 300,000 sorties were flown, and some 860,000 tons of bombs were dropped, on North Vietnam, three times the tonnage dropped on Europe, Asia, and Africa in World War II. Some 52,000 civilians were killed at a loss of 922 planes.

On 24 April, Johnson stepped up the bombing again, defending the decision on the 26th by saying 'Our restraint was viewed as weakness. We could no longer stand by as the attacks mounted.'

But the restraint continued throughout the war. The USAF never used the 'carpet bombing' that obliterated Dresden and Tokyo during World War II. Nor did it target the

A wrecked A-1E Skyraider in 1965. Skyraiders participated in the first air strikes against North Vietnam. They shot down at least three MiG-17s, but were later replaced by A-6A Intruders. The USAF lost 201 Skyraiders in Southeast Asia, while the Navy lost 65. Five were shot down by surface-to-air missiles and three in air-to-air combat – two of them accounted for by North Vietnamese MiGs.

arm badly burnt. After eight months she was discharged from hospital. Some years later, she went to Germany where her treatment was completed by a plastic surgeon. She went on to become a pharmacist in Ho Chi Minh City, as Saigon was renamed. She later visited the US and is now a Canadian citizen living in Ajax, Ontario.

The other enduring image of the war is of enormous B-52 Stratofortresses with their bomb bay doors open, dropping 500-pound bombs. Flying from Guam, Okinawa and Thailand, the huge bombers, 48 metres (157 feet) long and with a wing-span of 56.4 metres (185 feet), flew in a cell of three planes guided by ground-based radar stations. They would drop their 84 bombs simultaneously, completely obliterating everything in a 'box' measuring 1 x 3 kilometres (½ x 1¾ miles). Throughout the war, B-52s dropped a dykes along the Red River which, had they been breached, would have flooded the valley and killed hundreds of thousands of people. And for two years, the US did not even bomb the air bases, leaving the North Vietnamese Soviet-built MiG jet fighters free to attack incoming American aircraft, forcing bombers to jettison their bombs and return to base. While air strikes were authorized in South Vietnam, killing 70 Vietcong on 29 April, Johnson made the first of many bombing halts on 13 May 1965 to see if the Hanoi government was ready to parley. The Communist response was a daylight attack on a textile mill just five miles north of Saigon by theVietcong. The bombing was renewed on 19 May. By 22 June American planes were dropping bombs within 80 miles of the Chinese border, prompting the Chinese government to warn that it might send troops to aid its Communist ally to the south. And on 11 July the US

announced its intention to bomb all parts of North Vietnam. Later in the month US planes launched major strikes against Vietcong positions in South Vietnam as well and on 5 September US and ARVN planes flew a record 532 missions in one day. Another record was set on 20 September, when seven US planes were lost. Two more USAF jets were downed on last day of the month while bombing the Minh Binh bridge near Hanoi.

In October, the massive B-52s were deployed against targets inside South Vietnam – a friendly country – when the USAF began bombing Vietcong bases near the Cambodian border. The Vietcong responded by attacking American airbases and destroying US planes. But this did not discourage American fliers who, soon after, bombed a friendly Vietnamese village, killing 48 civilians and injuring 55 others.

Although protests against the war had already started in America, Johnson also faced pressure from those who wanted to escalate the war. On 22 November 1965, the chairman of the House Armed Services Committee, L. Mendel Rivers, called for bombing raids against Hanoi and North Vietnam's principal port Haiphong, saying it was 'folly to let the port of Haiphong and military targets of Hanoi remain untouched while war supplies being used against our troops are pouring into port'.

Upping the stakes yet again, the 7th Fleet sent two nuclear-powered ships – a guided-missile frigate and an aircraft carrier – to take up positions off Saigon. US A-1 Skyraiders, A-7 Corsairs and F-4 Phantoms were then sent

An F-4 Phantom II fighter circles over attack carrier USS Midway to which it was attached in the South China Sea in October 1965. The F-4 could carry up to 18,650 pounds of weapons, including air-to-air and air-to-ground missiles, and nuclear bombs, on nine external hardpoints.

to bomb, strafe and fire rockets at the Ho Chi Minh trail in an attempt to cut down on the amount of supplies getting through. But they did not go unopposed, the NVA responding with withering fire from anti-aircraft batteries.

On 9 December 1965, an article in *The New York Times* reported that the bombing had not succeeded in slowing the infiltration of NVA troops and supplies into South Vietnam. The USAF responded by turning their attention to industrial targets in the North, destroying a power plant in Uongbi.

A 37-day bombing halt over Christmas failed to bring Hanoi to the negotiating table and Rolling Thunder was resumed at the end of January. Its purpose, said Maxwell Taylor, the retiring ambassador to South Vietnam, was to 'change the will of the enemy leadership' and show others that 'wars of liberation' were 'costly, dangerous, and doomed to failure'. Rolling Thunder was stepped up again in March with USAF and USN flying two hundred sorties over North Vietnam in a single day. In April, F-4 Phantoms took out the road and rail bridges connecting North Vietnam to the city of Nanning in China. But these sorties took their toll on the fliers and the USAF imposed a limit of a hundred missions on flight crew. Nevertheless, in a concerted campaign against the Ho Chi Minh trail, B-52s dropped a million tons of bombs on the Mugia Pass, where the trail passes from North Vietnam into Laos. On 17 April the bombing campaign was escalated once again when USAF and USN planes began to close in on Hanoi and Haiphong. The North Vietnamese responded by sending up their MiGs, flown by Soviet-

DOWNED AMERICAN PILOTS WERE PARADED...WHILE BRITAIN, FRANCE AND OTHER FRIENDLY COUNTRIES CONDEMNED THE AIR RAIDS

trained pilots, in their first concerted effort to engage American planes in air combat. But in a raid on 29 June US bombers managed to destroy 50 per cent of North Vietnam's stock of fuel. This was the beginning of a campaign to knock out all the fuel installations in the Hanoi-Haiphong area, forcing the North Vietnamese to evacuate all but essential workers from the area. China denounced the bombing as 'barbarous and wanton acts that have further freed us from any bounds of restriction in helping North Vietnam'. They also claimed that US planes had hit Chinese fishing boats in international waters, killing three sailors.

Downed American pilots were paraded in front of angry crowds, while Britain, France and other friendly countries condemned the air raids. However, a Pentagon report claimed that some 80 to 90 per cent of North Vietnam's fuel supplies had come under attack and the raids were intensified. The raids on the Ho Chi Minh trail were intensified too, with over a hundred raids a day being flown over neutral Laos, and at the end of July, US planes also began bombing the DMZ. But more mistakes were made. USAF jets hit two villages 80 miles south of Saigon, killing 63 civilians and wounding over a hundred, and Prince Sihanouk, the leader of neutral Cambodia, complained about the

Sweeping over the tree-tops, this C-123 Ranch Hand aircraft sprays defoliant over a target area near Tay Ninh and An Loc, Vietnam, in January 1967 as part of the 'pink rose' test programme. Ten flights of B-52s each dropped 42 M-35 incendiary cluster bombs per aircraft into the target area, setting fires that burned the heavy undergrowth as well as enemy fortifications.

US bombing of the village of Thlock Track, situated near the South Vietnamese border. China complained that US planes had hit more of its shipping and attacked Chinese territory in its campaign against North Vietnamese coastal installations.

At the same time, Operation Ranch Hand was reaching its height. This was America's attempt to deny the Vietcong and NVA the protection of the forests. Several methods of jungle clearance had been used, including dropping napalm in an attempt to set the forest on fire. But in dense jungle, the canisters got caught in the canopy and burnt down just one tree, rather than beginning a self-sustaining fire. Roman Plows, huge Caterpillar tractors fitted with a 2.5-ton plough blade and 14 tons of armour plating, bulldozed 750,000

acres of forest, but this method could not be used on hilly terrain. Besides, it fertilized the ground very effectively and in the monsoon conditions of Vietnam dense undergrowth rapidly grew back. Instead, the US forces began using chemical herbicides, Agent White and Agent Purple, named for the colour of the can they came in. But none was as effective as Agent Orange.

Agent Orange was a growth hormone that made the trees shed their leaves prematurely. Converted C-123 transports sprayed 1000 cans at 280 gallons a minute from 200 feet above the jungle and in three-and-a-half minutes another 350 acres of jungle had been destroyed. The programme began in 1961, when American airmen dressed as civilians began spraying VC strongholds at the request of President Diem. The Ranch Hand fliers adopted the motto 'Only you can prevent forest'. In the nine years of Operation Ranch Hand, over eighteen million gallons of herbicide were used, laying waste 5.5 million acres: the area of Wales or Vermont. That was one-seventh of the area of the country, including 36 per cent of the coastal mangrove swamp, wiping out shellfish, cutting the production of the local fisheries, and driving several species into extinction.

In areas where it was sprayed, leaflets were dropped, warning local people. This gave the VC a chance to organize a hot reception committee and F-4 Phantoms had to rocket and strafe target areas before the spray planes went in. The VC distributed their own leaflets, telling local people to bury their food six feet below ground. To counter VC propaganda, South Vietnamese psychological warfare teams would eat bread soaked in Agent Orange and wash their faces in it. This failed to convince. Rumours that the Americans were trying to poison them spread among the peasants, who could not get used to evil-smelling fluid falling on them. Agent Blue was also used to destroy crops grown by the VC and crops that would be taken as 'taxes' by the Communists. This technique had been used effectively by the British against Communist insurgents in Malaya. But peasants hated seeing the crops that they had planted and trees they had tended for years killed overnight by a spray plane.

The use of herbicides helped drive the peasants off the land, into refugee camps, leaving free-fire zones where US forces could use their massive firepower with impunity. However, it was also a massive propaganda failure. It was a great recruiting sergeant for the Vietcong and also exposed the US to charges of using chemical warfare, causing protest at home in the United States and abroad. In 1969, the UN General Assembly found the use of herbicides illegal under the 1925 Geneva Protocol that outlawed the use of the poison gases used in World War I and 'all analogous liquids, materials, or devices'. The US protested. Herbicides were used in the US, USSR and other countries in order to eliminate unwanted vegetation. During 1961, forty million acres of agricultural land in the US, along with thousands of acres alongside freeways and railroads, were treated with the same herbicides and ten million acres, a quarter of the area of South Vietnam, were sprayed from the air. However, in 1969, the National Cancer Institute discovered that dioxin, an impurity created in the manufacture of Agent Orange, caused cancer and birth defects in laboratory animals. Over 32,000 disability claims have been filed by US servicemen exposed to Agent Orange (the Vietnamese had no legal redress) and in 1975 President Gerald Ford signed Executive Order 11850, renouncing the first use of herbicides in war.

Agent Orange was sprayed not only in Vietnam, but also in Laos and Cambodia to strip the Ho Chi Minh trail of its forest cover. Again this was ineffective as the trail was more a network of tracks than a two-lane blacktop and the supply lines could easily revert to a different route. One solution tried out was

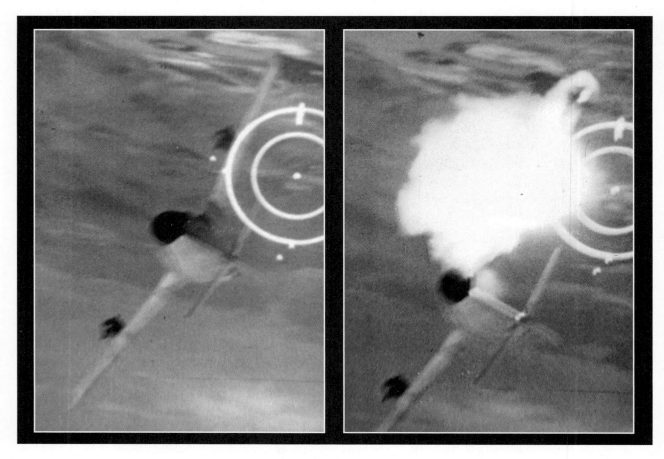

Death of a MiG – an F-105 closes in at a rate of 200 knots on a MiG-17 over Hanoi, its sights trained on the underside of the enemy aircraft's wing. Once hit, the MiG is engulfed by flames and disintegrates.

Operation Popeye, a weather-modification programme designed to intensify the monsoon and wash out the jungle trails. Their motto was 'make mud, not war'. It proved ineffective. In 1976, the UN banned weather modification as a weapon of war.

But still, for MACV, it was vital to know what was going on along the Ho Chi Minh trail. If they could monitor the amount of men and matériel heading down it, they would have a good idea of what the Communists were planning in the South. Special Forces trained the local primitive Meo tribesmen, but they proved unreliable, and the NVA soon became adept at tracking down the Green

Berets' A-Teams. The answer in 1966 – the year that saw the first broadcast of *Star Trek* – was more technology. The Spocks of the shadowy Institute of Defense Analysis came up with sensors that would detect movement along the trail. Manufactured by the Pentagon's little-known Defense Communications Planning Group, they were submarine passive sonar devices, modified for land use. Some were dropped by planes by parachute so they hung in the trees. Others were dropped free-fall so that the pointed body would bury itself in the ground, leaving only the antenna, often disguised as a jungle plant, above ground. These battery-powered devices picked up the sound and seismic vibrations of passing trucks or columns of troops, or the electrical inference given off by a truck's ignition system. Data from the sensors was collected by a Lockheed EC-121R Warning Star circling overhead and relayed back to the Infiltration Surveillance Center at Nakhon Phanom – NKP or Naked Fanny – in Thailand, also known as Dutch Mill after its windmill-shaped antenna.

The problem was that the aircraft dropping the sensors had to fly low and slow, otherwise the sensor would be smashed to bits when it hit the ground. Modified USN OP-2E Neptunes, usually used for tracking submarines, were used. They presented NVA anti-aircraft teams with an easy target, as did the circling Warning Stars. Later the QU-22B Pave Eagle II, a pilotless version of the Model 36 Beech Bonanza light aircraft, was used to relay data to the Warning Stars that stood off out of range. The trail surveillance programme, which was called Operation Igloo White, cost $725 million. As a result, as one air force officer put it, 'every fourth bush in the Ho Chi Minh trail had an antenna in it'.

The ISC in Nakhon Phanom had two IBM 360-65 computers – state of the art at that time – to process the data. In theory, they could pinpoint the position of any convoys and call in an air strike. But for all its sophisticated electronic equipment, the US could not stop men and supplies trundling down the Ho Chi Minh trail.

Another expensive failure was the 'people sniffer'. Originally designated the XM-2 airborne personnel detector, it was an electrochemical device made by GE that could detect tiny particles of human sweat or bodily wastes, both liquid and solid, in the air. In the pollution-free air of Vietnam, it was deployed to detect the VC. Mounted on a Huey helicopter, people-sniffer patrols would roam the countryside, searching for the enemy. Unfortunately, the people sniffer could not tell the difference between the sweat of troops or that of old men, women and children going about their business, and the flood of urine discharged by a water buffalo or jungle animals sent it off the scale. However, a modified version known as the E-63 which clipped onto the barrel of an M16 was used in Vietnam to limited effect.

By October 1966, the US was flying over 25,000 bombing missions a month over Vietnam. B-52s were pounding the NVA's supply and staging areas in the DMZ, in the belief that the 324B Division was building up to launch a major attack, and the bombing crept closer and closer to Hanoi. A Department of Defense report revealed that attacks on oil facilities in the North had done nothing to slow the infiltration of arms and supplies into South Vietnam. The Pentagon response was to intensify the raids, although three days before the November congressional elections, Secretary McNamara said that there had been no 'sharp increase' in the number of air strikes. On 2 December fuel depots were bombed once again and US Navy jets hit targets just five miles outside Hanoi. Eight US planes were lost that day. The Vietcong retaliated by attacking US aircraft inside Tan Son Nhut air base. By 14 December, US planes were bombing a truck depot two miles south of Hanoi. A French journalist reported that the village of Caudat, outside Hanoi, had been 'completely destroyed by bombs and fire'. The raid brought international condemnation.

General Westmoreland denied that US bombers had attacked nonmilitary targets in Hanoi, but on 25 December *The New York*

'WE OUTFLEW, OUTSHOT AND OUTFOUGHT THEM' – FLIGHT LEADER COLONEL ROBIN OLDS

Times published a report describing the wholesale damage done to various North Vietnamese cities by the bombing. The following day, the Pentagon was forced to admit that North Vietnamese civilians may have been killed accidentally in bombing raids against military targets. The year ended with US planes dropping hundreds of tons of high explosives and napalm on the Mekong Delta. Six thousand ARVN troops then moved in on the Vietcong bases in the U Minh forest, claiming a body count of 104 VC killed and eighteen captured.

In over eighteen months, Operation Rolling Thunder had not succeeded in stemming the flow of men and matériel from North Vietnam into the South, so it was decided to step up the bombing of the North once again. But first they had to take out the North Vietnamese Air Force and its Soviet-made MiGs in Operation Bolo. This began on 2 January 1967, when a force of eighty-four

F-4Cs of the 8th Tactical Fighter Wing ('the Wolfpack') took off from Ubon Royal Thai Air Force Base. They were equipped with new electronic jamming pods that could simulate the characteristics of other aircraft. The 8th TFW disguised themselves electronically as a pack of F-105 Thunderchiefs and refuelling tankers on a Rolling Thunder mission. They used the same approach routes, altitudes and Thunderchief call signs. From the east, more F-4s from the 366th TFW approached. They were to cover two of the NVAF's airfields and cut off the MiGs' escape route to the north.

Rising to the bait, the MiGs took off to attack what they thought were a wing of bombers as they crossed into North Vietnamese air space. Instead they found themselves up against Phantoms. Despite the new MiG Fishbed's superior manoeuvrability and its Atoll air-to-air missiles, the Phantoms shot seven of them down – half of the NVAF's operational inventory – without loss. The score would have been higher if the weather had not stopped more of the fourteen flights of Phantoms engaging them.

'We outflew, outshot and outfought them,' flight leader Colonel Robin Olds told news correspondents afterward.

While the American people were getting disillusioned with the war on the ground, fighter pilots such as Olds and the US Navy's Randy Cunningham became national heroes. Their pictures appeared on the covers of news magazines and they were fêted like movie stars. While grunts on the ground were pictured zipping the Vietnamese huts known as hootches, these men were portrayed as all-American heroes who took on the enemy one-to-one. Randy Cunningham is now a congressman.

On 6 January the Phantoms attacked again, this time disguised as an unarmed reconnaissance mission. This effectively cleared the skies of all enemy fighters and Operation Rolling Thunder progressed into Phase V. Attacks were authorized on the air base at Phuc Yen and the air fields at Hoa Loc, Kien An and Kep, along with the military facilities in Hanoi and along the Chinese border, all of which had previously been off-limits. The US was escalating the war once more.

During these raids, 52 NVAF aircraft were shot down, though the USAF also suffered heavy losses. Nine F-4s and 11 F-105s were shot down by MiGs, and 3 F-4s and 17 F-105s hit by surface-to-air (SAM) missiles. In all, in 1967, 294 USAF aircraft were lost to enemy action, along with 87 operational losses. The F-105 Thunderchiefs sustained the worst losses: 113 were downed. But they made 22 of the 59 MiG kills claimed by the USAF.

At the end of May, the new F-4D Phantom was introduced. On 24 August, the AGM-62A Walleye TV-guided missile made its debut and the AIM-4 Falcon air-to-air missile made its first kill on 26 October. Again the stakes were being raised relentlessly, but it did little good – the Soviets simply replaced the planes that were lost and upped the pilot training programme. The intensification of the bombing did little to impair the North's ability or willingness to fight.

While the US airmen were heroes at home, to the North Vietnamese they were air pirates. Downed pilots were attacked by angry mobs and had to be protected by the militia. Their capture was often re-enacted for the cameras. Once in captivity, they were held in solitary confinement for years and badly mistreated. Kept in vermin-infested cells, they were fed thin pumpkin or cabbage soup with maybe a little pig fat in it. The Hanoi government insisted that, as war had not been declared, the Geneva Convention did not apply, a misleading statement, as the Geneva Convention applies not only to declared wars, but to any armed conflict between parties to the Convention. The Democratic Republic of Vietnam – North Vietnam – had ratified the Convention in 1957. Nevertheless, the Hanoi government refused to provide the required lists of those men they held captive and allowed neither the International Red Cross nor the representatives of any neutral nation to inspect their prisoners. The American authorities had to

US Phantom jets prowl the skies during Operation Rolling Thunder. From 2 March 1965 to 1 November 1968 the USAF, US Navy and Republic of Vietnam Air Force pounded the North. The idea was to destroy North Vietnam's transportation system, manufacturing facilities and air defences, and hamper NVA soldiers moving south. It failed on all counts and was cancelled when President Johnson decided not to run again.

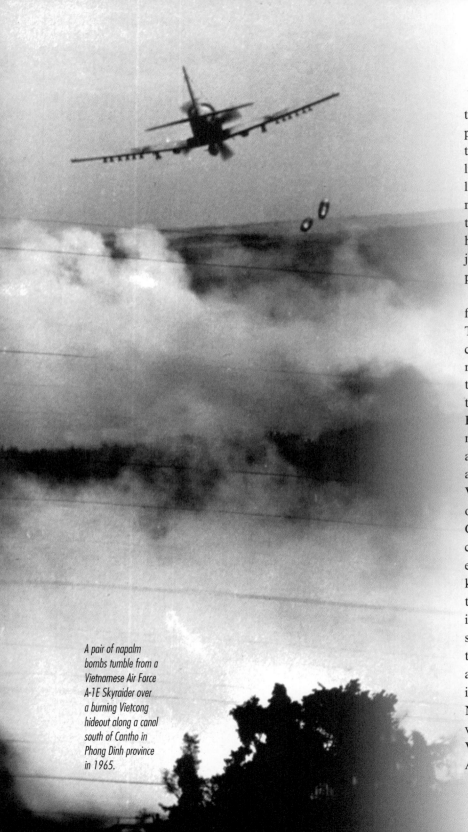

A pair of napalm bombs tumble from a Vietnamese Air Force A-1E Skyraider over a burning Vietcong hideout along a canal south of Cantho in Phong Dinh province in 1965.

trawl through North Vietnamese newspapers, propaganda movies and the publications of their Communist allies to built up their own list of captives. Fortunately, the Communists liked to show off their prisoners. One of the most frequently shown images of the war on the Communist side was a tall American with his head bowed being marched through the jungle by a small Vietnamese woman in black pyjamas carrying a rifle.

It had to be said that there was little regard for the Geneva Convention on either side. There were instances of Americans using coercion and torture on captured Communists, often 'interrogating' VC suspects with the aid of electric shocks generated by a field telephone in what was flippantly known as 'the Bell Telephone hour'. Geneva Convention III not only covered members of conventional armed forces but also militias, volunteer corps, and organized resistance groups, such as the Vietcong. Prisoners were regularly handed over to the ARVN – again in violation of the Convention – who had no scruples when it came to the maltreatment and summary execution of their fellow countrymen. Those kept alive were held in 'tiger cages' which were too small for them to stand up or lie down in. The South Vietnamese were accused of shooting Vietcong prisoners and throwing them out of helicopters. The Vietcong openly admitted executing US prisoners without trial in reprisal. When the US protested that the North Vietnamese had made numerous violations of the Convention in 1966, North Vietnam declared its intention of trying all American prisoners as war criminals. World opinion turned against this and the North Vietnamese dropped it, but continued to parade downed pilots through the streets of Hanoi where they were jeered at by angry crowds who had suffered American bombing.

American prisoners captured in the South were often held in the combat zone, a violation of Article 19 of the Geneva Convention. They were denied medicine and food – in breach of Article 33 – subjected to 're-education', and often held in inhuman conditions, frequently confined to tiny bamboo cages, in breach of Article 13. Few survived.

Airmen downed over the North were stripped of their clothing and possessions in breach of Article 18. They were regularly paraded through streets full of jeering crowds and threatened with 'war crime trials'. Many were kept shackled for long periods, alone, in the dark, left to wallow in their own excrement, and denied medical treatment. Those who refused to divulge more than their name, rank and serial number were brutally tortured in breach of Article 17, though rarely to extract any useful information. The idea was to break them and force them to make some propaganda statement. Eighty per cent of them did. Since the Vietnam War, the US military code of conduct has been changed so that prisoners of war are allowed to provide more than the name, rank, date of birth and serial number required by Article 17 of the Geneva Conventions if they face inhumane treatment. Once the Vietnamese had extracted statements or 'confessions' from the airmen, they paraded them in front of the world's television cameras – the final

humiliation for a courageous fighting man.

Most downed airmen ended up in Hoa Lo, the old French colonial prison in Hanoi, which inmates dubbed the 'Hanoi Hilton'. It was made up of a series of compounds. Each got a nickname. When prisoners first arrived, they went to 'New Guy Village', then to 'Las Vegas' and 'Heartbreak Hotel', where they were tortured. 'Camp Unity' was the compound where prisoners were allowed to meet after December 1970: until then, they would have been held in solitary confinement.

From 1965 to 1967, some US prisoners

AIRMEN…WERE PARADED THROUGH STREETS FULL OF JEERING CROWDS AND THREATENED WITH 'WAR CRIME TRIALS'

were held in a compound called the 'Briar-patch', some thirty miles to the northwest of Hanoi. After 1967, they were moved to the 'Zoo' at Cu Loc. There were other compounds outside Hanoi such as 'Camp Faith', 'Skid Row' and Son Tay. There were other smaller compounds in Hanoi, including one in the old movie studio. After 1967, 'Alcatraz' housed the prisoners who had given their captors particular problems. A 'model' prison was also constructed for the cooperative prisoners in the grounds of the mayor's house, where they could be inspected by visiting dignitaries.

The most famous prisoner of war was John McCain, who went on to become a US

An AH-1C Cobra gunship of D Troop, 3rd Squadron, 4th Cavalry, 25th Infantry Division, fires a rocket at a Vietcong position in 1968. Also manufactured by Bell, the Cobra was the attack version of the Huey. They provided fire support for ground forces, escorted transport helicopters and formed 'hunter-killer' teams when paired with Hughes OH-6A scout helicopters.

Senator and ran for the Republican presidential nomination in the 2000 AND 2008 elections. During the Vietnam War, McCain was a Navy flier. His father, an admiral, was commander of all US forces in the Pacific. McCain was shot down over Hanoi in 1967 and badly injured. When the Vietnamese realized that their prisoner was the son of a high-ranking officer, they offered to return him. But McCain refused early release, fearing it would be used to embarrass the US government. Instead, he insisted that standard military procedures be followed and prisoners of war be returned in the order of their date of capture. As a result, McCain was held in solitary confinement and tortured frequently. He was returned in 1973 with the other prisoners after five and a half years in

captivity. In 1982, he was elected to Congress as a Republican and in 1986 he became a US Senator for Arizona. *Time* magazine named him one of its 'Top 25 Most Influential People in America' in 1997.

Even though Rolling Thunder was intensified in 1967, the North Vietnamese were repeatedly offered an end to the bombing, if they would come to the conference table. They insisted that the bombing must end first. On 13 January, the US had to temporarily halt the bombing unilaterally during a controversy over civilian deaths following an air raid on the Yenvien marshalling yard. Nevertheless, after a truce for Tet, the lunar New Year, the US escalated the war yet again by permitting artillery bombardments of North Vietnamese territory and dropping mines in Northern rivers. In March, the USAF destroyed a steel works forty miles from Hanoi and the Thai government gave permission for B-52s to fly from their air bases, instead of coming all the way from Andersen Air Force Base on Guam in the Mariana Islands, a twelve-hour round trip. Even so, at a conference in Guam, Ky criticized US restraint, asking Johnson, 'How long can Hanoi enjoy the advantage of restricted bombing of military targets?'

In the South, nearly 180 fighter-bombers supported the US forces in Operation Junction City. In the battle at Ap Gu on 2 April, the Vietcong claimed to have downed 22 of them.

On 20 April, the port at Haiphong was bombed for the first time, while US Secretary of State Dean Rusk expressed 'regret' that civilian casualties might occur as a result of raids on 'essential military targets'. Five days later, US planes hit the British freighter *Dartford* in Haiphong harbor. But this did nothing to check the Pentagon's relentless escalation of the bombing. On 19 May central Hanoi was hit for the first time in an effort to take out the largest power plant in North Vietnam.

In August, President Johnson dropped most of the remaining restrictions on the bombing of the North, and North Vietnam became, essentially, a free-fire zone. US planes began bombing road and rail links in the Hanoi-Haiphong area and raids attacked targets just ten miles from the Chinese border. One Democrat congressman asked how the US would react to a Chinese bombing raid on

Mexico that hit targets ten miles from the Rio Grande. Despite this Ronald Reagan, then governor of California, complained that too many 'qualified targets' were off-limits to bombing. Meanwhile, the USAF Chief of Staff General John P. McConnell told a Senate Committee that the graduated escalation of the bombing begun in 1965 was a mistake. Rather they should have taken out 94 key targets in the first 16 days in one massive blow. Three days later, McNamara admitted that bombing the North had not materially affected the Communist's fighting capability, though Admiral Sharp claimed that it was causing Hanoi 'mounting logistic, management, and morale problems'. General Giap had his say in a Communist newspaper, declaring that President Johnson was using 'backward logic' if he thought that bombing the North would ease the pressure on the South. Nevertheless, the Senate Committee called for massive bombing raids on

Unidentified US POWs turn their backs on a North Vietnamese cameraman in their cells at the Nga Tu So prison camp in Hanoi. One airman explained: 'We object to pictures, because this is not the way we lived.'

Haiphong. Renewed raids were mounted on Hanoi and Haiphong, and on the dock area of Cam Pha. But by then the North Vietnamese MiGs were airborne again, this time flying from airfields in China and out of bounds to US air raids. Between 23 and 30 October, during heavy attacks on bridges, airfields and power plants in the Hanoi-Haiphong region, 13 US aircraft were shot down.

While Rolling Thunder was escalating, a huge tonnage of bombs was being dropped on South Vietnam. The statistics looked impressive. The US won numerous victories on the battlefield, inflicting huge losses on the enemy. In Operation Wheeler/Wallowa, the American Infantry Division claimed a body count of 8,188, but somehow this did not sap the Communists' will to fight. Meanwhile, US casualties continued to mount. On 11 December 1967, Johnson declared that 'our statesmen will press the search for peace to the corners of the earth' and suggested that peace talks be held on board a neutral ship at sea. Hanoi rejected this idea four days later.

However, the Christmas truce brought a ray of hope. The North Vietnamese Foreign Minister Nguyen Du Trinh announced that North Vietnam was willing to open talks if the US halted the bombing. But this was a ruse to lull the US authorities into a false sense of security. The Hanoi government was already planning the biggest offensive in the war so far – the offensive that would finally convince the American people that the war was unwinnable.

Napalm attack south of Saigon in 1965.

A S 1967 DREW to a close, the American people were told they were winning the war. On 17 November President Johnson told the television audience, 'We are inflicting greater losses than we're taking… We are making progress.'

Four days later, General Westmoreland told the press, 'I am absolutely certain that, whereas in 1965 the enemy was winning, today he is certainly losing.'

However, there was one man who was not convinced. His name was Robert McNamara, and as Secretary of Defense, he was well placed to judge: even a cursory look at the war would have shown that the US was in trouble. Despite repeated escalations in the American commitment, men and matériel continued to flow down the Ho Chi Minh trail. The Communists seemingly suffered no shortage of weapons or ammunition. The Vietcong mounted attacks throughout the country, seemingly at will. They even attacked well-protected air bases and destroyed planes. The NVA fought massed engagements, then withdrew and re-formed. American forces made repeated sweeps through hostile areas, only to find them reoccupied by the VC as soon as they were gone. With no front lines, no territory was being taken. American forces seemed to be committed to an endless round of piecemeal battles that never proved to be big enough to be decisive.

As Secretary of Defense in both the Kennedy and Johnson administrations, McNamara was one of the most relentless advocates of the war. It was McNamara who had presented the evidence of North Vietnamese aggression to Congress after the Gulf of Tonkin Incident in 1964. In February 1965, he backed the National Security Council's proposal for 'retaliatory' air strikes against the North and backed Westmoreland's repeated demands for more troops. But in October 1966, McNamara went to Vietnam. It was his eighth trip, but the first for over a year. On 14 October, he sent a memorandum to President Johnson suggesting 'stabilizing' the bombing campaign. In McNamara's opinion it had been a costly failure. Millions of tons of bombs had been dropped with no marked effect on the economy of the North, Hanoi's commitment to the war, or the infiltration into the South. The hi-tech McNamara Line was to be the alternative to bombing to prevent infiltration. He also recommended that there should be no further increase in troops and a greater commitment to 'pacification'. Only his idea for the McNamara Line – which soon proved to be another costly failure – was accepted. His other views found no support outside the State Department. But again in March 1967, he suggested limiting bombing to staging areas and infiltration routes.

McNamara was an alumnus of Harvard Business School. Regarded as a whizz kid, he was hired by the Ford Motor Company, where he set about the institution of strict cost-accounting methods and rose to become the first person outside the family to reach the position of company president, quitting after a month to join the Kennedy administration as Secretary of Defense. With his business school background, he had been taught to

Opposite: Walter Cronkite testifies on freedom of the press before a Senate subcommittee in Washington on 30 September 1971. The trusted anchorman of CBS Evening News, when he turned against the war after the Tet Offensive President Johnson knew the game was up.

Defense Secretary Robert McNamara and the Commander-in-Chief of US Forces President Lyndon Johnson confer. McNamara had also been Secretary of Defense under President Kennedy and was one of the the major architects of the war. But by 1967, he already knew it was unwinnable.

analyse problems dispassionately and follow the conclusion no matter where it led. In May 1967, the Department of Defense's Systems Analysis Office did the figures on the war and realized that the Communists were controlling the frequency, number, size, length and intensity of engagements. That way they controlled their casualties, which they were keeping just below their birth rate. This was a winning strategy. According to the DoD's report:

The VC and NVA started the shooting in over 90 per cent of company-sized firefights. Over 80 per cent began with a well-organized enemy attack. Since their losses rise – as in the first quarter of 1967 – and fall – as they have done since – with their choice of whether or not to fight, they can probably hold their losses to about two thousand a week regardless of our force levels. If their strategy is to wait us out, they will control their losses to a level low enough to be sustained indefinitely, but high enough to tempt us to increase our forces to the point of US rejection of the war.

As long as the North Vietnamese government were able to maintain their people's will to fight – and there were no signs of a crack in the Communists' morale – this strategy meant they could fight forever. The same could not be said of America. Public opinion, although hugely in favour of the war at the outset, was now fragmenting. Huge anti-war demonstrations were taking place across America. Even in Congress things were looking bad. The influential chairman of the Senate Foreign Relations Committee, William Fulbright, who had initially been a keen supporter of the war, had turned fervently against it, advocating talks between Saigon and the Vietcong.

To McNamara the war now seemed unwinnable. As it dragged on it was bound to become increasingly unpopular. In June 1967, he instituted a study of 'The History of the US Decision Making Process in Vietnam' – which would be leaked to the newspapers as the 'Pentagon Papers' – and in August he outlined his increasingly dovish views to the hawkish Preparedness Sub-committee of the Senate Armed Services

A UH-1D helicopter takes off after completing a resupply mission during Operation Pershing, a search and destroy mission approximately 31 miles northeast of An Khe in June 1967.

A Marine shooting at the enemy. Despite their expertise, training and exceptional esprit de corps, there was little the US Marines could do against an enemy who could melt away any time the going got rough.

Committee, who strongly favoured a further escalation in the bombing.

In a Draft Presidential Memorandum of 17 November 1967, McNamara recommended curtailment of the war rather than escalation. In his conclusion, he wrote, 'The picture of the world's greatest superpower killing or seriously injuring a thousand noncombatants a week, while trying to pound a tiny backward nation into submission on an issue whose merits are hotly disputed is not a pretty one.' This could have come straight from an anti-war pamphlet. It was a final break with Johnson's hardline policy. Close to a nervous breakdown, McNamara tendered his resignation in November 1967. After waiting for a suitable interval to elapse before leaving the administration, on 29 February 1968 he quit to become president of the World Bank. The official line was still that the war could be won, if Westmoreland were given enough men. By the end of 1967 there were half-a-million American troops in Vietnam and Senator Eugene McCarthy announced he would run for the presidency on an anti-war ticket. But neither the hawks or the doves predicted what would happen next.

They did know that something was going to happen, though. For six months there had been reports that Hanoi was planning a major offensive in the South. The truce for the Christmas and New Year period was punctuated by frequent outbreaks of violence and Ho Chi Minh announced that the forthcoming year would bring great victories for the Communist cause.

On 21 January 1968, four North Vietnamese Army infantry divisions, supported by two armoured regiments and two artillery regiments – 40,000 men in all – began converging on Khe Sanh, a US Marine Corps base just south of the DMZ. Westmoreland believed that the North Vietnamese intended to grab the northernmost provinces of South Vietnam, prior to opening peace negotiations – just as they had moved against the French at Dien Bien Phu to buttress their bargaining position at the Geneva Peace Conference in 1954. Peace feelers were out at that time. At a reception in Hanoi on 30 December 1967, less than a month earlier, North Vietnam's Foreign Minister Nguyen Duy Trinh dropped most of North Vietnam's preconditions on talks and said that Hanoi would enter peace talks with the US if the bombing was halted.

But peace was the last thing on Hanoi's mind. A massive offensive was planned for Tet, the Vietnamese new year festival which lasts for the first seven days of the lunar new year. In the first years of the war, Tet had been marked by a truce. For Westmoreland an attack during Tet was unthinkable. It would be like mounting an attack at Christmas and he did not think that the Communists would risk alienating the populace by violating their sacred holiday. But like most Americans, the general was unfamiliar with Vietnam's history:

in 1789 the Vietnamese had claimed one of their greatest victories during Tet, when the Emperor Quang Trung had routed the occupying Chinese army.

During the 1968 Tet Offensive, the whole of the South erupted. This took the US and the South Vietnamese completely by surprise. According to a West Point textbook published later, it was an 'intelligence failure ranking with Pearl Harbor'. American intelligence had its problems. MACV Combined Intelligence Center received around three million pages of captured documents every month, along with enormous quantities from electronic surveil-

AN ATTACK DURING TET WAS UNTHINKABLE. IT WOULD BE LIKE MOUNTING AN ATTACK AT CHRISTMAS

lance, intercepted signals, and information from prisoners, defectors and agents, far too much to evaluate. The attacks at Khe Sanh, Con Thien, Loc Ninh and other places along the DMZ had encouraged Westmoreland to send his forces north. Indeed, Westmoreland considered the Tet Offensive a diversion. As far as he was concerned, the battle for Khe Sanh was the real thing. Meanwhile, South Vietnamese President Nguyen Van Thieu had furloughed most of his troops for the holiday. Thieu himself was vacationing at his wife's family home in the Mekong Delta. Even those at the State Department Vietnam desk in Washington, DC, had taken the opportunity to go skiing in New Hampshire or Vermont. However the Communists had been planning their offensive since July 1967, with top-level planning conferences being held in Hanoi, chaired by Ho Chi Minh and General Giap. They told the world that the offensive was to 'punish the US aggressors'. Their aim was to fatally weaken the South Vietnamese army and with it the Saigon government. They hoped to provoke a spontaneous uprising and the installation of a neutralist government run by Communist agents. Failing that, they hoped to drive a wedge between the US and the Saigon government. Offering peace talks with the US was part of this strategy: Thieu lived in constant fear that the US would abandon South Vietnam.

In 1967, the North Vietnamese strategist General Giap, like his American counterparts, felt that the war on the battlefield was deadlocked. The Communists did not have the strength to overcome America's superior firepower, but the Americans were dispersed too thinly across the country to deliver the final blow to the elusive Communist forces. However, this deadlock favoured the Commu-

A wounded Vietnamese civilian beside his seriously injured wife in a crowded Saigon hospital, following a rocket attack by the Vietcong in August 1968. Although civilian casualties were caused by both sides, it was always the Americans who got the blame.

nists. America could not commit more men and matériel to Vietnam without reducing its global defence commitments and damaging its social and economic programmes at home. So the Communists could continue to bleed the US until it was forced to meet Hanoi's terms at the negotiating table. Giap could lose every battle and still win the war.

THE TET OFFENSIVE: 1968

Until January 1968 the fighting in Vietnam had taken place in the countryside. The Communists would now take it to the cities. Tet was the perfect time to do this as it was a time when Vietnamese people honoured their ancestors and many people travelled to visit their families. It would not be unusual for city hotels to be full of people from the countryside and it was easy to infiltrate guerrillas. The Vietnamese also took their dead home to be buried in ancestral plots and arms were smuggled into the cities in coffins. On the evening of 31 January 1968, some 84,000 Vietcong and NVA troops suddenly emerged in more than a hundred South Vietnamese cities and towns, including the capital Saigon. Da Nang, Hoi An, and Qui Nhon, coastal enclaves thought to be beyond the reach of the

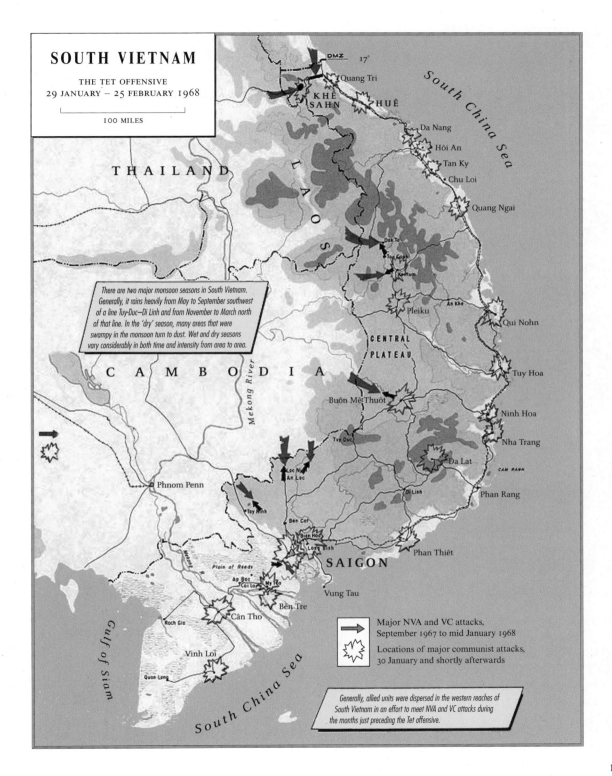

SOUTH VIETNAM

THE TET OFFENSIVE
29 JANUARY – 25 FEBRUARY 1968

|———————————————|
100 MILES

DMZ   17°

Quang Tri

KHÉ
SAHN   HUÉ

Da Nang

Hôi An

Tan Ky

Chu Loi

Quang Ngai

T H A I L A N D

L A O S

South China Sea

Dak To

Tan Canh

Kontum

There are two major monsoon seasons in South Vietnam.
Generally, it rains heavily from May to September southwest
of a line Tuy-Duc–Di Linh and from November to March north
of that line. In the 'dry' season, many areas that were
swampy in the monsoon turn to dust. Wet and dry seasons
vary considerably in both time and intensity from area to area.

Pleiku

An Khé

Qui Nohn

C A M B O D I A

Mekong River

CENTRAL

PLATEAU

Tuy Hoa

Buôn Mê Thuôt

Ninh Hoa

Nha Trang

Tuy Duc

CAM RANH

Phnom Penn

Loc Ninh

An Loc

Da Lat

Di Linh

Phan Rang

Tay Ninh

Ben Cat

Biên Hoa

Long Binh

SAIGON

Phan Thiêt

Plain of Reeds

Ap Bac

Cai Lay

My Tho

Vung Tau

Bên Tre

Cân Tho

Roch Gia

Vinh Loi

Quan Long

Gulf of Siam

South China Sea

→ Major NVA and VC attacks,
September 1967 to mid January 1968

✷ Locations of major communist attacks,
30 January and shortly afterwards

Generally, allied units were dispersed in the western reaches of
South Vietnam in an effort to meet NVA and VC attacks during
the months just preceding the Tet offensive.

Saigon citizens return to the remains of their burnt-out homes after Vietcong rockets struck a mile-wide section of the Vietnamese city in August 1968.

Communists, came under attack. They even rocketed the well-defended US Navy base at Cam Ranh Bay. Thirty-six of the forty-four provincial capitals were hit and the mountain resort of Dalat, previously spared by tacit agreement, was stormed.

The start of the uprising in Saigon was masked by the firecrackers set off to welcome the Year of the Monkey. But when the racket continued and people realized that it was the sound of small-arms they were hearing, they imagined that the fighting heralded a palace coup with Vice President Ky finally moving against President Thieu, though Thieu was more than 60 miles away in My Tho. In fact, Saigon was under attack by more than 4,000 Communists deployed in small teams. In the early hours of 31 January they hit their first

compound wall, killed five GIs on guard there, and held the compound for six and a half hours, to the consternation of the American public who saw the battle for the Embassy on TV. By the end of the battle the beautiful white walls of the six-storey Embassy building – a symbol of American power and prestige which dominated downtown Saigon – were riddled with bullet holes. Its green manicured lawns were stained red with blood, and its flower beds piled with corpses.

Youthful hard-core Vietcong fighters, heavily guarded, await interrogation following capture in the attacks on the capital city during the Tet holiday period in 1968.

target, the Presidential Palace. Other public buildings came under attack and the Vietcong swept through the Chinese quarter of Cholon.

At 0300hrs a nineteen-man VC suicide squad seized the compound of the US Embassy with the aid of a chauffeur nick-named Satchmo who had worked for the US mission for years. They arrived in a truck and a taxi, blasted their way through the

A second suicide squad took over Saigon's radio station. But the plug was pulled on them so they could not broadcast the propaganda tapes they had brought with them. When they ran out of ammunition, they blew up the building and themselves. American TV audiences saw grinning South Vietnamese soldiers searching their bodies for valuables. They were also shocked to see chief of police General Nguyen Ngoc Loan casually blow the brains out of a bound Vietcong suspect in the streets of Saigon.

No planes could take off or land at the Bien Hoa air base for 48 hours and the Communists held some areas of the city for ten days. For the first couple of days, US forces were confined to barracks in case the street fighting in Saigon was part of a popular uprising. But the ARVN were supplied with M16 automatic rifles for the first time. Eleven thousand ground troops were committed to fight just 1,000 VC on the streets of Saigon. The ARVN fought well, but the VC proved hard to dislodge, so the US Marines were brought in to blast the place. They brought in helicopter gunships, firing rockets that demolished whole rows of houses. Recoilless rifles took out houses where the VC were holed up. Civilians were killed and streets set ablaze. The homeless were forced to seek shelter in shanty towns made out of packing cases and drainage pipes.

In most places the offensive was quickly put down, but often at massive cost. The provincial town of Ben Tre was reduced to

Marines of D company, 1st Battalion, 5th Marine Corps, in the streets of Hué on the north side of the Perfume River on 24 February 1968.

Refugees flee the Communist-controlled sectors of Hué during the Tet New Year period. The Communists committed atrocities before they withdrew, slaughtering some 3,000 civilians.

rubble and ashes. 'It became necessary to destroy the town in order to save it,' a US spokesman explained.

Some of the worst damage occurred in the old imperial capital of Hué, where the Communists held out for twenty-five days. The battle for the Citadel there was one of the bitterest, and the city suffered one of the worst atrocities of the war. During the early hours of 31 January, Communist forces had poured into the city, meeting little resistance. They ran up the Vietcong flag on top of the Citadel, the ancient fortress in the centre. Armed with lists

drawn up months before, the Communists began a house-to-house search of the city, rounding up government employees, however minor, along with merchants, teachers, doctors, clergymen and foreigners. Around 3,000 people were shot, clubbed to death or buried alive in mass graves. A janitor who worked part-time in a government office was shot with his two children; a cigarette vendor was executed because her sister worked for the government. The dead included three German doctors, two French missionaries and Stephen Miller of the US Information Service.

Over the next 25 days, US Marines and ARVN troops fought their way back into the city, street by street, inflicting terrible damage. Nearly 150 Marines were killed, along with 400 South Vietnamese and an estimated 5,000 Communists. During the battle the 1st Air Cavalry prevented the infiltration of three fresh NVA regiments. But the Communist troops inside the city did not melt away as before. Despite their reluctance to use huge firepower inside the historic city, the Marines eventually deployed their deadly Ontos. The city was also hit by 5,191 naval rounds,

18,091 artillery rounds and 290,877 pounds of bombs, including 500-pound napalm canisters and 250-pound 'Snakeye' bombs. As a result, nearly three-quarters of the city was destroyed, including many of the former royal buildings, museums, libraries and Buddhist shrines, most notably, the Temple of Heaven.

During Tet some 2,000 Americans lost their lives, along with 4,000 ARVN and maybe as many as 50,000 NVA and VC. The massive Allied response had also wreaked havoc among the non-combatants, leaving 14,000 civilians dead, 24,000 injured, and 800,000

Marines of the second platoon of F Company, 2nd Battalion, 5th Marine Corps take cover behind a wall in the Citadel during the Battle of Hué. At last, the Marines could fight an old-fashioned battle against fixed positions, but at a terrible cost.

homeless. Nevertheless, the US considered Tet a military victory. Most of the Communist gains had been quickly reversed. Westmoreland even began to consider the Communists a spent force, while the ARVN had acquitted itself well. However, the Hanoi government had something to celebrate too. The Tet Offensive killed off much of the South Vietnamese component of the Vietcong, regarded by Hanoi as unreliable, picking up their news from the BBC World

'I SHALL NOT SEEK, AND WILL NOT ACCEPT, THE NOMINATION OF MY PARTY FOR ANOTHER TERM AS YOUR PRESIDENT'

Service instead of Radio Hanoi or Radio Moscow. The resulting decimation of the Vietcong allowed Northerners to take total control when Saigon eventually fell.

Tet had not finished off the ARVN, as Hanoi had been hoping, nor had it destabilized the South Vietnamese regime. But it had been an astonishing propaganda victory. Until the Tet Offensive no one in America had thought that the Communists were capable of staging a coordinated attack across the country on such a scale. Back home many people concluded that, after three years of fighting, if the US could not hold its own Embassy it could not hold the country. One of those to voice their disquiet was influential CBS TV news anchor Walter Cronkite. A Missouri boy and a former World War II war

correspondent, Cronkite was one of the most trusted men in America, who, according to one politician, could change the way thousands of Americans voted 'by a mere inflection of his deep baritone voice, or by a lifting of his well-known bushy eyebrows'.

From 1965 to 1968, he was evenhanded in his coverage of the war, reflecting the networks' caution not to show the Johnson administration's handling of the war in a bad light. But when news of the Vietcong's assault on the US embassy in Saigon reached New York just before the evening news, Cronkite exploded.

'What the hell's going on?' he yelled. 'I thought we were winning this war!'

When, on 2 February, President Johnson announced that the Tet Offensive was 'a complete failure', the veteran newsman decided to go to Vietnam to see for himself. This was his first visit since 1965. On 27 February 1968 he made a rare personal report on CBS, saying that it was now 'more certain than ever that the bloody experience of Vietnam is to end in stalemate'. He saw just one way out: negotiations with Hanoi, and he said so. Johnson, who was watching the broadcast, turned to an aide and said, 'If I've lost Walter, I've lost Mr Average Citizen.'

But Cronkite was merely reflecting public opinion rather than leading it. On 20 February the Senate Foreign Relations Committee had begun televised hearings which were openly critical of the war. Two days later, the US military authorities in Vietnam released the weekly total of combat deaths – 543, the highest yet. Public opinion would not stand for that rate of loss when the American people had been told that their technologically superior army was only facing a bunch of poorly-armed peasants.

Worse was to come. On 12 March the peace candidate Senator Eugene McCarthy, a virtual unknown, took 42 per cent of the poll in the New Hampshire primary with only 300 votes less than Johnson, the incumbent. Four days later, Senator Robert Kennedy, brother of the late President John F. Kennedy, entered the race for the presidential nomination, also on a peace platform. On 18 March 139 Congressmen – including 41 Democrats – sponsored a resolution calling for an immediate congressional review of the administration's Vietnam policy. Johnson's approval rating plummeted from 48 per cent to 36 per cent. In a dramatic TV broadcast on 31 March, Johnson announced a limitation of air strikes against the North to below the 20th parallel, stopping the bombing of Hanoi and Haiphong and limiting it to the border region, and he offered peace talks. Although this seemed like a magnanimous gesture, Johnson was in fact caving into the Communists' strategy. Johnson then dropped the bombshell:

'I shall not seek, and will not accept, the nomination of my party for another term as your president,' he said. Instead he would 'rise above partisan divisions' and devote himself to the pursuit of an honourable peace.

Cronkite was invited to visit Hanoi, but declined in case it was perceived as a reward

A Chinook helicopter comes in to land while marines cover with M-60, location HMM-46 just west of Khe Sanh. The hill fort there was supposed to prevent the NVA coming over the DMZ. It failed. Instead, in 1968, it found itself surrounded and many feared that the Americans were about to face their Dien Bien Phu.

for his criticism of the war. Another seasoned CBS correspondent, Charles Collingwood, went instead. In an interview with Collingwood on 5 April, North Vietnamese Foreign Minister Nguyen Duy Trinh formally agreed to open talks and on 3 May Paris was chosen as the venue.

THE SIEGE OF KHE SANH

While all this was going on, the American people were treated to nightly reports from the bunkers of Khe Sanh, which remained under siege for 77 days. Fifteen miles south of the DMZ and near to the Laotian border, this forward base straddled Route 9, an old French road that linked the Laotian towns along the Mekong to the coast, and it had become a major infiltration route. A base had first been established around a French airstrip there by the Green Berets so that they could recruit and train local hill tribesman. At that time, the rolling hills around the little village of Khe Sanh were considered one of the most beautiful places on earth, but all that was about to change. In the summer of 1966, General Westmoreland strengthened the base at Khe Sanh as a springboard for operations into Laos, which

President Johnson later vetoed. Bulldozers were brought in to extend the French airstrip, which was carpeted with metal planking, while engineers built a huge new combat base. Tons of ammunition and matériel were stockpiled there, and a battalion of US Marines was sent in to defend it.

Throughout 1967, the Marines met the North Vietnamese Army in a number of pitched battles in the surrounding hills. Then in late 1967, intelligence reports indicated the Communists were gearing up for a major attack. Sensors on the Ho Chi Minh trail picked up just over 1,000 truck movements around Khe Sanh. By December that number had increased to 6,500 and in early January 1968 there were reports of large-scale NVA troop movements in the area between Route 9 and the DMZ. By that time there were 6,000 Marines at Khe Sanh. On 10 January, a Marine detachment patrolling the surrounding hills ran into a battalion of NVA. The ensuing firefight convinced the base commander Colonel David E. Lownds that the long-awaited attack was now on its way. A showing of the Elvis Presley movie *Paradise Hawaiian Style* was cancelled and the Officers' Club closed until further notice. Marines cleared their small arms with short bursts of fire. The 105mm artillery guns were readied. The barbed wire defensive perimeter was checked and extra claymore mines and trip flares were laid.

NVA gunners began to lob range-finding shells into the compound and the Marines started wearing their flak jackets at all times. The Marine artillery returned H&I (harassment and interdiction fire), though they had problems identifying their targets, the low cloud and dense fog that shrouded the surrounding hills making it impossible for airborne observers to 'walk' the Marine's gunfire onto the NVA artillery positions. The various electronic sensors in the area were too inaccurate to tell if the Marines had hit anything, and to send observations teams out into the NVA-infested territory would be the same as handing the spotters their death certificates at the gates of the camp.

On nearby Hill 881S (881 South), Captain Bill Dabney and India Company met an NVA lieutenant who strolled up to the patrol waving a white flag. He told Marine interrogators that the NVA planned to attack at 0030hrs that night. After overrunning the base at Khe Sanh and the surrounding hills, they would go on to take the cities of Quang Tri province and Hué. Although the man could have been a plant to spook the Marines, Lownds decided that he had nothing to lose by believing him. Exactly as the deserter had predicted, Hill 861 to the east came under heavy rocket, mortar and machine-gun fire and a fierce battle for the possession of the hill broke out. Five hours later, the base itself came under fire. Hundreds of 122mm rockets, each of them weighing over 100 pounds, screamed into the Marine positions. One of the first hit a large ammunition bunker, and the whole plateau was lit up as 1,500 tons of ammunition went sky high. Shells of every description came raining down, some exploding on impact, others 'cooking off' in the intense fires caused as the oil and aviation fuel dumps ignited. Buildings were blown away and the helicopters parked on the airstrip were knocked over like nine-pins. The explosion reduced the length of the runway to 2,000 feet, which meant that four-engined C-130 Hercules aircraft were unable to land. Only smaller twin-engined C-123 Providers with one-third the cargo capacity could get in. They had to be turned around within three minutes. Meanwhile, more rockets, artillery shells and heavy-mortar rounds came screaming into the compound.

On the morning of 21 January, the sun

A SHOWING OF THE ELVIS PRESLEY MOVIE PARADISE HAWAIIAN STYLE WAS CANCELLED AND THE OFFICERS' CLUB CLOSED

came up to reveal what was left of the base. Fires were still burning. There was blackened debris everywhere and the compound was full of unexploded ordinance and shrapnel. As the tired and shell-shocked Marines struggled to put the base back onto a war footing, they were constantly harassed by more incoming fire. For the rest of the month, the NVA kept up its pressure on Khe Sanh and the surrounding hills. But abandoning the battle-scarred base was not an option. Westmoreland had gone on TV, telling the American people how important it was to hold Khe Sanh and there was no chance of the world being allowed to see Marines retreating down Route 9 with their tails between their legs. Westmoreland believed that the battle for Khe Sanh would be as

The Marines did not want to hold Khe Sanh, seeing it as of little strategic importance. But hold it they did, losing 204 men doing so. Some 1,622 NVA bodies were left on the battlefield, though Westmoreland reckoned between 10,000 and 15,000 had been killed.

decisive as the battle for Dien Bien Phu. Walter Cronkite agreed.

'The parallels were there for all to see,' he told a CBS radio audience.

Even the formidable 304th Division that had won the day at Dien Bien Phu turned up on the battlefield. During the siege, President Johnson had a sand-table model of the base built in the basement of the White House and, expressing his fear that Khe Sanh might turn into another Dien Bien Phu, took the unprece-

dented step of having a declaration that they would hold Khe Sanh 'signed in blood' by the entire Joint Chiefs of Staff. On 10 February a North Vietnamese newspaper also picked up on the analogy. But the analogy was wrong.

At Dien Bien Phu the French had been caught in a remote valley where they could not be resupplied and were outgunned by superior Vietnamese artillery. Throughout the siege at Khe Sanh the Marines were resupplied by parachute drops and landings on the airstrip,

January, when 600 tactical air strikes were flown against enemy bunkers, trench and tunnel networks, supply depots, assembly areas, and forward units. The French fort at Dien Bien Phu also lay in a valley, while the Vietminh occupied the surrounding hills, while at Khe Sanh, the Marines held onto the surrounding hills, despite intense fighting.

At Dien Bien Phu, both the Vietminh and French had massed themselves for a final battle: at Khe Sanh, both sides knew that was not on the cards. A Communist victory could not be decisive, as the US was still entrenched throughout the South. Besides, the French had lost at Dien Bien Phu; Westmoreland was determined to win. He had moved 6,000 Marines into the area and initiated Operation Niagara, the campaign of tactical air strikes against the NVA that would break up enemy concentrations and make an organized attack on the Marine base impossible. Westmoreland even drew up plans to use tactical nuclear weapons, arguing that this would force the Communists to capitulate. Fearing protests at home, Washington issued a directive ordering him to halt these plans in case the press found out. On 16 February, after much public speculation, President Johnson denied that he ever considered using nuclear weapons in Vietnam.

Some 2,000 French and 8,000 Vietminh troops died in the 54-day siege at Dien Bien Phu. At Khe Sanh, just 204 Marines died during the siege and, although only 1,622 NVA bodies were left on the battlefield, Westmoreland reckoned between 10,000 and 15,000 were killed. Some Communist units had losses of 90 per cent. Even the NVA

which had been repaired, though planes landing there were shot at and hit by rockets. Three C-123s and two C-130s were lost, and a Marine was killed when a pallet from an air drop crashed onto his bunker. Neither was Khe Sanh outgunned. It had artillery support from the Rockpile and Camp Carroll, and more than 75,000 tons of high explosives were dropped on the NVA formations – the largest aerial assault on a tactical target in the history of warfare. This had begun as early as 6 commander, General Giap, almost lost his life at Khe Sanh, when 36 B-52s bombarded his field headquarters with 1000 tons of high explosives after intelligence intercepts revealed that a high-ranking Communist was in the area. But despite their losses, the NVA and Vietcong had good strategic reasons to continue their assault. America had made the battle a test of its prestige and the fighting there diverted 30,000 US troops away from the South Vietnamese cities that were the targets of the Tet Offensive.

Throughout the siege, Westmoreland maintained that the Tet Offensive was just a feint to distract the American forces from the main struggle at Khe Sanh. Khe Sanh was the feint. However, had Khe Sanh fallen after the US humiliation at its Embassy in Saigon it is unlikely that the American people would have allowed the war to continue.

The US Marine Corps itself was not happy about defending Khe Sanh. Marine commander Major-General Lowell English described Khe Sanh as 'a trap' which forced Westmoreland to expend 'absolutely unreasonable amounts of men and matériel to defend a piece of terrain that wasn't worth a damn'. He had not wanted to defend it in the first place, and General Westmoreland used the siege as an excuse to put the Corps under army command and its air wing under the control of the air force.

As the siege continued into February, the base continued to be pounded daily by enemy fire and the Marines were constantly on the alert for the unstoppable human-wave assaults that the NVA mounted. Ditches regularly snaked their way up toward the perimeter wire and the NVA constantly probed the defences. But the Marines drew comfort from the amount of firepower they could call in. The base itself had plenty of heavy mortars and batteries of 105 and 155mm guns, and barrages from the sixteen huge 175mms at the Rockpile and Camp Carroll to the northeast could be called in. B-52s, along with 350 fighter-bombers from the USAF, navy, and Marine Corps, would pound everything from the NVA positions just outside the wire to their supply areas and long-range gun platforms over in Laos. Poor visibility hampered air support, but low-level bombers would go right down through the ack-ack fire into the soup and hope that during bombing runs they did not fly into one of the hills in the area that rose to 1000 feet. Over hot targets, the bombing runs came in so thick and fast that the planes would stack up in a holding pattern, which one pilot compared to the traffic pattern at O'Hare on a foggy day. Pilots of the A-4 Skyhawk, A-6 Intruder, F-4 Phantom, and F-8 Crusader strike aircraft had to make instant decisions in cloud cover, dodging enemy fire, whether the people on the ground were a formation of NVA or a group of refugees fleeing the area, while the B-52s bombed up to within 1,000 feet of the Marines, though 3,000 was considered the safe distance. Closer than that, 500-pound high-explosive bombs would burst eardrums, at the very least. Up to 108 were dropped at a time. In all 2,700 B-52 missions and 24,000 tactical air strikes were made during the defence of Khe Sanh, while AC-47 'Puff the Magic Dragon' gunships maintained the pressure on the NVA at night. Despite the appalling weather conditions only one F-4 Phantom and one A-4 Skyhawk were lost, though the Marines also lost seventeen helicopters that resupplied positions on the outlying hills.

Living conditions inside the base became intolerable. The constant noise of incoming and outgoing artillery shells and the scream of jets overhead meant the men got little sleep. Piles of garbage mouldered around the base. Human excrement had to be doused in black oil and burned in oil drums. The stench was sickening. The Marines lived in underground bunkers that reeked of sweat and urine, plagued by rats that would jump on them from the rafters at night. Men trying to sleep would cover their faces to prevent them being bitten. Bites developed into ugly infections and

US Marines at Khe Sanh prepare defences during the siege in 1968.

running sores, which some men encouraged by smearing their toes with peanut butter – a bad rat bite was a ticket out of Khe Sanh.

The base was hit by over 1,000 rounds of incoming fire some days. Any movement above ground attracted the attention of snipers. On 23 February, 29 men from Bravo company under Lieutenant Jacques went out to deal with an NVA mortar position that was pounding the base with uncanny accuracy. They walked straight into a wave of rifle fire and only four of them made it back to the perimeter. The remains of the other 25 lay outside the wire for four weeks before they could be retrieved.

BITES DEVELOPED INTO… RUNNING SORES, WHICH SOME MEN ENCOURAGED BY SMEARING THEIR TOES WITH PEANUT BUTTER

Each morning a tattered Stars and Stripes would be hauled up the flagpole on Hill 881S to show that the Marines still occupied it. Captain Dabney ordered his men to stand to attention until the last note of the bugle had sounded, despite being in the enemy line of fire. Some days the battle became so intense that men had to stand in line to piss on the mortar tubes to keep them cool. On Hill 881, the casualty rate was 50 per cent and the men got down to a one-quart canteen of water a day. Marines were constantly in danger of being shot by snipers and medevac helicopters carrying the wounded were brought down. However, only small-scale attacks were launched against the base itself:

Westmoreland never got the full-scale battle that he craved.

Slowly, as the weather improved, more supplies got through and the men on Hill 881S could see well enough to call down accurate air strikes on the NVA. They knew they were winning when, on 1 April, two naked NVA soldiers ran up to their positions in broad daylight, asking to surrender. One was shot in the back by his own troops; Marines crawled out under heavy fire to retrieve the other one. Back in the trench, he seemed calm, until a Marine jet passed overhead, when he threw himself into the corner of the trench quivering uncontrollably. The air strikes were plainly taking their toll.

Although the Marines held on to the high ground overlooking Khe Sanh, which they had taken from the NVA in April and May 1967, the Special Forces camp at Lang Vei, eight miles southwest of Khe Sanh down Route 9, was overrun. It had been manned by twenty-two Green Berets and 400 CIDGs when, on 7 February, NVA tanks rolled in across the wire, the first time the North Vietnamese had used armour. The defenders stood no chance. The camp had been established as a base for guerrilla operations against the Ho Chi Minh trail across the border in Laos, not as a defensive position. There was a rudimentary defence plan, though. The commander, Captain Frank C. Willoughby, could call in artillery support from Khe Sanh, Camp Carroll and the Rockpile, whose guns were pre-registered on positions around the camp. Forward Air Controllers could call in USAF and Marine ground-attack aeroplanes and, if all else failed,

Colonel Lownds was to send two rifle companies by helicopter or by foot to Lang Vei.

When the NVA tanks came in, Willoughby called for artillery and air support. None came. He called Lownds, but his request for infantry reinforcements was refused. Lownds thought that the attack might be a feint to draw men away from the defence of Khe Sanh itself and his men were not equipped to fight tanks. Lang Vei was on its own.

As two Soviet-made PT-76 tanks, followed by two platoons of infantry crashed through the perimeter, Sergeant James Holt knocked them out with one of the base's two 105mm recoilless rifles. The tanks' crews, which included three women, bailed out of the burning vehicles. Then Holt spotted a third PT-76 blasting one of the bunkers, traversed the gun, and hit it with his last shot. Minutes later, two more tanks appeared and destroyed the abandoned gun.

Fifteen minutes after the attack had begun, the Special Forces base received some artillery support. The first shells came crashing down outside the perimeter. Willoughby called through corrections to the line of fire and zeroed the artillery on to the main assault. Ten minutes later a Spooky gunship arrived. The tanks pressed on regardless, shelling the emergency medical bunker, taking out a mortar position, and blasting their way into the inner compound. One tank was destroyed with grenades and an LAW rocket fired by an ad hoc tank-killer team under Lieutenant-Colonel Daniel F. Schungel, who had been visiting the base. Seeing their comrades incinerated in the burning PT-76, another crew abandoned their

tank, only to be shot as they fled.

Even so the NVA took the camp, all except for the command bunker where Willoughby, seven other Green Berets, the South Vietnamese camp commander, and twenty-five CIDGs held out. The NVA tried to destroy the bunker by driving their tanks over it, then blasting it with grenades, explosives, tear gas, and small-arms fire. Willoughby began destroying documents.

Then the words, 'We are going to blow up the bunker, give up now' in Vietnamese came echoing down the stairwell. After an animated discussion, the CIDGs ran out – only to be cut down by machine-gun fire. There were just eight Americans left alive now, six of whom were wounded. It was then that the NVA began digging their way into the bunker.

Help, however, was at hand. Half a mile to the east was an older camp, manned by Sergeants Richard Allen and Eugene Ashley, and Specialist Joel Johnson, along with around a hundred Lao. They called in strafing runs over the camp, then moved in on foot. They were met with mortar and machine-gun fire, and called in more air strikes. Runners went back to get their 51mm recoilless rifle. With this they breached the bunker line before being halted again. A shell killed Ashley and Johnson and the rest of the men withdrew.

After eighteen hours of siege, Willoughby and his men had run out of food and water. The situation was desperate, so he took desperate measures: he called in an air strike on his own position. This was followed by numerous dummy runs, during which the survivors managed to slip out of the camp, hampered only by gunfire from one bunker. When they reached the old camp they found Colonel Schungel who, despite being wounded three times, was trying to organize another rescue mission. Willoughby told him not to bother – everyone was dead – and called in more air strikes on Lang Vei. More than 200 of Lang Vei's defenders were killed or missing and the camp was lost. On 7 February, Marine helicopters brought out the survivors.

Back at Khe Sanh, the Marines clinging on by their fingertips feared the lifting of the siege, however. If it seemed like they were being rescued by an outside force, the Corps would be humiliated in front of the world. Worse, while the Marines sat watching the remains of 25 of their buddies rotting outside the wire for four weeks, 50 more leathernecks of Bravo Company had been killed and 135 wounded, few of whom had even seen the enemy. Morale in the Marine Corps was at an all-time low. When Lieutenant-General John J. Tolson, the commander of the 1st Air Cavalry, visited Khe Sanh to plan its relief, he said that the base was 'the most depressing and demoralizing place I have ever visited. It was a very depressing sight, completely unpoliced, strewn with rubble, duds and damaged equipment, and with troops living a life more similar to rats than to humans'.

But the honour of the Corps had to be upheld and Marine commander General Robert E. Cushman insisted, 'I want no implication of a rescue or breaking the siege by an outside force.'

First the Marine Corps had a score to settle. At 0800 on 30 March, in a thick fog, the men of Bravo Company climbed out of their bunkers and fixed bayonets. While 105mm recoilless rifles poured fire onto the enemy's position, they advanced inside a double box of artillery and mortar fire that kicked up the red earth all around them. But as they reached the enemy lines, the fog lifted and NVA mortar rounds came raining down on them. One of the first to be hit was the command group. The forward observers and the radio operator were killed. A fragment of shrapnel lodged in Captain Pipes two inches from his heart. But he stayed on his feet and urged his men forward. They used automatic fire, satchel charges, grenades, and flame-throwers to clear the enemy trenches. It took three hours. At the end, 115 NVA lay dead. Then Bravo Company returned to Khe Sanh, taking the 25 bodies of their lost patrol with them. While the dead Marines lay outside the wire, the NVA had not had time to pick over the remains and their watches, rings, wallets, and dog tags were still in place. The honour of the Corps had been redeemed on the battlefield.

Two days later, the Marines were allowed to lead the relief operation, Operation Pegasus, when two battalions moved down Route 9 from the east. But even the name of the operation seemed to be designed to humiliate the Marines, as Pegasus, the mythical flying horse, was an insignia of the Air Cavalry. Later that day, the 1st Air Cavalry began its much-publicized leapfrog down Route 9. There were no NVA in the area, but there were plenty of pressmen and TV crews present. As they neared the base, landing zones came

under fire and at one point the NVA staged a counter-attack, but this was quickly suppressed by a massive air and artillery assault. By 8 April, the road was clear and the Marines had to put on a brave smiles for the TV cameras as lead elements of the Air Cav arrived. To add insult to injury, it was an ARVN company that eventually reached Khe Sanh in force. Then a cocky young Air Cav trooper hung a sign on a Marines' bunker which read: 'Khe Sanh – Under new management, Delta Co, 2/7 Cav'.

By then, the area around Khe Sanh, once compared to the lush hills of Tuscany, was a barren moonscape. Where once there had been forests full of game and streams full of trout, there was no game, no trees, no trout and no streams. Nevertheless, Westmoreland would appear on the White House lawn and proclaim, 'Victory at Khe Sanh'.

This fooled no one. Although the NVA had been badly mauled, Khe Sanh had shown that the US forces were in fact vulnerable both in conventional warfare and guerrilla warfare,

Members of 101st Airborne Division pass a partially destroyed enemy hut next to a trail in jungle-covered mountains 15 miles southwest of Phu Bai in September 1968.

147

and Khe Sanh was ultimately seen by the American people as a victory for the Communists. Even at the time, it was a hollow victory for the Marines. Two months after it had been relieved, Khe Sanh was abandoned, though it was briefly re-established as logistics base for a disastrous incursion into Laos in 1971. The Hanoi government called the withdrawal from Khe Sanh the US's 'gravest defeat' so far. That same month, June 1968, Westmoreland was rotated home and kicked upstairs to become Army Chief of Staff after a report leaked to *The New York Times* revealed that, even in January, he had no idea that the Tet Offensive was imminent. He was replaced as commander in Vietnam by his deputy General Creighton W. Abrams.

THE **BEGINNING** OF **VIETNAMIZATION**

Abrams abandoned Westmoreland's strategy of trying to trap the enemy into large-scale engagements and began a policy of what would be known as Vietnamization – that is, the replacement of US troops with the

Tan Son Nhut – an ARVN soldier holds a Chicom machine-gun captured by his unit while on a sweep near the old French cemetery on Plantation Road on 7 May 1968.

ARVN and other South Vietnamese forces. Part of this programme was to encourage the CIDG programme. The loss of Lang Vei was a setback. Then on 12 May 1968, the CIDG camp at Kham Duc was overrun by elements of the 2nd NVA Division. The Green Berets A-105 Detachment there was decimated and a relieving force from the American Division suffered heavy casualties. As a result there was a rout of the CIDGs. With CIDG detachments now under attack from the NVA main force, their casualties grew and they soon ran out of trained and experienced men. The Green Berets could then find little use for them. The mountain tribes who made up the CIDGs had little love for the ethnic Vietnamese and when they were handed over to the ARVN they effectively disappeared.

By the time Abrams took over, the 82nd Airborne had arrived in Vietnam and US troops in country topped 495,000 men. Despite the fact that General Westmoreland had declared that the Communists had suffered a 'military defeat' at Tet, they continue to shell South Vietnamese cities and, on 2 March, succeeded in killing 48 men of the US 25th Infantry Division in an ambush at Tan Son Nhut. The body counts continued to climb, showing the Communists' strength had not been diminished.

The ARVN had mobilized an extra 11,000 troops and announced that they planned to invade the North with a 'volunteer force'. The idea was immediately quashed by Washington, who were making peace overtures. Although on 3 May Hanoi agreed that Paris would be the venue for the peace talks, this did not diminish the Vietcong's willingness to fight. Two days later 'mini-Tet' began with ground assaults in Saigon and the shelling of 119 towns, cities and barracks. The Paris peace talks opened on 10 May amid an air of optimism. The US delegation was headed by 77-year-old Averell Harriman, former Assistant Secretary of State for Far Eastern affairs in the Kennedy administration, while the North Vietnamese negotiators were led by Xuan Thuy, a former foreign minister. The Americans had checked into hotels, rather than arranging more permanent accommoda-

THE COMMUNISTS REFUSED EVEN TO DISCUSS THE MATTER

tion, believing that a settlement was only months away. Almost as soon as the talks opened, however, they were deadlocked. The US delegation demanded a withdrawal of the North Vietnamese troops from South Vietnam. The Communists refused even to discuss the matter. Instead, the North Vietnamese insisted that the Saigon government be re-formed to include representatives of the Vietcong, but the Americans rejected this. This stand-off lasted for another five years. During that time, more Americans would be killed in Vietnam than had been lost previously and the US would be torn apart by internal dissent. Meanwhile, the fighting in Saigon had spread to the Tan Son Nhut airbase, the Phu Tho race track and the Cholon district, where the battle climaxed on 12 May with US jets dropping high explosives

Representatives of the governments of the United States and North Vietnam meet in Paris in May 1968 for preliminary talks.

and napalm. In the countryside, fresh search-and-destroy operations claimed more enemy casualties. In Saigon, a third battle for the city broke out on 25 May. It lasted eleven days with, once again, the heaviest fighting taking place in Cholon.

July began with a lull in attacks by the North, but the VC managed yet another assault on Saigon. Meanwhile Hanoi released three US airmen as a gesture of good will. At the same time in Paris, Xuan Thuy denounced US participation in the war. Despite the talks, Johnson reassured President Thieu that talk of a major change in US policy was 'absolute tommyrot and fiction'.

Vice-President Ky clarified South Vietnam's position, saying, 'The only way to win over the Communists is by military strength. We cannot have a coalition with them.'

The ARVN stepped up its own search-and-

on a state of maximum readiness.

In August, Johnson urged Hanoi to respond to the limits he had put on the bombing. In September, the nine hundredth US plane was shot down over the North and, on 11 October, *The New York Times* revealed that the US had offered to halt the bombing of the North completely if Hanoi would make concessions. Three days later, the US released 14 North Vietnamese sailors in its own goodwill gesture. US forces continued fighting on the ground but, on 31 October, just five days before the US election, President Johnson tried to jump-start the talks again. He went on national TV to announce a complete halt to the bombing campaign against the North. All naval and artillery bombardments would also cease as part of his policy of 'de-escalating the war and moving seriously toward peace'. Bombing had ended at 0800 Eastern Standard Time that morning. Since 1965, over 2.5 million tons of bombs had been dropped on the North, and over 300,000 sorties flown, with nearly half a ton of explosives being dropped each minute for three-and-a-half years, with no notable effect. Indeed, during that time infiltration down the Ho Chi Minh trail had soared and the NVA strength south of the DMZ had increased by an estimated 75 per cent. Rolling Thunder may have stiffened morale in the South, but it also hardened the attitude to the war in the North.

Johnson told the TV audience that he had halted the bombing because of favourable developments in Paris. The North Vietnamese delegation took the hint and, in

destroy missions, claiming dizzying body counts. The response was renewed attacks by the NVA, who besieged the US Special Forces camp in Duc Lap, while the VC once again shelled Saigon. Even Thieu himself seemed to be under threat. After rumours of an attempted coup, he appeared on national TV on 10 October to assure viewers that his government was under no threat. The day before, though, he had put his troops in Saigon

Richard Nixon enjoying his triumph in the 1968 presidential election. He promised 'peace with honour'. Instead, he extended the war with illegal incursions into Cambodia and Laos.

exchange for the bombing halt, agreed to enter into more meaningful discussions in Paris. To find a way around the impasse, it was suggested that the talks be widened to include delegations from the South Vietnamese government and the Vietcong. If this was designed to swing the election it failed. The Democratic candidate in 1968 was Hubert Humphrey, Johnson's vice president. Although by this time the Democrats had

turned sharply against the war, it was hard for Humphrey to distance himself from the policies of the Johnson administration that had got America into the war in the first place. On the other hand, the Republicans had picked Richard Nixon, a former hawk who now promised to 'bring an honourable end to the war'. However, he failed to bring an honourable end to the election. Behind the scenes, a prominent supporter of Richard

Nixon offered South Vietnam's President Thieu better terms if they stayed out of the talks in Paris. On 2 November, the Saigon government announced they would boycott the talks because of the presence of the NLF. Explaining Saigon's position, Vice-President Ky said, 'We can no longer trust the Americans: they are just a band of crooks'. On 5 November, six years after losing the gubernatorial race in his native California and dropping out of politics, former vice president in the Eisenhower administration Richard Nixon was elected 37th President of the United States.

After a situation briefing at the White House on 11 November, Nixon said that Johnson spoke for him on the war until he assumed office in January. Meanwhile, on the ground, the Communists made a mad scramble to improve their position in the South prior to Nixon's inauguration. The US announced that the movement of military vehicles in southern North Vietnam had increased three-fold since the bombing ended. The NVA moved back into the DMZ and the Vietcong High Command ordered an all-out effort to smash the Phoenix Program. Although targets in the North were now off limits, B-52s were used to bomb Communist bases near the Cambodian border and to stifle any renewed attack on Saigon.

However, to the end, Johnson tried to sue for peace. After heavy US pressure, the Saigon government agreed to join the peace talks, despite the presence of the NLF. But when the South Vietnamese delegation under Vice President Ky arrived in Paris on 26 November, the talks immediately hit a snag again over the shape of the table. The Hanoi government wanted a square table, while the US wanted it oblong. Eventually, they compromised on a round one.

M113 armoured personnel carriers from 1st Squadron, 11th Armour Cavalry wait for the order to advance against a suspected Vietcong position at Long Bin on 23 February 1969. Although both sides resorted to armour, it was of little use until the dying days of the war.

7

THE WAR
AT HOME

ROTESTS ABOUT the US involvement in Vietnam began before the large-scale commitment of American ground troops in March 1965. The early protesters were for the most part old-fashioned pacifists and liberal intellectuals, but when the war started in earnest, student activists already committed to the civil rights movement and other radical causes soon began coming out against it.

In April 1965 Students for a Democratic Society, the student civil rights organization under Tom Hayden, mobilized a 25,000-strong national march on Washington, DC. What impact it had was largely negative. In January 1965 a Harris poll showed that 59 per cent of Americans were cool on the Johnson administration's policy in Vietnam. By the summer, in contrast, a solid two-thirds majority backed the administration. The anti-war movement intensified in parallel with the intensification of the conflict, however, and over time, that majority was gradually eroded.

There were good reasons for students to take a stand against the Vietnam War. One was that the young men who actually had to go and fight the war had cause to question its purpose. This was especially true on campus, where the civil rights movement had familiarized students with the effectiveness of protest. At the time, there was a moral battle going on for the heart of America that was being fought and won by committed pacifists. Since the early 1960s, nonviolent civil rights marchers – both black and white – had been abused, beaten and even killed, protesting against segregated schools, housing, transportation, and unfair literacy and civics tests that barred many African-Americans in the southern states from voting. Despite baton-wielding state troopers, Ku Klux Klan bombers, White supremacist snipers, rock-throwing racists and the murderous assaults of police chiefs such as Bull Connor in Birmingham, Alabama, who set dogs on child protesters, nonviolent tactics were seen to triumph. With the passing of the Voting Rights Act in August 1965, the civil rights protesters felt they had won the first round in the civil rights struggle. This left a large number of radical activists with a wealth of organizational ability and the feeling that they could win any battle, whatever was ranged against them. Soon the anti-war movement and the civil rights movement became closely intertwined.

Many of the civil rights leaders were committed pacifists. Martin Luther King Jr spoke out against the war, bringing to bear his enormous moral authority. The war itself was racially divisive. African-Americans did not find it as easy as middle-class white youths to evade the draft. Under the Selective Service Act of 1948, 26,800,000 young American males were eligible for military service. Of these, 8,720,000 volunteered for military service and 2,215,000 were drafted. Those who volunteered could often wangle a non-combatant job, or they could join the National Guard, spending six months on active duty training before returning to civilian life, though for the next six years, they would have to attend a two-week summer camp and meetings every other weekend. This was the path favoured by George W. Bush. Only 2.5

Opposite: Kent State, Ohio, in the aftermath of the shootings on 4 May 1970. One of the four students shot dead by the Ohio National Guard lies in a pool of blood. This was the final straw. Although President Nixon dismissed the protesters as bums, middle-class parents were now seeing their children shot down by their own government.

per cent of those eligible for the draft, 570,000 in all, became 'draft dodgers'. They avoided the call-up by failing to register or by moving abroad. Canada, Mexico, and Sweden provided havens for those avoiding conscription. The Canadian immigration authorities registered some 30,000 draft dodgers, but it is thought another 50,000 settled there illegally. Bill Clinton sat out the war in Britain, but this option became unpopular when, controversially, some US citizens were deported back to America to face military service. However, the problem of draft dodgers was tiny compared with the 15,410,000 men who were disqualified or obtained some exemption or deferment more or less legitimately. The sons of well-off white families could easily get a deferment by staying on at college, getting married, feigning homosexuality, or faking a medical condition. Some took drugs to raise their blood pressure, others punctured their arms to simulate needle tracks. Doctors – usually middle-class white men themselves – were often sympathetic. 'I save lives by keeping people out of the army,' said one.

President Johnson introduced a policy that drafted African-Americans preferentially. He did this not for racist reasons, but because he felt that, by putting deprived black men in the armed services, he could provide them with improved health care and education, and promote their social advancement. Many African-Americans were not opposed to this, to start with. After centuries of discrimina-

Some African-Americans saw the war as an opportunity to demonstrate their full citizenship. Others saw it as a conspiracy to get rid of them.

tion, they saw fighting in the war as a chance to prove their worth to their country. Others thought that the war in Vietnam had nothing to do with them. The real enemy was back home. Al Harrison, civil rights organizer at Detroit's Wayne State University, said, 'We got no business fighting a yellow man's war to save the white man.'

In April 1967, the heavyweight boxing champion of the world Muhammad Ali refused to be inducted into the armed forces on religious grounds: in 1964, he had joined the Nation of Islam, better known then as the Black Muslims. He was stripped of his title and prosecuted. He was sentenced to five years in jail and fined $10,000 for draft evasion, though the conviction was overturned by the US Supreme Court in 1971. He won his title back by beating George Foreman in 1974.

It was indisputable that African-Americans bore an unfair burden in Vietnam. While just 8 per cent of the military were black, in 1965 African-Americans made up some 23 per cent of the enlisted soldiers killed in action. There were few black officers, though Major-General Beauregarde Brown III was made head of MACV logistics. Since Vietnam, many African-Americans have been promoted to the highest ranks of the US Army. Colin Powell and others started their careers in Vietnam. But at that time, medals and stripes came easier to whites. Less than 3 per cent of the officers in the Army were black, less than 1 per cent in the Marines. The feeling that African-

Thieb Tieu Dieu, a Buddhist priest, burns himself to death in protest against South Vietnamese government policies in Hué in 1965.

Americans were being unfairly sacrificed in a foreign war helped foment further racial conflict at home. It was only after the beginning of the Vietnam War that rioting spread to the black ghettos of the northern cities and those of the West Coast. In 1967, the 82nd Airborne had to be sent into Detroit's Twelfth Street ghetto to restore order, and the assassination of Malcolm X in 1965 and Martin Luther King in 1968 cranked up race tension to a level where groups such as the Black Panthers were openly advocating insurrection.

On 21 April 1965, a Buddhist monk publicly burnt himself to death in Saigon as a protest against the war. Television pictures of the ritual suicide were relayed around the world. Other Vietnamese monks and a young girl followed suit.

This potent form of protest was brought horrifyingly home to America on 2 November when Norman Morrison, a 31-year-old Quaker and father of three, burnt himself to death outside the Pentagon. He was holding his three-year-old daughter when his clothes caught fire, but dropped her just in time. She was rescued unharmed by a passer-by. A week later, on 9 November, Roger Allen LaPorte of the Catholic Workers movement burnt himself to death outside the United Nations building in New York. The impact was enormous. Ninety-three per cent of American homes had a TV and Americans could witness these self-immolations in their own front rooms. Fortunately, they were few and far between; mass protest, sit-ins and, ultimately, full-scale riots were found to be a more effective tactic.

Anti-war activists also tried to halt troop trains. In June 1965 protesters held up the 173rd Airborne Brigade who were en route to Saigon. Later that summer the Vietnam Day Committee, formed on the campus of the University of California at Berkeley in the spring, organized further attempts to stop trains. These were unsuccessful, as only a handful of hard-core radicals were prepared to stand in front of a train full of armed troops. Most protesters would only picket local induction centres or join marches.

On 27 November 1965, a demonstration of 30,000 of the older, quieter protesters took

ON 9 NOVEMBER, ROGER ALLEN LAPORTE OF THE CATHOLIC WORKERS MOVEMENT BURNT HIMSELF TO DEATH

place in Washington, DC. It was organized by SANE, the Committee for a Sane Nuclear Policy. Its most famous member was Dr Benjamin Spock, whose best-selling book *Common Sense Book of Baby and Child Care* was the paediatric bible to the parents of the Vietnam War generation. His presence was a major boost to the anti-war movement's respectability in the public's eyes and attracted many other older liberals. The more radical protesters carrying banners calling for the immediate withdrawal of US troops from Vietnam were persuaded to keep a low profile. The march's leaders made speeches calling for an end to the American troop build-up and condemning both sides for not making any

Anti-Vietnam War campaigners staged a protest march in New York on 17 April 1965, with young men of draft age making clear their determination not to fight.

serious effort to find a negotiated settlement.

As these so-called 'peaceniks', later known as 'Vietniks', marched around the White House, their moderate banners called for a 'Supervised Ceasefire' and claimed that 'War Erodes The Great Society'. President Johnson issued a statement the next day saying: 'Dissent is a sign of political vigour'. However, the vigour came, not from the liberals who protested outside the White House, but radicals across the country who had already adopted a new and dramatic form of protest.

In mid-October 1965 David Millar, a 22-year-old Jesuit charity worker in a Bowery soup kitchen, held up his draft card at an anti-war rally in New York City.

'I believe the napalming of villages is an immoral act,' he declared, holding a match to the corner of the card. 'I hope this is a significant act – so here goes.'

He lit it and was arrested by the FBI. At the end of October, he became the first American to be arraigned under a new law that made draft-card burning a federal offence with a maximum penalty of five years in jail and a $10,000 fine. The pacifist Terry Sullivan was sent to jail for a year for destroying his draft card. Millar was certainly right in one respect – it was a significant act. Draft-card burning became a regular feature of anti-war demonstrations and the nightly news. The cameras would also capture infuriated onlookers attacking the protesters or dousing the flames with water or fire extinguishers. The leading ranks of a New York march were drenched with red paint; in Chicago and Oakland, demonstrators were pelted with eggs. In Detroit, marchers chanting 'Hey, hey, LBJ! How many kids did you kill today?' were drowned out by pro-war protesters singing 'The Star Spangled Banner'. When leading pacifist David Dellinger visited North Vietnam in 1966, he was denounced as a traitor.

Despite the opposition of a great many ordinary people, the protests continued. In New York and Chicago, students seized university administration buildings in protest. At New York University, 130 students and members of the faculty walked out when Defense Secretary Robert McNamara turned up to collect an honourary degree. Although attitudes towards the war were often split along the generation line, teachers soon began to support their students, whose leaders were calling for an end to the draft. In June 1966, *The New York Times* ran an anti-war ad signed by 6,400 academics, and on 13 November, 138 prominent Americans signed

a document urging 'men of stature in the intellectual, religious, and public service communities' to withdraw their support for America's policy in Vietnam, although five days later the American National Conference of Catholic Bishops confirmed its support of US actions in Southeast Asia.

By 1967 American society was becoming increasingly divided. The anti-war movement now embraced a broad coalition of radical groups. The anti-war intellectuals, notably Dr Spock, the novelist Norman Mailer, and MIT linguistics professor Noam Chomsky, had been addressing 'teach-ins' at colleges organized by Students for a Democratic Society. This caused problems among pro-war parents. One mother asked for her son's college scholarship to be revoked after he was shown Vietcong propaganda movies at school. But in 1967, these leading anti-war activists began to appear on television. Even on Johnny Carson's *Tonight* show, guests openly expressed anti-war sentiments, though Carson kept his views to himself.

Television played a key role in the war. Vietnam was the first televised war. As well as giving the protesters a voice, it showed vivid scenes of the fighting every evening on the nightly news. Unlike wars before and since, in Vietnam the military had no chance to restrict TV crews' access to the war zone or censor their coverage. American viewers could witness every mistake and reverse. They could see grunts zipping hootches, or Americans bombing and shelling Vietnamese homes in Saigon after the Tet Offensive. The American custom of shipping their dead home in body bags also damaged domestic morale. The British, by contrast, like to bury their dead on the battlefield – it is considered an honour so 'that there's some corner of a foreign field that is forever England'. In America, consignments of coffins arriving at airports and endless hometown funerals made the nation's losses very public.

In January 1967, the US Court of Appeal ruled unanimously that local draft boards could not punish anti-war protesters by reclassifying them 1-A. On 31 January 2,000 clergymen marched on Washington, DC, demanding an end to the bombing of North Vietnam. In February, there was a three-day 'Fast for Peace' by Christians and Jews and, in March, Martin Luther King told 5,000 demonstrators in Chicago that the war in Vietnam was a 'blasphemy against all that America stands for'.

On the weekend of 15–16 April 1967, 125,000 anti-war demonstrators gathered in New York, with another 5,000 in San Francisco as part of the 'Spring Mobilization to End the War in Vietnam'. At a demonstration in Central Park, protesters in bizarre costumes carried placards that said 'Draft beer, not boys' and 'I don't give a damn for Uncle Sam'. One African-American held a sign that pointed out 'No Vietcong ever called me Nigger'. Dr King delivered a statement to the United Nations, accusing the US of violating its charter. However, protesters outside the UN building still had to be protected from pro-war demonstrators by mounted policemen. These protests were condemned by the House Un-American Activities Committee, who claimed that they were inspired by Communists. Their report was, in turn, condemned by Reverend James L. Bevel, a prominent anti-war cleric and Dr King's adviser. Senator Robert Kennedy spoke out defending 'the right to criticize and dissent' and said that those donating blood to North Vietnam were maintaining 'the oldest tradition of this country'.

The anti-war protests were already having an effect. Nixon, who was criticizing the Johnson administration for taking a soft line on Vietnam, claimed on a visit to Saigon that 'this apparent division at home' was 'prolonging the war'. Westmoreland said that anti-war activity in the US 'gives him [the enemy] hope that he can win politically that which he cannot accomplish militarily'. He went on to say that his troops in Vietnam were 'dismayed, and so am I, by recent unpatriotic acts at home'. And on a visit home in April 1967, he addressed Congress in an attempt to stiffen the resolve of the American people.

'Backed at home by resolve, confidence, patience, we will prevail in Vietnam over the Communist aggressor,' he said. Johnson agreed that 'protest will not produce surrender'. But on 27 September 1967, an advertisement appeared in the press, signed by 300 influential Americans, asking for funds to support an organization helping young men dodge the draft. Johnson could not help but acknowledge that the war was becoming unpopular. Speaking in Washington on 7 October 1967, he said that he was not going to court cheap popularity 'by renouncing the struggle in Vietnam or escalating it to the red line of danger'.

Former President Dwight D. Eisenhower said, 'America doesn't have to apologize for her part in the war. She can be proud of it.' But the youth of America were far from proud of what was being done in their name. On 21 October 1967, some 50,000 demonstrators marched on the Pentagon. It was the biggest anti-war demonstration to date. In a televised showdown, they faced 10,000 US Army troops and National Guardsmen drawn up to defend the building. The soldiers had rifles though no ammunition, but were authorized to break up the demonstration by force. At first the confrontation was peaceful. Demonstrators

came up to the soldiers and poked flowers down the barrels of their guns, while another group attempted to mystically levitate the building. But as night drew on it was broken up with considerable brutality.

The March on the Pentagon was the idea of the National Mobilization Committee to End the War in Vietnam (MOBE), formed in 1966 to coordinate anti-war demonstrations. In the spring of 1967, they decided to hold a protest in Washington, DC, aiming to attract one million protesters. But MOBE director James Bevel fell ill and their chairman David Dellinger was abroad, so former Berkeley

Dr Benjamin Spock and Dr Martin Luther King lead a 3,000-strong anti-war demonstration in Chicago on 25 March 1967.

Vietnam Day Committee organizer Jerry Rubin was called in. However, he had changed since his VDC days and MOBE members were shocked to find he was now into hallucinogenic drugs and Native American religion. He also asserted the five-sided pentagon was a symbol of evil that had to be 'exorcized'. Nevertheless, on 26 August 1967, MOBE agreed to hold a protest at the Pentagon.

Two days later, at a press conference in New York, Rubin announced that protesters would shut down the Pentagon by blocking its entrances and halls on 21–22 October. This was perfectly feasible, as in those days there were no security checks and anyone could walk into the Pentagon. Then Rubin's sidekick, former civil-rights activist Abbie Hoffman, told the nation that they were going to 'raise the Pentagon 300 feet in the air'. Dellinger urged protesters to attack other federal buildings.

'There will be no government building unattacked,' he said.

Many of MOBE's more conservative supporters were put off by these outspoken tactics, but Dellinger said that it marked the anti-war movement's transition 'from protest to resistance'.

The administration was frightened that the demonstration might turn violent and threatened to ban it unless MOBE leaders renounced their threat of civil disobedience. This would prove counterproductive, as the threat of a ban was regarded as political repression and many disparate groups rallied to MOBE's cause. The administration was forced to let the demonstration go ahead, but confined the route to narrow side roads and the Pentagon's parking lot, over a thousand feet away from the building.

On 20 October protesters began pouring into Washington. Washington reacted as if it were facing a full-scale revolution. Access to all government buildings was restricted. The speaker ordered the House of Representatives locked and Congress passed a bill to protect the Capitol from armed intruders. Wire barriers were erected down Pennsylvania Avenue outside the White House, with tours being limited to VIPs. The president's wife, Lady Bird Johnson, wrote in her diary that it was like being in a state of siege.

Six thousand soldiers were at hand. Shortly after dark on 20 October, troops in full kit, carrying rifles, C-rations and teargas, moved into the Pentagon. Jeeps and trucks of the First Army sat bumper to bumper in four underground tunnels, the lead vehicles draped with beige cloths to conceal their identity. Across the country another 20,000 troops were put on alert in case there was an uprising in the ghettos. Two thousand National Servicemen were mobilized to support Washington's 2,000 policemen, 800 of whom were protecting the Capitol. More 'special policemen' were hidden in the Executive Office Building. Blankets were concealed along the route of the march to snuff out anyone who might try to set themselves on fire. However, arrests were to be kept to a minimum to avoid attracting more national and international attention to the protest.

On the morning of the 21st, over 100,000 gathered at the Lincoln Memorial. Placard slogans ranged from 'Negotiate' to 'Where Is Oswald When We Need Him?' – a reference to Lee Harvey Oswald, the accused assassin of President Kennedy. Then, with helicopters buzzing overhead, they headed off towards Arlington Bridge. Meanwhile, with a secret service helicopter hovering over the White House, President Johnson invited journalists to watch him working in the Rose Garden. He made a show of being unconcerned, believing the demonstration would be broken up too late to get much coverage in the Sunday papers.

Once the march reached the other side of the bridge, a group carrying a Vietcong flag peeled off and made a dash through the woods to the Pentagon, where they were surrounded by MPs and US Marshals. Another group tore down a barrier and got into the building, only to be beaten up by waiting troops.

When the main group reached the building they appealed to the troops guarding it to join them. A protester from Berkeley put flowers down the barrels of their guns. Abbie Hoffman and his wife, high on acid and wearing tall Uncle Sam hats, made love in front of the troops. Others followed suit shouting, 'We'd rather f*** than fight'.

Young women clawed at the zippers of the soldiers and offered to take them into the woods if they changed sides. One reportedly accepted this offer, but was bundled away by officers. More than 200 draft cards were burnt.

Sharpshooters lined the Pentagon roof and, watching from their office windows, were Secretary of Defense Robert McNamara, who by that time was regularly seen weeping in his office, and defence analyst Daniel Ellsberg, the man who leaked the 'Pentagon Papers'. Many of the Pentagon officials were unnerved by the situation, knowing their own children were among the demonstrators.

As dusk fell, most protesters began to drift away, but around 400 stayed. Shortly before midnight, a V-shaped phalanx of troops came out kicking and clubbing the protesters. Women were beaten in the face with rifle butts. Rubin urged the protesters to fight back and they began setting fire to pieces of wood and

YOUNG WOMEN CLAWED AT THE ZIPPERS OF THE SOLDIERS AND OFFERED TO TAKE THEM INTO THE WOODS IF THEY CHANGED SIDES

hurling them at the Marshals. Though more moderate voices spoke up and some protesters withdrew, others who had been camping out in the woods returned. The following day some 2,000 protesters were still besieging the Pentagon. Rioting continued sporadically for two days. TV viewers saw coverage of the 82nd Airborne's action on the Potomac interspersed with the 1st Air Cavalry's action in Vietnam on the nightly news.

In all 683 people were arrested, including two UPI reporters and the novelist Norman Mailer, who immortalized the event in his book *The Armies of the Night*. Fifty-one were given jail terms ranging up to 35 days and fined $8,000 in all. There were numerous

Even those who had fought in the war turned against it, later returning their medals and despoiling their uniforms in protest. The disillusion soon spread to the Army, badly damaging morale and undermining discipline.

injuries but no deaths. Mailer's presence in the anti-war movement was important. He was no pacifist and had come to prominence with his first novel *The Naked and the Dead*, based on his experiences in the Pacific, hailed as one of the finest novels to come out of World War II. With the death of Ernest Hemingway in 1961, Mailer had inherited his macho mantle. But instead of celebrating this war he became deeply pessimistic about it. In 1967, he published the novel *Why Are We in Vietnam?* Strangely, it is not set in Vietnam at all. The action takes place on a hunting trip in Alaska. However, the book explores men's quest to prove their masculinity and the relish that human beings take in killing – issues that seemed to be possessing America as a nation in its attitude to the war at the time.

In *The Armies of the Night*, published in 1968, Mailer got more direct. The first half of the book records his first-hand experiences during the anti-war demonstration in Washington, DC in October 1967. The second half gives a detailed history of the origins and organization of the demonstration. Although this book could be dismissed as a piece of supercharged journalism, Mailer lent his intellectual authority to the fight against the war in the most public way he knew. But he was preaching to the choir. His influence extended only to the students and intellectuals who were already opposed to America's intervention in Vietnam. Support for the war came from blue-collar workers and middle America, who neither read nor cared about the musings of Norman Mailer.

The television and newspapers were still largely pro-war and the media roundly condemned the protesters as 'extremists' and 'troublemakers', insisting that, as a whole, the demonstration would stiffen Hanoi's resolve. Johnson claimed that he had a secret report showing that the demonstration had been choreographed by Communists. Indeed, some of its leaders had met with Vietcong and North Vietnamese delegates at a conference in Bratislava, Czechoslovakia in September. But the demonstration had already been planned by then, and when Johnson asked the FBI and CIA to substantiate his claims, they came up with nothing.

The march on the Pentagon was only one of many protests that broke out across the US in 1967. There were more violent clashes in

New York City, and Oakland, now the home of the militant African-American separatist Black Panther Party, continued to be a centre of protest with 125 demonstrators arrested on 21 October and a further 268 on 19 December. Anti-war demonstrations were not confined to the US: protest spread around the world, with anti-war feeling running especially high in Britain. On 4 July 1965, after a demonstration in London's Trafalgar Square, a homemade bomb exploded against the back door of the American Express offices in the Haymarket, less than half a mile away. In October, two days of protest in London led to a march on the US Embassy in Grosvenor Square, where 78 were arrested. Thousands more protested in Trafalgar Square. In July 1966, the British House of Commons passed a motion supporting American policy in Vietnam, but disassociating Britain from the bombing raids on Hanoi and Haiphong. But, while the government were equivocal, young people were vehemently opposed to the war and a full-scale riot took place in Grosvenor Square in March 1968 when 50 protesters were injured and 300 arrested. Undeterred, 50,000 anti-war protesters took to the streets of London in October after a heated row had developed in the United Nations when Secretary General U Thant backed a seemingly anti-US resolution.

In May 1965 in Sydney, Australia, 50 demonstrators were arrested just days after Australia had increased its contingent fighting in Vietnam to 1,300. Whenever President Johnson travelled abroad, he was met with protest, with demonstrations in Berlin, Rome,

Brussels, Copenhagen, Stockholm, Paris and Tokyo. When Johnson visited Australia in December 1967, the authorities were barely able to guarantee his safety. On one occasion, his car was splashed with green paint. Violent anti-war demonstrations broke out in January 1967 when South Vietnam's President Ky visited Australia and New Zealand, who had also sent troops to Vietnam, and in Sweden, an International War Crimes Tribunal, backed financially by British philosopher Bertrand Russell, condemned the US for war crimes.

IN SWEDEN, AN INTERNATIONAL WAR CRIMES TRIBUNAL... CONDEMNED THE US FOR WAR CRIMES

Another key element in the growth of the anti-war movement, both internationally and domestically, was the hippies. Also known as flower children, adherents wore their hair long, smoked marijuana, dropped LSD, believed in peace and free love, and wore colourful and eccentric clothes. Although they seemed to burst upon the world fully formed in 1967, the summer of love, they were a development of an older American youth movement that had been subsumed by the invasion of British music and fashions in 1963. Hippies had their roots in the Beat Generation of the late 1940s and 1950s whose rootless, bohemian philosophy was summed up by Jack Kerouac's 1957 novel *On the Road*. The book, which details free-wheeling journeys across America, ends in San Francisco, where Kerouac moved to live with Neal Cassady, the model for Dean Moriarty, the hero of the novel. And the poet Alan Ginsberg wrote the quintessential Beat poem 'Howl' in San Francisco.

In 1961, Neal Cassady hitched up with another novelist, Ken Kesey, who was living in Palo Alto. Together they began experimenting with the drug lysergic acid diathylamide (LSD or acid) a hallucinogenic drug synthesized by Swiss chemist Albert Hoffman in 1938 as a possible cure for migraine (it was not illegal at the time). In the summer of 1963, with the royalties from Kesey's novel *One Flew Over the Cuckoo's Nest* – later made into a successful film starring Jack Nicholson – Kesey and his circle moved to a big log house in the hills of La Honda, northwest of Palo Alto, where they continued their experiments with drugs.

In 1964, Cassady, Kesey and Kesey's pal Ken Babbs – recently returned from active service as a helicopter pilot in Vietnam – began calling themselves the Merry Pranksters and decided to take their drug-fuelled philosophy on the road. They bought an old school bus, painted it with swirling 'psychedelic' patterns, and renamed it 'The Magic Bus'. On the rear of the bus was a sign reading: 'CAUTION: WEIRD LOAD'. On the front the destination board read: 'FURTHUR' – with two 'U's. They set off across America, with Kesey and Babbs playing whistles and flutes on the roof, filming their journey as they went.

In Millbrook, New York, they dropped in unannounced on acid-guru Timothy Leary. A former Harvard lecturer and author of *The*

Psychedelic Experience, he advised his followers to 'turn on, tune in, drop out'. However, the Merry Pranksters found Leary and his League for Spiritual Discovery altogether too solemn and headed back to San Francisco, where the use of LSD was spreading throughout the city. Folk music, which had been the standard fare of the Beats, was overtaken by the sound of the Beatles and the Rolling Stones. Young acid-users shed their sombre beatnik garb for the crazier clothes and long hairstyles imported by the British bands. As LSD seemed to offer some sort of spiritual enlightenment, a Christ-like look with flowing locks and robes became fashionable.

San Francisco bands such as Jefferson Airplane and the Flamin' Groovies took LSD and developed the psychedelic sound of Acid Rock. A band called the Warlocks took LSD at the Pranksters 'Acid Tests' at La Honda in 1964 and became the Grateful Dead. These Acid Tests were prolonged parties that attracted a mixed group: a gay New York Jewish intellectual such as Alan Ginsberg could be seen dropping acid with Hell's Angels from Oakland. The scene was recorded in Tom Wolfe's 1968 book of new journalism *The Electric Kool-Aid Acid Test*.

Beat veterans used the pejorative term 'hippies' – a term used by African-American musicians to described white beatnik hangers-ons on the jazz scene – to dismiss the middle-class drop-outs slumming it in North Beach, a term the hippies embraced. Their burgeoning counter-culture spread across the Bay to Berkeley, where the Free Speech Movement was under way. When Ken Kesey was invited to speak at the anti-war demonstration in Berkeley on 16 October 1965, he turned up in the Magic Bus covered in military symbols and outraged the earnest anti-war protesters with a mocking speech. However, the Berkeley band Country Joe and the Fish, who became famous for the anti-Vietnam song 'Feel-Like-I'm-Fixin'-to-Die Rag', embraced the psychedelic music of San Francisco and hippie-ness spread to the campus.

The hippies borrowed their 'peace' philosophy from Martin Luther King and the anti-war movement. They looked to the East for enlightenment after the Beatles went there to meditate with the Maharishi Mahesh Yogi in 1968. Marijuana use came from the Beats and the philosophy 'free love' came from utopian religious groups of the nineteenth century, the modernist movement of the early twentieth century, and the availability of reliable contraception in the form of the recently introduced pill. Hippies summed up their philosophy in the slogan 'Make Love Not War'.

Hippie culture began to find expression in 'underground' magazines and newspapers and celebrated at 'Be-In' in San Francisco's Golden Gate park on 14 January 1967, where thousands of young people openly took drugs and bands played for free. Similar events were organized across America and around the world in the summer of 1967.

The 'Death of the Hippie' in San Francisco was prematurely announced in October 1966 with a march down Haight Street. Elsewhere hippies were very much alive. In 1968, hippies went mainstream with the musical *Hair* and declared independence with the founding of the 'Woodstock Nation' at a free music festival in upstate New York in August 1969. Hippies believed that they lived at the dawning of a new age – the age of Aquarius, dedicated to peace and love, a dream which would be soured when a young black man was stabbed to death just four months later at a free festival given by the Rolling Stones at Altamont, California, and the nightmare hippie Charles Manson and his murderous 'family' moved into the limelight. Nevertheless, the hippie creed of peace, love and nonviolent protests was a focus for young people who found themselves alienated from their parent's support of the war and it briefly found political expression in the Youth International Party – the Yippies – founded by the organizers of the march on the Pentagon, Rubin and Hoffman.

Although most people in America still condemned the anti-war protesters, the demonstrations began to have a political effect. Chairman of the Senate Foreign Relations Committee William Fulbright, Senator Robert Kennedy and Senator Eugene McCarthy began to express their doubts about the war. President Johnson held firm, but his Secretary of Defense Robert McNamara, the chief architect of the war, turned against it. The commander on the ground in Vietnam, General William Westmoreland, insisted the war could not be won without a massive escalation, which would involve an extension of the already unpopular draft. With rioting on the streets, it seemed plain that this was an

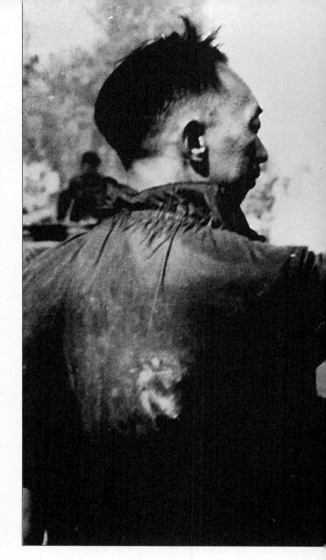

escalation that the country would not bear. McNamara decided that there was no alternative but to withdraw. He tendered his resignation in November 1967, but agreed to stay on until February 1968 to maintain the illusion of loyalty. But Fulbright was free to speak out, and on 8 December 1967 he did so, denouncing the conflict as an 'immoral and unnecessary war', adding, 'Far from demonstrating America's willingness and ability to save beleaguered governments from communist insurgencies, all that we are demonstrating

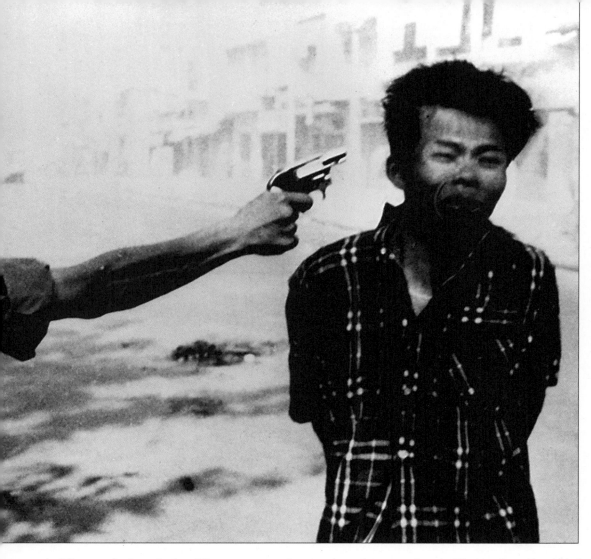

Saigon Chief of Police Van Ngoc Loan's shooting of a vc suspect was captured live on camera by cbs, shocking US TV viewers back home. Scenes like this on the nightly news helped to turn the nation against the war. It is arguable that the Communists won the war not on the battlefields of South Vietnam but on the TV screens of America.

in Vietnam is America's willingness to use its B-52s, its napalm, and all other ingenious weapons of "counter-insurgency" to turn a small country into a charnel house.'

American public opinion turned decisively against the war following the Tet Offensive in January 1968. Although the Vietcong's six-hour occupation of the compound of the US Embassy in Saigon was a suicide mission, it showed the American people that, after nearly three years of war, no progress had been made. People were particularly appalled when they saw South Vietnam's police chief Van Ngoc Loan blow a Vietcong suspect's brains out on the TV news. If Loan was an example of the kind of people that they were supporting in the Saigon government, perhaps America was on the wrong side. In fact, the victim had just murdered one of Loan's best friends and had knifed his entire family. Loan was to end up in the US, running a pizza parlour in the Burke suburb of Washington, DC.

Walter Cronkite's public reassessment of

Burning your draft card became a very potent symbol of opposition to the war. It was, of course, illegal, but it was a very public way for those liable to get drafted into the military and sent to fight in Vietnam to show that they would not go.

the war put the final nail in Johnson's coffin. When Senator Robert Kennedy declared he would run for the Democratic presidential nomination four days after Senator Eugene McCarthy's spectacular showing in the New Hampshire primary, both the peace protesters and, to some extent, middle America breathed a collective sigh of relief. Here was another charismatic Kennedy who might just be able to free them from the Vietnam debacle and reunite the country. But Robert Kennedy was assassinated in Los Angeles on 6 June. As a result, Johnson's vice president Hubert Humphrey got the nomination, but not before the Democratic convention in Chicago had turned into a riot with running battles between anti-war protesters and the police of Mayor Richard Daley, the last of the big-city bosses. Norman Mailer again immortalized the event in his book *Miami and the Siege of Chicago* – the Republican convention was held in Miami. It nominated former hawk Richard Nixon, who, after a political volte face, now promised peace with honour. After

the Chicago convention, Rubin, Hoffman and five others – the 'Chicago Seven' – were tried on charges of conspiracy to incite violence and crossing state lines with intent to riot. After a long trial punctuated with taunts and outbursts from the defendants, they were acquitted of conspiracy, although five were convicted of incitement, and all of them, plus their lawyers, were cited for contempt a total of some 200 times. The convictions were later overturned.

In the election in November, Nixon beat Humphrey in a close vote. America now found it had a right-wing Republican president who had run on a peace ticket. This split the anti-war movement. But it soon became clear that, rather than ending the war, Nixon was expanding it and the peace lobby had to start up all over again. In September 1969 a former McCarthy campaign worker, Sam Brown, began the Vietnam Moratorium Committee with the intention of showing that anti-war protest was not just confined to students. The date of 15 October 1969 was declared National Moratorium Day and some 250,000 people from all walks of life took to the streets of Washington, DC to protest. Between 13 and 15 November a further 500,000 demonstrated in response to the committee's call. By then the anti-war movement commanded popular support.

The Moratorium demonstrations had a great effect on the Pentagon defence analyst Daniel Ellsberg, one of thirty-six who had produced a massive report on the conduct of the war which became known as the 'Pentagon Papers'. Although the publication of the Pentagon Papers did not take place until the 1970s, the report was written in the 1960s and had an effect behind the scenes. In June 1967, at the behest of Secretary of Defense Robert McNamara, Ellsberg and his colleagues began reviewing America's policy in Vietnam, beginning in 1954. The resulting report took eight months to compile. Officially called 'The History of the Decision Making Process on Vietnam,' it ran to 47 volumes, 7,100 pages in all, cataloguing systematic government deception, cynicism and incompetence in the handling of the war. Only 15 copies were printed. There were rumours that McNamara planned to leak the report to his friend Robert Kennedy to help him in his bid for the Presidency.

Ellsberg had been a keen supporter of McNamara and US involvement in Vietnam, but he was disillusioned by what he learnt while compiling the report. After the National Moratorium on 15 October 1969, he began secretly photocopying the study and passing pages to Senator William Fulbright, chairman of the Senate Foreign Relations Committee and a prominent critic of the war. Later, he sent copies to *The New York Times*, which began publication on 13 June 1971. President Nixon slapped an injunction on the *Times*, but then the *Washington Post* began printing more extracts. When the *Post* in turn was silenced by an injunction, other newspapers in Chicago, Los Angeles, St Louis and Boston took up the challenge. On 30 June the Supreme Court quashed the injunctions, condemning Nixon's attempt to gag the press. In the meantime, Ellsberg had given himself up to the police. He and another colleague, Anthony J. Russo, were indicted for theft but the charges were dropped in May 1973 when it was revealed that Nixon had authorized the burglary of the offices of Ellsberg's psychiatrist in an attempt to find evidence to smear him. The burglary was carried out by members of the White House staff in a sinister precursor to the Watergate break-in which would take place in 1972.

While they now commanded national support, some protests began to take a more violent turn. The SDS had grown increasingly militant, and by 1969 it had split into several factions, the most notorious of which was the Weathermen, or Weather Underground, which began planting bombs. Over 5,000 bombs went off in all, including one that wrecked a bathroom in the Pentagon.

In 1970, protests against the incursion into Vietnam's neighbour Cambodia swept the universities. Conservative politicians demanded an end to the campus unrest: California's Governor Ronald Reagan said, 'If it takes a bloodbath, then let's get it over with.'

His words came true on the campus of the traditionally politically apathetic Kent State University. When protests broke out there, the Governor of Ohio came to the campus and described the demonstrators as 'trouble-makers' who were 'worse than the brown shirts' (Hitler's early followers in Nazi Germany) and the Communist elements, and also the Night Riders and the vigilantes. 'They are the worse type of people that we harbour in America,' he said. He was standing in the primaries for the Republican senate nomination the following week.

The Ohio National Guard was called in. The protesters sang John Lennon's 'Give Peace a Chance' and the Riot Act was read. A campus policeman with a bullhorn ordered the crowd to disperse. They answered with cries of 'Pigs off campus' and 'Sieg Heil'. The National Guard commander, General Canterbury, ordered his men to load their rifles with live ammunition and don gas masks. From the top of a grassy knoll, 100 state troopers fired tear gas canisters into the crowd. The protesters hurled them back, along with rocks, lumps of concrete, and obscenities. Around 40 of the National Guardsmen moved down the hill to confront the crowd. A couple of times, they assumed firing positions to scare the demonstrators, but were eventually forced back. Then a single shot rang out, followed by a salvo from the troopers on the grassy knoll. Sixty-one shots were fired in all. No warning had been given.

Flowers and 'flower power' became the very antithesis of the military-industrial complex that backed the war.

FREE YAWF LEADERS
JAILED FOR AIDING
ANTI-WAR G.I.s

The protesters had no idea that the troopers were armed with live ammunition. One demonstrator said that they were firing blanks, otherwise they would be shooting in the air or at the ground. But four students died. There was no indication that they were regular SDS activists. One of them, Sandra Lee Sheuer, was passing by on the way to class. Jeffrey Miller was a registered Republican and William Schroeder was a member of the university's Reserve Officer's Training Corps. The fourth victim was Allison Krause. Ten more students lay wounded, one paralysed

THE LADIES' ROOM IN THE US SENATE WAS BLOWN UP

from the waist down by a bullet lodged in his spine. Ignoring cries for help from the crowd, the National Guardsmen shouldered their arms and marched away.

Attempts to justify the actions of the National Guard as self-defence were dented when the results of the FBI investigation into the shootings were leaked. The report concluded, 'The shootings were not necessary and not in order.' It also stated, 'We have some reason to believe that the claim by the National Guard that their lives were endangered by the students was fabricated subsequent to the event.'

Even so, when the National Guardsmen were brought to trial they were found not guilty. However, eight-and-a-half years later the defendants issued a statement admitting responsibility for the shootings and expressing their regret, and in January 1979, the parents and students received $675,000 from the State of Ohio in an out-of-court settlement.

The shootings at Kent State brought the war home to white middle class America. The victims were not little yellow men on the other side of the world, or blacks in the ghetto, or student radicals from Berkeley. These were their sons and daughters, middle-class kids attending a relatively quiet campus in middle America. Over 150 colleges were closed or went on strike in the days following the killings. One hundred thousand protestors marched in Washington, DC, though construction workers broke up a demonstration on Wall Street while the NYPD looked on.

Although Nixon dismissed the protesters as bums, America was shocked. Even the Education Secretary Robert Finch condemned the rhetoric that had heated the climate which led to the Kent State slayings. The days when hippie protesters put flowers in the barrels of soldier's guns were gone. The Weathermen set up a National War Council. The ladies' room in the US Senate was blown up. The home of a judge trying African-American radicals was bombed, as was the New York Police Department. An attack on an army dance at Fort Dix was planned. More seriously, one person was killed and three wounded by a bomb attack on the army's Mathematics Research Center in Wisconsin. But the outrage of middle America meant that mainstream politicians were now forced to tackle the issue. Nixon was forced to withdraw American troops from Cambodia and funding for the war was cut by Congress.

But the protests continued. In May 1971, 12,000 demonstrators were arrested in Washington, DC. In November that year there were large-scale rallies in 16 cities. By then Nixon, the man who had come to power offering 'peace with honour', was the focus of the protests.

One of the most powerful propaganda weapons the anti-war movement had was the group Vietnam Veterans Against the War. These men could hardly be accused of being cowards or Communists, accusations regularly hurled at student protesters. They had served their country in Vietnam, and decided the war there was wrong. They turned up to demonstrations in uniform, though they often threw away their medals. The injured – amputees and men in wheelchairs – added a powerful wordless protest to student chanting. No New York hardhat was going to beat them up. They even defied a Supreme Court ban on demonstrating in Washington, DC, with impunity.

On 28 December, 1971, sixteen Vietnam veterans occupied the Statue of Liberty, hung the Stars and Stripes upside down from the observation platform and sent an open letter to President Nixon, saying, 'We can no longer tolerate the war in Southeast Asia regardless of the colour of its dead or the method of its implementation.'

In 1972, wheelchair-bound Vietnam veteran Ron Kovic gatecrashed the Republican convention on the night of Nixon's speech accepting the presidential nomination, telling the guards who attempted to throw him out, 'I'm a Vietnam veteran... I've got just as much right to be here as any of these delegates.

I fought for that right and I was born on the Fourth of July.'

For two minutes, he condemned the war on national television. Kovic's story was later immortalized in Oliver Stone's controversial film *Born on the Fourth of July*.

Quite apart from the demonstrations, opinion polls revealed disillusionment with the war throughout the nation, and it was clear that one way or the other the US had to extricate itself from what was graphically called the 'Vietnam quagmire'. Bowing to the inevitable, Nixon concluded a negotiated settlement to the Vietnam War, which was signed in Paris in January 1973.

A member of the Vietnam Veterans Against the War group (VVAW) wields a plastic gun as the group march from New Jersey to Pennsylvannia in June 1970. Although a lot of the protests had a comic or play-acting quality, the protesters were in deadly earnest.

8

THE COLLAPSE OF MORALE

A soldier of 198th Light Infantry Brigade shows support for Moratorium Day by wearing a black armband on 15 October 1969. It was impossible to maintain discipline when even the troops sided with the protesters.

182

THE WAR was not universally popular even among the military. On 8 July 1965 a US captain was court-martialled in Okinawa for feigning mental illness while serving in Vietnam. On 11 June 1966, Private Adam R. Weber, an African-American soldier in the 25th Infantry Division, was sentenced to one year's hard labour for refusing to carry a rifle because of his pacifist convictions. In September, three army privates were court-martialled for refusing to go to Vietnam. The court rejected the defence argument that the war was immoral and illegal. In March 1967, USAF Captain Dale E. Noyd sued in court to have himself reclassified as a conscientious objector to the Vietnam conflict. His petition was denied in June. In August, the US Court of Military Appeals upheld a sentence of one year's hard labour on a soldier found guilty of demonstrating against the war.

To start with, these military objectors were few and far between. On the other hand, by September 1965, over 100 US servicemen were volunteering for service in Vietnam every day, although the enthusiasm for the war did not last long, even among the professional soldiers who longed for combat experience. The cherished discipline of the army and the Marine Corps was soon corrupted by exposure to the delights of Saigon and the other cities of the east.

Before the war Saigon had been known as the 'Paris of the Orient'. Like Paris, Saigon was famous for its prostitutes. During their occupation, the French had both legalized and profited from it, and had developed a system of military brothels. Mobile brothels followed the troops and at Dien Bien Phu in 1954 Vietnamese and North African prostitutes acted as nurses and even frontline fighters. The South Vietnamese army inherited the system but, under the Diem regime, the president's sister-in-law Madame Nhu, known for her tight dresses and expensive jewellery, tried unsuccessfully to clean up the city, banning all overt forms of licentious behaviour including the

A rifleman with A Company, 1st Battalion, 8th Cavalry, 1st Brigade, takes a break from the search and destroy mission against the VC to freshen up, but there was little relief from the war itself.

latest American dance craze, the Twist, which was condemned by many as lewd. Madame Nhu had people arrested for wearing 'cowboy clothes', and she and her husband, warlord Ngo Dinh Nhu, took out full-page newspaper ads denying their involvement in illegal activities – an attempt doomed to failure.

However, when the Americans arrived in force in 1965, Diem was dead and Madame Nhu's puritanism was on the retreat. Soon the black market was flourishing, selling everything from jeeps and fridges to hairspray and pantyhose, much of it direct from the US commissary. Cigarettes were another major item on the black market, with some American brands sold at $1 a pack with the tax seal apparently intact: in fact, the tobacco had often been taken out and marijuana had been substituted. Other cigarettes were painted with opium and sold singly. Much of the drug supply was brought into the city by the Vietcong, who quickly realized the debilitating effect it had on US morale. Drug abuse was a central theme of 1960s music and culture, and was associated with the hippie movement and its anti-war stance.

By 1967, there were 50,000 US troops stationed in Saigon, with huge numbers moving through Tan Son Nhut Airport. Thousands more came into the city on three-day passes from the fighting in the surrounding countryside, and thousands of US and foreign journalists packed into Saigon for what they called the 'five o'clock follies', the regular afternoon press briefings held in the US Information Service auditorium. By then, much of the French flavour of the city had been lost.

The US troops brought their own radio and TV stations. Traditional Vietnamese cafés began selling hamburgers, fries and milkshakes. Tailor shops sprung up providing safari suits and other American-style civilian clothing so that the troops could get out of uniform, while others specialized in military insignia and other souvenirs of the war. To cater to this huge influx of foreigners, there were bars, brothels, opium dens and massage parlours. Girls came pouring into Saigon from the countryside: a prostitute in Saigon could earn more than a cabinet minister. The streets were full of military jeeps, official Ford sedans, and the motor scooters and Japanese motorbikes of the Saigon Cowboys (pimps) and black marketeers.

There were 'Turkish baths' where a soldier could pay to be bathed by a pretty young woman, 'magic finger' massage parlours and 'steam and cream' joints; oral sex was freely available under bar-room tables. You could buy a hostess and take her away for sex, provided you paid the mama-san for the number of 'Saigon teas' she would have consumed. You could pay in US dollars or military script that was supposed to be spent only on military posts but was widely traded outside at a 40 per cent discount. Prostitutes were often working for the Vietcong and used to wheedle information out of GIs. This was widely known, but the authorities could do nothing about it. Although US soldiers were banned from carrying weapons in Saigon or wearing camouflage fatigues, many did. The South Vietnamese police were supposed to enforce the law, but few risked their lives trying

to disarm a heavily armed Green Beret or prevent him taking his pleasures with a bar girl, even if she was VC. There was a ready supply of new girls among those driven off the land by search-and-destroy missions, but still there was the ever-present danger of contracting a sexually transmitted disease. An especially pernicious strain that was doing the rounds was called the Heinz 57 variety, for which there was no known cure and sufferers had to endure an endless drip.

WHEN ONE AFRICAN-AMERICAN APPEARED ON THE COVER OF TIME, HE WOKE UP TO FIND A BURNING CROSS OUTSIDE HIS TENT

Servicemen on liberty in Saigon separated largely along racial lines, largely because of music. White GIs went to the bars along the Tu Do where rock music was played. African-American servicemen established a separate quarter, known as 'Soulsville', behind the docks in Khanh Hoi, where soul music was played, and many of the prostitutes were darker-skinned Khmer women from Cambodia or the daughters of Senegalese soldiers brought to Vietnam by the French. This racial division became such a sore point that after the assassination of Martin Luther King the Armed Forces TV station screened nothing but his picture for three whole days. The soul singer James Brown, Soul Brother Number One, the Godfather of Soul, came to Vietnam to perform for the troops; Whitey got Bob Hope and Jayne Mansfield. After the death of King, Brown had to go on TV in the US to help quell the ensuing riots. As a result, he was accused of being an 'Uncle Tom,' but answered his critics in 1969 with his number one R&B hit 'Say It Loud, I'm Black and Proud'. However, he drew more flak in 1972 when he endorsed the re-election campaign of President Nixon.

The racial tensions that were tearing apart the ghettoes back home in the US also infused the armed forces. In July 1969, there was a race riot in Lejeune Marine Camp in North Carolina. The Marines did not admit African-Americans until World War II, and the first black Leatherneck, Sergeant-Major Edgar A. Huff, was regularly arrested for impersonating a Marine – on the grounds that there 'weren't no coloureds in the Marines'. During World War II 'Negroes' were restricted to separate units. Although the US Army had been integrated in 1949, Vietnam was essentially the first war where blacks and whites fought side by side. African-Americans called themselves 'Negroes' or 'coloured people' until 1966 when the term 'black' was coined by the activist Stokely Carmichael. After that 'black' as in 'black power' became a political statement, particularly when two African-American athletes competing at the 1968 Mexico Olympics raised gloved fists on the podium in a black power salute. In Vietnam, fights erupted between blacks and whites. Sometimes guns were used. And the walls of latrines were scrawled with racist graffiti, such as, 'Better a gook [a derogatory term used for the Vietnamese] than a nigger.'

When one African-American patrol leader appeared on the cover of *Time* magazine, he woke up to find a burning cross outside his tent – the traditional warning from the Ku Klux Klan to any African-American who sought to better themselves. The day before Captain Lewis, an African-American officer later caught on film setting light to a hootch in the Kim Son Valley, was due to go to Vietnam he was in a phone booth in Montgomery, Alabama saying goodbye to his wife when he was shot in the back by a Klansman. The army's response was to make him commanding officer of an almost exclusively white unit. This was rare, but as the war dragged on African-Americans in the Marines won the rights to grow their hair in Afros. However, it was noted that there was one time when blacks and whites were comfortable with each other in Vietnam – that was when they were smoking marijuana.

Since the Korean War, GIs had been given a week's R&R (rest and recreation) during a tour of duty. Among the troops R&R was known as I&I – intoxication and intercourse. From Vietnam, troops were sent to Bangkok, Penang, Hong Kong, Hawaii, Taipei or Sydney on a week's pass. Grunts also got three-day passes to Saigon or one of the in-country beach resorts at Nha Trang, Vung Tau, Chu Lai, Qui Nhon or Cam Ranh. The most famous, China Beach, was the Marine enclave just outside Da Nang.

Three-day passes were used as an incentive to capture enemy prisoners. As the war dragged on, the number of POWs being taken dropped off dramatically. GIs were sick of seeing their buddies blown apart by booby traps and mines, mutilated by an unseen enemy and sent home in body bags. As a result, they simply killed any Communist that fell into their hands. But as this wasted valuable intelligence, orders were issued that more live prisoners were to be taken and when whole companies were offered R&R as a reward, the POW count quickly improved.

At these beach resorts, the grunts found that sea water was the perfect cure for the terrible conditions they picked up in the jungle. China Beach offered five klicks (kilometres) of white sand, though swimmers and sunbathers had to keep a weather eye out for snipers. There was fresh lobster, fish, and beer flown in from the States and Australia. Australian troops got a tinny for every day they spent in the field. The beach resorts also offered beautiful young Vietnamese women in scanty bikinis, discreet massage parlours, illicit brothels that masqueraded as coffee shops, car washes where a grunt could pull over and get a complete service, and a corpsman who specialized in treating the clap. From the old French villas at Nha Trang, Special Forces would go scuba diving, snorkelling and surfing in the same waters where they dumped double agents in chains from helicopters.

As a result of the American troops' free-spending ways, the Vietnamese economy boomed. Everyone had jobs. Boys shined shoes. Women found jobs as hootch girls, cleaning barracks and, often, reporting anything of interest to the local VC. Taxi-drivers, black marketeers, bar owners, brothel keepers, pimps, shopkeepers and waiters made small fortunes. But the influx of dollars caused inflation in the Vietnamese piastre that was soon running at 170 per cent, which meant that ordinary Vietnamese struggled with deprivation as they watched Americans living in unimaginable luxury, causing untold resentment. Many Vietnamese felt that if the US government did not spend so much on amenities for the troops there would be more to spend on the victims of war.

The GIS were also largely ignorant of, and indifferent to, local customs. Despite the widespread prostitution, the Vietnamese had puritanical courtship codes for which the Americans showed no respect, and respectable Vietnamese women were shamelessly harassed. Americans' conspicuous consumption also offended the sensibilities of the fastidious Vietnamese. While bar owners and shopkeepers happily raked in the Yankee dollar, they made only the flimsiest attempt to disguise the contempt they felt for their American customers. After all, they had been educated by the French.

This all took a terrible toll on American morale, with the people they were supposed to be defending looking down on them. As well as defending the people, the GIS were also supposed to be in Vietnam to defend democracy, but there was precious little democracy to defend. The 1966 election for the constitutional assembly was boycotted by the Buddhists and two and a half million people in Vietcong-controlled areas were prevented from voting. When the Buddhists of Hué and Da Nang called for the resignation of Premier Ky's military government, Ky denounced them as communists and used the army to smash all opposition to his government. Even though Ky was persuaded to stand aside and run for vice-president on Thieu's ticket, it was widely rumoured that the 1967 election was rigged. The GIS' own newspapers ran stories about corruption in the South Vietnamese government. The *Grunt Free Press* – an in-country version of the hippy underground press that was flourishing in the rest of the world – carried the story of a man who became a province chief by getting his wife to lose $45,000 at poker to the wife of the party boss. It also investigated the crooked NCO club stewards, smugglers, Indian moneychangers, mafiosi, local gangsters, drug dealers, surplus arms dealers, and crooked contractors who were milking $20 million a year out of Vietnam.

The *Grunt Free Press* began in 1967 as a glossy magazine. It sold in Stars and Stripes bookstores as an in-country alternative to the military's official publication. In 1969, it went hippy. The nudes were more explicit, the humour blacker, the op-ed pieces more critical. One article noted that you could bomb North Vietnam back into the Stone Age, even nuke it, but that still would not get rid of the sniper at the end of the runway at Tan Son Nhut, who probably worked as a barber by day, cutting the hair of the US troops. *Grunt Free Press* had only one editorial rule: no one was ever allowed to die in its pages – not in the stories, pictures or cartoons. Circulation climbed to 30,000 and each issue contained a double-page centrefold poster, usually with an anti-war theme. They all contained a nude – an Asian girl:

Grunt Free Press left the round-eyes to *Playboy*. She would be surrounded by peace symbols – the stylized cross in a circle borrowed from the British Campaign for Nuclear Disarmament – and cryptic messages in psychedelic calligraphy.

These posters adorned walls the length of South Vietnam. The principal artist was Tran Dinh Thuc, a South Vietnamese student who had strong peacenik leanings. When the Vietnamese authorities found he was responsible, they tried to draft him, but appreciative readers smuggled him on board a plane to Darwin.

The editor of *Grunt Free Press*, Ken Sams, was chief of USAF CHECO (Contemporary Historical Evaluation of Combat Operations) in Vietnam. His editorial line reflected much of the grunts' disillusionment with the war and brought him to the attention of the authorities, especially as he liked to include items that he thought would give the enemy a laugh or two. MACV made several attempts to ban *Grunt Free Press* and a powerful underground syndicate tried to take it over, but Sams managed to keep it going by having it printed by a moonlighting ARVN Air Force officer with access to a USAID printing press. The magazine also popularized graffiti such as: 'This is a war of the unwilling led by the unqualified, dying for the ungrateful' and the ubiquitous 'IHTFP' (I Hate This Fucking Place). Vietnam was full of sardonic graffiti. Some simply said: 'Fuck Communism' or 'Fuck Vietnam'. Ho Chi Minh, apparently, was born out of wedlock and was gay and every motherfucker knew 'Ho Chi Minh ain't gonna win'. There were many variations on

the grunts' prayer: 'Yea, though I walk through the valley of the shadow of death, I shall fear no evil, for I am the meanest motherfucker in the valley'. A sign appeared in Vietnamese on a pile of four bullet-riddled VC corpses left to rot by the side of Route 13, which said: 'Vietcong meat – 300 piastres a kilo'. As the war dragged on one slogan summed up the grunts' evaluation of MACV's tactics: 'Kill them all and let God sort them out'. And peace symbols and marijuana leaves sprouted on helmets on the sides of APCs, and in other unlikely places.

PEACE SYMBOLS AND MARIJUANA LEAVES SPROUTED ON HELMETS ON THE SIDES OF APCS, AND IN OTHER UNLIKELY PLACES

Units also had their own in-country insignia run up, incorporating the ubiquitous peace signs and marijuana leaves. They also contained their own jaundiced mottoes. The Special Forces' unofficial insignia carried the legend 'We kill for peace'. Other units considered themselves to be mushrooms – 'kept in the dark and fed on horseshit'. And it was not uncommon to see a soldier wearing an anti-war badge, particularly those that were provided by Vietnam Veterans Against the War. GIs would also flick peace signs, the two-fingered V borrowed from Winston Churchill, whose 'victory' sign was a simple reversal of the traditional, offensive English V-sign said to have originated at the Battle of

Agincourt in 1415, where English archers showed the French that they still had their two bow fingers.

The *Grunt Free Press* became popular among anti-war students in Saigon, who believed that before the Americans started bombing the North there were no North Vietnamese in the South, so when the Americans went away so would the NVA. These proto-hippies would congregate in Ken Sams' apartment to dance to the latest Beatles and Rolling Stones records that Sams' son sent from London. They started their own band called CBC – a Vietnamese code for peace. Complete with long hair, hippy beads and peace symbols, they played for an appreciative audience of grunts at a club on Plantation Road outside Tan Son Nhut air base, until a bomb went off under the bandstand while they were performing and their girl singer lost a leg. Sams kept *Grunt Free Press* going until 1971, when he was rotated back to 'The World'. Long after the war, he maintained that you are more likely to find the reason why the US lost the war in Vietnam in the pages of *Grunt Free Press* than in anything he wrote for CHECO.

A deep disillusionment with the war had set in by 1969. The Paris peace talks were underway, Nixon had been elected on the promise of ending the war, and no one wanted to be the last GI to die in Vietnam. Despite his hawkish credentials, Nixon himself seemed to

President Richard Nixon visits soldiers of the American 1st Infantry Division based at Di An, 11 miles north of Saigon 1969, during a brief stopover on 30 July 1969. It did little to boost morale.

have decided that the war could not be won by military might in the paddy fields of Vietnam. Instead he called for 'days and even years of patient and prolonged diplomacy'. This gave no one any incentive to fight. Already America's war in Vietnam had lasted longer than its involvement in World War II. The validity of the war had been undermined in the minds of the men sent to fight there. The anti-war movement now had the support of every respected figure both at home in the US and internationally. The TV no longer reported victories, but night after night the evening news carried pictures of small, squalid engagements. Meanwhile, the grunts sweated it out on gruelling jungle patrols and watched their buddies being sent home in body bags.

Each man sent to Vietnam was on a strict 365-day tour. Towards the end of the year, when a man was 'short' – counting off the days on the notches of a 'short-time stick' – he would be unwilling to risk his life out on patrol and ceased to be an effective soldier. When he was sent home, all the expertise he had built up over his year in Vietnam went with him. He would then be replaced with an FNG (Fucking New Guy). FNGs were considered a liability as out on patrol they tended to talk too loudly, made too much noise when they moved around, failed to respond to basic commands, fired off too much ammo, packed the wrong kit, wore deodorant or used American soap which the VC could smell a mile off, flaked out after a ten-klick diddy bop in the boonies and got homesick. Veterans considered them to be as much use, in the phrase of the time, as 'tits on a boar hog'.

Men consigned to Vietnam felt that they were missing out on everything that was going on in the world. The miniskirt came to America in 1966. There were new movies, new music, new fashions. A youth revolution and a sexual revolution was going on at home while they were out patrolling the jungles in a part of the world few of them knew or cared anything about, and thanks to the miracle of TV they could see what they were missing. Even the moon landings in 1969 were a cause of aggravation.

'I remember July 20, 1969. I sat in my hootch and watched the satellite relay of the astronauts landing on the moon and saw Neil Armstrong's first step on the surface,' said one war-weary Marine. 'When I heard that fucking bullshit-nonsense phrase, "One small step for man, a giant leap for mankind", I was so angry. I thought to myself, "Come here and step with me for a day, motherfucker."'

The US build-up had ended in April 1968, when Johnson's new Secretary of Defense Clark Clifford rejected the request from Westmoreland and the Joint Chiefs of Staff for another 206,000 men to be added to the army worldwide. Clifford also initiated 'Vietnamization', though the term was coined by Nixon's Secretary of Defense Melvin Laird. Once Nixon was in the White House, he was committed to making troop withdrawals to cut expenditure and phase out the draft. In June 1969, Nixon had discussions with President Thieu on the Pacific Island of Midway. Afterwards, on 8 June, he announced that 25,000 men would be withdrawn by 31 August. This policy of withdrawal was consolidated into

Opposite: President of the Republic of Vietnam Nguyen Van Thieu with President Richard Nixon and entourage in 1969. Behind them are two arch-hawks, US National Security Advisor Henry Kissinger and South Vietnam's Vice-President Nguyen Cao Ky.

the 'Nixon Doctrine,' proclaimed on Guam on 25 July. Another withdrawal of 35,000 men was announced on 16 September, a further 50,000 on 15 December. But at the same time, he began the secret bombing of Cambodia.

In 1969, men began to refuse to fight. Even the elite 1st Air Cav notched up 35 'wilful refusals' that year, and those were only the reported cases. More often patrols did not bother to go out, or when they did, they would pretend that they had contacted a VC patrol and call down an artillery strike on an empty piece of jungle. Between 1968 and 1970, there were 350 convictions in cases of 'combat refusal'. But after that no figures are included in official army statistics on 'Insubordination, mutiny, and other acts involving wilful refusal to perform a lawful order', because there were so many of them. In 1971, there were full-scale mutinies. In September, 14 of the 35th Engineer group barricaded themselves in a bunker and refused to come out. At Fire Support Base Mary Ann in Quang Tin province, discipline had collapsed to the point where no one would even do sentry duty. About 50 NVA infiltrated one night and knifed or shot over 100 of the 196th Infantry Brigade while they slept. Eventually whole units would refuse to go into action. When they were ordered out, a 1st Air Cavalry patrol 'expressed a desire not to go'. The 196th Infantry Brigade refused en masse to go out on patrols in support of the ARVN.

Until 1968, the desertion rate among US troops in Vietnam had been lower than for previous wars, but after 1969, it soared. Some men would go underground in Saigon, while others would disappear while on R&R in Toyko and Hong Kong, and resurface in Sweden or Canada. Underground GI newspapers were full of contacts for organizations that ran escape routes, and some even ran escape routes themselves. AWOLS ran at 78 per 1,000 in 1967, with 21 desertions. This increased to 112.3 per 1,000 AWOL and 42.4 per 1,000 desertion. By 1971, the figures stood at 177 per 1,000 AWOL and 74 per 1,000 desertion; by 1973 even the Marines were suffering 234 per 1,000 AWOL.

Most GIS simply strove to survive their tour, whatever the dangers. In a country where nowhere was safe, paranoia became the order of the day. They came to see even friendly Vietnamese – even woman and children – as their enemy. It seemed quite legitimate to kill children as they would one day grow up to be Vietcong. The random massacre of Vietnamese civilians became commonplace. One incident, however, was to hit headlines across the world in 1969, and significantly weaken support for the war in America and further demoralize the troops.

Anti-war activists had repeatedly accused the US of committing atrocities in Vietnam. This infuriated the hawks, who accused them of being anti-American and unpatriotic. But in this one case the facts were undeniable. The incident concerned had occurred the previous year during a routine search-and-destroy operation. Compared with atrocities before and since, the numbers who lost their lives were small, but because it was perpetrated by Americans, the name of the village where it took place has taken its place in the annals of infamy. That name is My Lai.

THE MASSACRE AT MY LAI

On the morning of 16 March 1968, three companies of American troops were sent into the My Son area near Quang Ngai, 62 miles south of Da Nang. Their job was to seek out the enemy and kill them. The soldiers were from the 11th Infantry Brigade, American Division. C Company's target was the Vietcong's 48th Battalion, which intelligence believed was operating out of a hamlet marked on American maps as My-Lai 4. Helicopters set Charlie Company down nearby. There was no resistance at the landing zone. This was because they were at the wrong village. Nevertheless, the company commander Captain Ernest L. Medina sent the 1st and 2nd Platoons into the village. Seeing Americans coming, some villagers ran away and were gunned down. The 2nd Platoon swept through the northern part of the village, hurling grenades into the huts and killing anyone who came out. They raped and murdered village girls, rounded up civilians and shot them. There was no resistance. After half an hour, Medina ordered the 2nd Platoon

on to the hamlet of Binh Tay, where they gang-raped several more young women and rounded up some 20 women and children and shot them.

Appalling though this was, the name most closely associated with the massacre was that of Lieutenant William L. Calley. He was in command of the 1st Platoon which swept through the south of the village, shooting anyone who tried to escape, bayoneting others, raping women, shooting livestock and destroying crops and houses. Survivors were rounded up and herded into a drainage ditch. Lieutenant Calley opened fire on the hapless villagers and ordered his men to join in. They emptied clip after clip into the tangled heap of human flesh until all the bodies lay motionless. When they stopped firing, miraculously, a two-year-old boy crawled out of the carnage, crying. He tried to climb out of the ditch and run away. Calley grabbed him, pushed him back and shot him.

Half an hour later, the 3rd Platoon moved in to mop up. They shot wounded villagers to 'put them out of their misery', burnt houses, killed the remaining livestock, shot anyone trying to escape, and rounded up a group of women and children and sprayed them with bullets. No one is sure how many died, but estimates put the death toll at anywhere between 172 and 347 people. They were unarmed old men, women and children. Only three of them were known members of the Vietcong. Captain Medina reported a body count of 90 dead: all enemy soldiers, no civilians. The divisional press officer announced 128 enemy killed.

CWO Hugh Thompson speaking during the re-investigation of the My Lai massacre on 4 December 1969. His eyewitness testimony helped convict platoon commander Lieutenant William Calley.

taken. That only three weapons were being shared among 141 enemy soldiers should have alerted someone that something was wrong. But it was just another day in Vietnam.

The reason that, on this occasion, things came unravelled was that two pressmen, combat photographer Ronald Haeberle and army reporter Jay Roberts, had been assigned to Calley's platoon, and had witnessed the appalling carnage. One woman had been hit by such ferocious, continuous fire that bone flew off chip by chip. Another woman was shot and her baby cut down with an assault rifle. Another baby was slashed with a bay-onet. One GI who had just finished raping a girl put his rifle into her vagina and pulled the trigger. An old man was thrown down a well and a grenade was dropped in afterwards. A child escaping from the carnage was brought down with a single shot.

There was another appalled witness. Warrant Officer Hugh C. Thompson, the pilot of a small observation helicopter circling the village, had begun dropping smoke flares to mark the position of wounded civilians so they could be medevacked out. He was horri-fied to see American foot soldiers follow the smoke and shoot the casualties.

Gradually, the news leaked out. The men of C Company were not shy about boasting of their great victory at My Lai. Meanwhile the Vietcong distributed pamphlets denouncing it as an atrocity. The US Army half-heartedly investigated the rumours of a massacre that had eventually spread up the chain of command, but decided there was no basis for an official enquiry. However, another soldier

The My Lai Massacre neatly summed up everything that was going wrong in Vietnam. The war that had begun with a lie continued with lies. Patrols were reporting nonexistent contacts and officers were inflating body counts until no one in the Pentagon or in the US government had any idea what was really going on. At My Lai, there was just one American casualty, a self-inflicted wound. Thirteen Vietcong suspects, a press officer said, had been captured and three weapons named Ronald Ridenhour who had ambitions to be a journalist heard about the massacre and took an interest. He made it his business to meet the men from C Company, especially Michael Bernhardt, who had refused to participate in the killing. The other members of C Company were beginning to get uneasy about what they had done too. They were about to be rotated back to America and realized that the rest of the world did not operate in the same moral vacuum as Vietnam. They knew that there was nothing they could do without inviting murder charges, but they were happy to unburden themselves to Ridenhour.

He compiled what they told him, but took things no further while in Vietnam, realizing that if he took his evidence to the army, they would stage a summary investigation, which would result in another whitewash. On his return to America, however, he could not forget what he had been told, so he drew up a letter outlining his evidence and sent out 30 copies to prominent politicians. One of them was Congressman Morris Udall of Arizona, who pressed the Pentagon to interview Ridenhour. Six months later, and nearly 18 months after the event, Lieutenant Calley was charged with murder.

This posed a problem for the US military. What they needed was a scapegoat who could be branded a madman or psychopath. That way they could assure the world that the My Lai massacre was a one-off. But Calley was just an ordinary man. He had been working as an insurance appraiser in San Francisco when he had been called up in his home state of Miami. He started to drive home, but ran out

of money just outside Albuquerque, New Mexico, so he enlisted right there. He was sent to Fort Bliss, Texas, for basic training and went on to clerical school at Fort Lewis, Washington. By this time, the US Army had a severe shortage of officers. The extension of the draft meant that the army did not have enough West Point graduates to command its rapidly swelling ranks. As the war grew unpopular, the numbers joining the Reserve Officer Training Corps at universities and colleges declined rapidly. Consequently, poorly educated men such as Calley were picked for officer training. After a so-called 'Shake 'n' Bake' course at the Officer Candidate School at Fort Benning, Georgia, Calley graduated without even being able to read a map properly. Certainly the ethics of war was not a subject the course dwelt on. Before graduating, Calley was asked to deliver a speech on 'Vietnam Our Host'. At his trial, he recalled saying that American troops should not insult or assault Vietnamese women, but the rest he was foggy on.

Nothing could have prepared Calley for the moral morass that was Vietnam, certainly not his sketchy training. He found himself unable to control his own men and incapable of resisting the mounting pressure from his superiors for a 'body count'. As the war in Vietnam had no clear military objectives, the 'body count' had become all important. The problem was that Calley and his men could not find any Vietcong. In his own book on the My Lai massacre Calley described how, when he went with a prostitute who showed Communist leanings, he wondered whether he should have shot her. But she was the only 'enemy' he ever even clapped eyes on. His inept attempts at ambush were noisy enough to alert the enemy miles away. Out in the paddy fields, he could find no one. But the enemy were out there all right, invisible in the jungle, and close enough to pick off Calley's men with rifle shots, seemingly at will.

Patrolling near My Son in the My Lai area in February 1969, Calley's radioman was shot. For three days the company tried to penetrate My Son but were driven back. Two men were killed by booby traps. Another was hit by sniper fire. The patrol then blundered into a nest of booby traps, but when they extricated themselves unscathed, two more men were cut down by sniper fire.

On their next assignment, they were heading for the rendezvous point when an explosion tore through the early morning still-ness and a man screamed. There was another explosion and another scream. Then another explosion and another and another and another. They had stumbled into a minefield and, as men rushed forward to rescue their wounded buddies, there were more and more explosions. Severed limbs flew through the air, medics crawled from body to body and there were still more explosions. It lasted for almost two hours, leaving 32 men killed or wounded.

On 4 March the company was mortared and most of the men's personal possessions were destroyed. Two days before the assault on My Lai, four men – including the last of the company's experienced NCOs – were blown to bits by a booby trap. In 32 days, C Company, whose field strength was between 90 and 100, had suffered 42 casualties, a 40 per cent casualty rate, without ever even seeing the enemy.

Calley had had evidence of atrocities committed by the Vietcong, though. One night, the VC had captured one of his men and they heard him screaming all night. He was 4½ miles away. The screams were so loud that Calley thought the Vietcong must have had a PA system and amplifiers. They didn't. They had skinned the GI alive, leaving only the skin on his face. They then bathed his raw flesh with salt water. Calley's platoon recovered the body the next morning. Such mutilation was commonplace. Calley had seen a village elder broken in spirit when the VC delivered an earthenware jar containing what looked like stewed tomatoes to his door one morning. There were fragments of bone in it, and hair, and lumps of floating flesh. It was what remained of his son. He had seen GIS shooting down civilians for fun or target practice. He had heard of helicopter gunships hired out for human turkey shoots and bored GIS going 'squirrel hunting' in civilian areas. He had seen US soldiers casually fire on each other for no reason at all, and he had heard of fragmen-tation grenades being tossed into officers' quarters when their men did not want to go out on patrol.

'I look at Communism the same way a Southerner looks at a Negro,' he said in an interview. 'As for me, killing those men in My Lai didn't haunt me. I didn't – I couldn't kill for the pleasure of it. We weren't in My Lai to kill human beings, really. We were there to kill ideology that is carried by, I don't know –

pawns, blobs, pieces of flesh. And I wasn't in My Lai to destroy intelligent men. I was there to destroy an intangible idea.'

He even wished, humanely, that he could shoot the philosophy part out of people's heads. Besides, it wasn't even really him doing it. 'Personally, I didn't kill any Vietnamese that day, I mean personally. I represented the United States of America. My country,' he said.

Calley believed that he should put his duty to his country above his own conscience. He was not even worried about killing the aged, the women, the children. He had heard of mama-sans throwing grenades, children laying mines, girls carrying AK-47s. Besides, when the children grew up they would be VC, like their fathers and mothers. And where were all the men? My Lai was full of women and kids, but no young men. To Calley that meant their fathers were away fighting. They must be VC. Anyway, Calley reasoned, was what he had done any worse than dropping 500-pound bombs on them from a B-52 or frying them with napalm? The US had killed women and children in Hiroshima and Nagasaki by dropping an atomic bomb on them, hadn't it? And as a Southerner he wondered what these damn Yankees – the Pentagon, the media, the anti-war protesters – were getting so worked up about. He had done nothing worse than General Sherman had done in his march to the sea during the Civil War. Calley noted that the wisdom of the times was: 'The only way to end the war in Vietnam was to put all the dinks [South Vietnamese] in boats and take them out to sea, kill all the North Viet-

namese…then sink the boats.'

Like many American servicemen, Calley eventually stopped believing in the war. He came round to the opinion that to argue that Communism had to be stopped in Vietnam before it spread to Thailand, Indonesia, Australia and finally the US – the domino theory was then still the nearest thing the US had to a strategic aim – was like a man coming around to your house to murder his wife because he did not want blood on his carpet, then murdering your wife for good measure. He knew that it was the Vietcong who were winning the hearts and minds of the Viet-

'PERSONALLY, I DIDN'T KILL ANY VIETNAMESE… I REPRESENTED THE UNITED STATES OF AMERICA'

namese people, not the Americans. After My Lai, Calley became a welfare officer who bought pigs for peasant farmers, arranged sewing lessons for prostitutes, and took sick children to hospital. But he began to realize that even these laudable efforts were wasted. The Vietnamese people did not want his help. They did not care about democracy or totalitarianism, capitalism or Communism. They just wanted to be left alone.

When Calley was called to Washington, he thought he was going to be given a medal. He was shocked when he was arrested and charged. Calley's trial split America. Those who supported the war protested that he was only doing his duty. Those against it said that Calley was a scapegoat. Massacres like that at

My Lai were happening every day and it was Johnson, McNamara and Westmoreland who should be in the dock. Eighty per cent of those polled were against his conviction.

In all 16 men were charged in connection with the massacre at My Lai. Calley went on trial at Fort Benning with six other defendants, including his commanding officer Captain Ernest Medina. The jury went out on 16 March 1971, the third anniversary of the massacre at My Lai. They deliberated for two weeks. In the end, they found Lieutenant William L. Calley guilty of murdering at least 22 civilians. He was sentenced to life imprisonment with hard labour. On review this was reduced to 20, then 10 years. He was finally paroled on 19 November 1974, after serving three and a half years under house arrest: less than two months for each murder he was found guilty of and less than four days for each of the civilians killed at My Lai.

Charges of premeditated murder and ordering an unlawful act, homicide, against Captain Medina were reduced to involuntary manslaughter for failing to exercise proper control over his men. Not convinced that Captain Medina actually knew what his men were doing in My Lai 4, the jury acquitted him. Charges including the Nuremberg indictment of violating the laws and customs of war were brought against 12 other officers and men. Only five were tried. None were found guilty. A dozen officers, including Calley's divisional commander Major-General Samuel W. Koster, were charged with participation in

Marines of E Company carry another fallen comrade.

the cover-up. None were found guilty.

Calley himself believes that he was no worse than most, and better than many, of the officers and men who served in Vietnam. 'I was like a boy scout,' he said, 'and I went by *The Boy Scout Handbook*.'

He believed that he did his duty to God and country, that he was trustworthy, loyal, helpful, friendly, courteous, kind, obedient, cheerful, thrifty, brave, clean and reverent. And still there were 347 civilians lying dead after the atrocity at My Lai. One hundred were slaughtered in a ditch. One of them was a two-year-old child.

Despite the blustering of the hawks, My Lai sickened the American people. In its wake came a wave of other atrocity reports, 242 in all. In 1971, it was adjudged unconstitutional to prosecute former servicemen once they had left the service. However, 78 atrocity cases were substantiated. Thirty-six cases were prosecuted successfully and 61 individuals found guilty of war crimes. In all, 201 army personnel were convicted of serious offences against civilians. Ninety Marines were also found guilty of such offences, although Marine records do not distinguish between crimes committed in combat and those committed while off duty. It was plain that the US forces in Vietnam were on the verge of anarchy. Discipline broke down almost completely:

We had a sense that we were no longer GIs who had to march, who had to salute [said one veteran]. That was shit. We didn't have to salute nobody. We dressed the way we wanted to dress. If I wanted one sleeve up
and one sleeve down then I did it. If I didn't want to shave I didn't. Nobody fucked with nobody in the field. An officer knew that if he messed with you, in a firefight you could shoot him in the head. That was standard procedure in any infantry unit. Anybody tells you differently, he's shitting you. If you mess with my partner as an NCO or something like that, in the unwritten code there, I had the right to blow your brains out.

This collapse of military discipline brought into currency a new word – fragging. Initially it meant the murder of an officer with a frag-mentation grenade, often casually tossed into their hootch. But soon it came to cover any method of doing away with any inconvenient officer – one who made life difficult for his men, was gung-ho or incompetent and exposed his men to unnecessary risks. In the field there were plenty of opportunities to shoot an officer in the back. Company scout Mike Beaman said, 'We were aware that officers were being fragged and the officers knew it too.'

Fraggings followed two basic patterns. The first gave the officer a couple of warnings, so that he had a chance to change his ways. First, a smoke grenade was tossed into his hootch. If that did not convince, he got a CS gas grenade. 'When they put the gas on you, yeah, you know they mean you no good,' said one GI. If that warning was not heeded, the officer in question would get the real thing.

There were also 'bounty' fraggings that could come at any time with no warning given. Money changed hands for the removal of an officer. The underground newspaper *GI Says* posted a $10,000 reward for the death of Lieutenant-Colonel Weldon Honeycutt, the man responsible for the disastrous attack on Hamburger Hill in 1969. An ex-Leatherneck admitted to contributing to a bounty on a hated sergeant in the 3rd Marine Division. 'The first man with a witness who blew his ass away with a round across his eyeballs in a fire-fight would get $1,000,' he said. 'I personally offered approximately $25 for his head.'

Another Marine named Charles Anderson, while stressing that no fraggings had occurred in his particular company, knew of another incident concerning an old-time gung-ho sergeant who gave Anderson's buddies a hard time over spit and polish. One day the company was caught in an ambush. According to Anderson, 'When they found the sergeant there were more holes in his back than in his front.'

Incompetent officers, such as those who got their men lost because they were not able to read a map, were in constant danger. Out on patrol, no one would sleep near them in case a grenade was tossed in their foxhole. These officers could only be saved if their superiors spotted that they were not up to scratch and removed them. Many were threatened by their own men. In October 1972, the military police had to be flown into a camp near Da Lat to protect the commanding officer. Fraggings there had reached such epidemic proportions that attempts had been made on the officer's life two nights running and the MPs had to be in residence for a week before discipline was restored.

Of course, soldiers have always used such methods to rid themselves of officers and NCOs who needlessly put them in danger, but by 1969, it was so commonplace that its victims could not be hidden among battlefield casualties. According to a Congressional investigation there were 239 incidents in 1969, 383 in 1970, 333 in 1971 and 58 in 1972. Roughly 3 per cent of the 3,269 officer deaths in Vietnam are attributed to fragging. But these figures include only those who died by grenade and omit those who were shot, stabbed or disposed of some other way.

'WE WERE AWARE THAT OFFICERS WERE BEING FRAGGED AND THE OFFICERS KNEW IT TOO'

According to the Judge Advocate General's Corps it was estimated that only 10 per cent of fragging attempts resulted in the perpetrator coming to trial. And, like all figures from Vietnam, these statistics are highly debatable.

Another symptom of the collapse of American military morale was the widespread abuse of drugs. In 1969 and 1970 alone, around 16,000 GIs received a dishonourable discharge for possession. Although the overwhelmingly favourite drug was marijuana, amphetamines, barbiturates and opium were all widely used. A report issued by the Pentagon in 1973 estimated that 35 per cent of all enlisted men in the Army who had served in Vietnam had tried heroin and 20 per cent had been addicted at some point during their tour. Varieties of marijuana grew wild

Marines from G Company, 2nd Battalion, 4th Marine Regiment cross a stream on 17 July 1966 en route to their objective in Quang Tri province, northeast of Dong Ha, Vietnam, during Operation Hastings.

in Vietnam and Laos. Nearby is the 'Golden Triangle', the area of the Shan province in Burma which, at that time, was the source of most of the opium in the world. And you could get practically any pill you liked in a Saigon pharmacy.

For $10 you could get a coffee jar full of grass that GIS smoked in old corncob pipes, or for $15 you could get a carton of ready-rolled joints, packaged to look exactly like Winstons or some other American proprietary brand of cigarettes. For a few bucks extra a mama-san would paint opium on the paper.

Some restricted their smoking to off-duty hours, while others began smoking dope as soon as they woke. Men would run the risk of going out on patrol high, hallucinating, or paranoid on weed, or even tripping out on acid. Regular potheads grew their hair long, giving birth to the hippy GI. There was the occasional shakedown, but by and large NCOS turned a blind eye, only too well aware that drugs helped their men get through their year in the 'Nam.

Many took their drug habit with them back to the US, where they were confronted

1963. Even out of uniform, they found it hard to blend in. Combat veterans were distinguished by a distant look in the eye known as the 'thousand-yard stare'.

One veteran who later was to become the lieutenant-governor of Massachusetts recalled waking up yelling while on a domestic flight soon after returning home. 'The other passengers moved away from me – a reaction I noticed more and more in the months ahead,' he said. 'The country didn't give a shit about the guys who had come back, or what they'd gone through. The feeling toward them was "Stay away – don't contaminate us with whatever you've brought back from Vietnam."'

Public hostility and rejection made it hard for Vietnam veterans to reassimilate. They felt that they were being forced to shoulder the nation's collective guilt, shame and humiliation, with very little sympathy or understanding even from friends and family. The result was that as many as 700,000 veterans experienced some sort of emotional or psychological problems after their return, finally recognized in 1980 as Post Traumatic Stress Disorder.

Even the Vietnam Memorial in Washington, DC, unveiled in November 1982, had to be paid for by public subscription rather than government funds. Undoubtedly impressive though it is, visitors often note that the black marble wall carrying the names of all those listed KIA and MIA (killed in action and missing in action) is practically underground and cannot be seen from any major thoroughfare of the capital city.

with a world that they barely recognized. The pace of change in fashion, behaviour and attitude was so fast in the 1960s that even those who had not spent a year in Vietnam found it hard to keep up. Soldiers returning to the States would be greeted by stoned hippies asking, 'Howzit goin', baby killer?' or taunting them as 'army motherfuckers'. They would see protestors burning the American flag. The flag that they had fought to defend had become as debased as the Union Jack, which had sprung up everywhere since the invasion of British bands and fashions in

9

THE EXPANDING WAR

NIXON'S STATED policy was that the war was going to be concluded by diplomacy, not on the battlefield. After his inauguration on 20 January 1969, he set about marrying diplomatic activity to troop withdrawals to bring 'peace with honour'. He brought in Harvard professor Henry Kissinger as assistant National Security Adviser to handle the diplomacy, while Secretary of Defense Melvin Laird would deliver on Nixon's campaign promise to withdraw troops, despite the protests of MACV.

General Abrams was to press ahead with Vietnamization and produced a 'glide path' of fourteen incremental withdrawals which would extricate US ground troops completely by November 1972. The first phase would remove 25,000 men, largely the 9th Infantry Division, between 1 July and 31 August 1969. The 3rd Division of the Marine Corps and the 3rd Brigade of the 82nd Airborne Division – some 40,500 – were withdrawn in phase two between 18 September and 19 December. By the end of 1969, some 51,670 men had left Vietnam. For those who remained behind, of course, the fighting became more intense. With the Americans going home, the Communists now knew they were winning. But America was not about to give up without a fight and Nixon was determined to keep up the pressure on Hanoi by intensifying the bombing campaign.

'I would rather be a one-term president than see America accept the first defeat in its 190-year history,' Nixon told a TV audience.

Even before President Nixon entered the

White House, it soon became clear to the Communists that he was going to play hardball. He believed that the Soviet Union and Red China wanted the North Vietnamese to enter into constructive negotiations. So, while widening the war in Southeast Asia, he would put pressure on the Soviet Union – and later the Chinese – to abandon their North Vietnamese ally. Both Communist powers sought to improve relations with the US. Nixon also toyed with the idea of what he called the 'Madman Theory' – hinting that he might be crazy enough to use nuclear weapons in Vietnam in order to encourage the Communists to negotiate.

However, once in power, Nixon found that the Soviets exerted no influence over the North Vietnamese. On 4 August Nixon's National Security Adviser Henry Kissinger held a secret meeting with Xuan Thuy in Paris. He restated America's position that the North Vietnamese should withdraw and allow the Saigon government to come to some compromise with the Vietcong. Xuan Thuy

A US Air Force CH3E helicopter approaches a landing zone in the jungle during Operation Pony Express in June 1968. This was an entirely illegal incursion into neighbouring Cambodia and Laos which had remained ostensibly neutral throughout the war.

Opposite: In North Vietnam a statue of a god stands undamaged amidst the ruins of his temple, destroyed by US B-52 attacks. Under Nixon the bombs would rain down again.

insisted that the Saigon government be dissolved. Nixon tried appealing to Ho Chi Minh directly, but was rebuffed. The war on the battlefield would continue.

In March 1969, the Vietnam War had turned, briefly, into a conventional conflict when an armoured column pushed up Route 9 to Khe Sanh, which had been virtually a no-go area since the Marines had pulled out in July 1968. The road was in a terrible state. In places it was washed out and NVA sappers had left hardly a bridge or culvert intact. The 1st Battalion of the 77th Armored Regiment took with them armoured vehicles carrying bridges to cross ravines and giant bulldozers to cut away cliffs where mountain roads were too narrow for tanks to pass. The column was supplied by a shuttle service of CH-47 Chinook helicopters and CH-54 Skycranes. On 18 March, lead elements reached what had once been one of the most beautiful valleys in Vietnam, now a moonscape honeycombed by B-52 raids: a wasteland of unexploded bombs, mines, abandoned fortifications, barbed wire, rotting parachutes, devoid of vegetation. The armoured column arrived in the ruins of Khe Sanh at 1300hrs, taking the NVA completely by surprise. They fled into Laos. Lieutenant-Colonel Carmen P. Milia, commanding the armoured column, wanted to follow and engage the enemy in conventional tank warfare. Instead, he was ordered to cut south across country to interdict traffic on the Communist-controlled Route 926. The bulldozers went first, cutting a path through the jungle. The column reached Route 926 five days later on 26 March. But on 30 March, it

was ordered to withdraw. The operation was declared a success. In 43 days, it had swept 38 square miles of 'injun country'. However, only 73 enemy had been killed.

HAMBURGER HILL

To the south, the US Army's last large-scale action of the war was about to get underway. In the aftermath of the Tet Offensive, Westmoreland had committed forces to the A Shau valley on the Lao border, one of the least hospitable parts of South Vietnam. The valley was a 30-mile-long funnel which connected the Ho Chi Minh trail to Thua Thien province in the northwest. Its rolling terrain was covered with 8-foot-high elephant grass and the hills around its rim were lush with triple-canopy jungle. This had been one of the major staging areas for Tet. In April 1968, the 1st Cavalry Division (Airmobile) and the ARVN had helicoptered deep into the valley. They encountered heavy antiaircraft fire but little resistance on the ground. In August, the 101st Airborne Division swept along the valley floor. They uncovered supply caches but the NVA melted away, leaving their anti-aircraft guns behind them.

Early in 1969, MACV intelligence discovered activity in the valley again, and the 101st were sent back. This time, they established firebases along the edge of the valley and helicoptered men in. Again they uncovered supplies but the enemy proved elusive. In May, the 101st, the 9th Marines and the 3rd ARVN regiment planned a number of hit and run raids. This time they were in for a surprise. On the morning of 11 May, B Company of the 3rd Battalion, 187th Infantry – part of the 101st – landed at the foot of Hill 937. Covered in lush green vegetation and spiked bamboo, this rugged peak was known to the Vietnamese as Dong Ap Bia or Ap Bia mountain. Americans would learn to call it Hamburger Hill.

Bravo Company were on a routine search-and-locate operation. They knew that the enemy were in the area, but expected them to melt away as they always had before. As they moved cautiously up the north slope of Hill 937, the undergrowth suddenly erupted with machine-gun fire from hidden bunkers. Those a fraction slow in hitting the deck were cut down. Survivors returned fire with M16s and light anti-tank weapons, then retreated down the hill with the wounded, their job done. They had located the enemy: the rest was up to the artillery and air support. Within minutes the firebase at Ta Bat opened up, then the USAF pummelled the bunkers with high explosives and incendiaries.

When the smoke died down, Bravo Company advanced up the hill again to mop up, but once again they came under withering fire. Again they withdrew and more fire support was called in. For the rest of the afternoon and the following night, bombs and shells pounded the NVA positions until logic

PFC David S. Whitmen, a member of the Leathernecks rifle company that in 1969 fought its way to the top of a mountain near the Laos border and, with wounded comrades, back down to the valley below in heavy fog and rain.

demanded that, if there were any enemy left on the slopes, they would be in no condition to fight. Logic was wrong. One of the GIS on the next advance was Spec 4 Jimmy Spears. He recalled that they ran 'into garbage' – automatic fire, rocket grenades and lethal claymore mines hanging from the undergrowth. Again B Company was forced to withdraw. As they prepared a new LZ to medevac their growing casualties out, more air and artillery support was called in and the enemy position was pounded for another day and night.

It did no good. At Hamburger Hill an irre-

'THERE'D BEEN LOW MORALE, BUT NEVER BEFORE SO LOW – BECAUSE WE FELT IT WAS ALL SO SENSELESS'

sistible force had met an immovable object. The irresistible force was the commander of the 3rd Battalion Lieutenant-Colonel Weldon Honeycutt. Codenamed Blackjack, he was a tough son-of-a-bitch who liked nothing better than walking point. His determination to shift the NVA from Hamburger Hill whatever the cost earned him a price on his head. The immovable object was the NVA's fortifications. The 7th and 8th Battalions of the 29th Regiment had built bunkers flush to the ground, hidden by dense undergrowth. They were practically indestructible and their interlocking fire converged on every approach to the hill. What's more, the air and artillery support was systematically stripping the hill

of any cover and it soon became clear to the men of the 187th that, if they continued to attack up the denuded slopes, it was not a question of if they were going to die but when. But attack they did.

On 12 May, B and C Companies made another attempt on the blasted hill. The attack lasted just 30 minutes before it was decisively repulsed. Rocket and automatic fire accounted for another 37 casualties. The following day, B, C, and D Companies went up the hill in separate lines of attack. Charlie Company was in the lead, but their commander fell wounded, his radio fell silent, C Company fell back, and the attack fell apart. The hill was blasted with artillery shells and bombs once again. The night was spent listening for activity, but the men who advanced again the following dawn expected a bullet with their name on it.

The attack on the morning of 15 May was reinforced by elements of the 3rd ARVN Brigade. But the thinned ranks of Bravo Company, supported by A Company, moved out again. With helicopter gunships rocketing the enemy positions, they inched forward desperately searching for any scrap of cover. Even the odd patch of undergrowth provided no haven: the NVA had spent the night rigging up more claymores. However, this time the grunts broke through and began clearing out the bunkers, slowly, one by one. But then disaster struck. Lead elements of B Company were strung out across the exposed hillside in sight of the crest of Hill 937 when a helicopter gunship bore down on them and let rip with its rockets and machine guns. Bodies flew through the air. The mutilated lay there screaming. After everything they had suffered the last four days, the last thing B Company needed was 'friendly fire'.

Later that afternoon, battalion headquarters came under fire by enemy RPGs. Honeycutt was wounded for the third time in the battle. He refused to be medevacked out. Many of his men wanted to see him go – in a body bag, preferably.

There were no attacks on 17 May. For 36 solid hours, the hill was bombarded with high explosives, napalm and CS gas. The GIs were issued extra-heavy flak jackets. They were almost unbearable to wear in the heat, but everyone cursed that they had not been issued a week earlier. On 18 May, two full battalions attacked with the 3/187th being joined by the 1st Battalion of the 506th Infantry. Amid desperate fighting the grunts reached the summit of Hamburger Hill. Then the heavens opened. Visibility dropped to zero and the thunderstorm turned the soil of the slopes, already churned up and loosened by repeated bombardment, into mud chutes where men could not keep their footing. They were bombarded with grenades and mines that were detonated within the enemy's perimeter. Another retreat was ordered.

By this point, 3/187th were on the brink of mutiny.

'There were lots of people in Bravo Company who were going to refuse to go up again,' recalled one GI. 'There'd been low morale, but never before so low – because we felt it was all so senseless.'

Despite this, on 20 May, a four-battalion attack was organized with the 2nd Battalion of the 501st Infantry and the 2nd Battalion of the 3rd ARVN joining the assault. They fought from bunker to bunker in combat so close that air support was out of the question. But, by the end of the day, the men of the 187th were in control of what was left of Hamburger Hill. Lieutenant-Colonel Honeycutt could not praise his men enough.

'My boys were really doing their jobs,' he said. 'I love every one of them.'

It was not reciprocated. Some 50 GIs had lost their lives on Hamburger Hill, and 40 had been wounded. And after the hill had been secured and the bunker complexes searched and destroyed, the peak was abandoned. On a piece of cardboard pinned to a tree along with a black 101st neckerchief, an unknown GI left the scrawled message: 'Hamburger Hill. Was it worth it?'

Back in Washington, DC, Senator Edward Kennedy did not think so. He pointed out that Hamburger Hill had no strategic value and he called the attack 'senseless and irresponsible'.

Soon after, *Life* magazine published the photographs of the 242 young Americans killed in a single week in the war that the Nixon administration was committed to ending. After Hamburger Hill, General Abrams ordered that American troops should instigate no more full-scale actions. For different reasons Hanoi issued similar orders.

If Hamburger Hill proved anything it was that Westmoreland's concept of 'big unit' engagement had finally been discredited. Vietnamization was proceeding apace. Between 1968 and 1971, the ARVN grew from 820,000 to over a million men. Their heavy World War II-vintage M1 rifles were replaced by lightweight M16s, which were a reasonable match for the Communists' outstanding AK-47s. While the ARVN performed well on incursions into Cambodian territory, they did less well at home where the largely city-dwelling ARVN did not win the hearts and minds of the villagers, who they often stole from. A 1969 study found that ARVN soldiers had upset the civilian population in almost half of South Vietnam's hamlets. Their attempts to move peasants into safe areas to limit VC influence were also heavy-handed.

'Putting the people behind barbed wire against their will is not the first step to earning loyalty and support, especially if there is no concentrated effort at political education and village development,' one US study said.

The ARVN also suffered a huge number of desertions. In 1970, over 100,000 men, more than 10 per cent of its strength, deserted, failed to return from leave, or defected to the Vietcong. On the other hand, the VC was not what it had been. Attacks by Communist units fell from 318 in 1969 to 295 in 1970 and 187 in 1971. By 1971, the insurgency was largely confined to ten provinces and more than one million refugees had been able to return home. The Tet Offensive and the Phoenix Program had destroyed the VC command structure – along with a great many innocent people – and with peace talks going on in Paris the Communist soldiers, like their American counterparts, did not want to be the last one to die in the conflict. During 1969–70, the number of VC taking advantage of the amnesty offered by

the South Vietnamese government soared. Only a small percentage of these deserters were genuine, according to the US head of the pacification programme William Colby, but even this small number marked significant progress. Even so Communist forces kept up the pressure in Vietnam despite the death of Ho Chi Minh in September 1969. President Thieu attempted to sue for peace by offering elections that would include the NLF, but Vice-President Ky warned that any attempt to form a coalition with the NLF would result in another military coup.

In America, the split in public opinion over the war became further entrenched when Lieutenant Calley was charged with murder over the My Lai Massacre. Nixon announced the withdrawal of a further 35,000 troops but on 15 October 1969, 'Moratorium Day', hundreds of thousands of Americans demonstrated against the seemingly endless war. To still the protest Nixon made a televised speech promising an 'orderly scheduled timetable' for US troop withdrawals. It did little to quell public feeling. Two weeks later, a quarter of a million people attended an anti-war demonstration in Washington. Despite continuing troop withdrawals, US casualties continued to rise, topping 40,000 by the end of 1969.

The morale of the US troops was now at breaking point. At the beginning of the war, they had faced a guerrilla army, who hit then ran away, and they had longed for a conventional battle where they could use their superior firepower to defeat the enemy. But when they did meet the NVA in set-piece battles, they found that the enemy could suffer enormous casualties without breaking. The Communists mounted a new offensive in January 1970, attacking over a hundred bases with missile fire. Nixon responded by pounding the Ho Chi Minh trail with B-52s. The NVA began a major offensive in Laos and reports circulated that the US was bombing Laos in support of the anti-Communist government there. Many feared Nixon intended to extend the war, although Secretary of Defense Melvin Laird stated that the President would ask for Congressional approval if US ground troops were to be sent into Laos. This was disingenuous. The country had been politically unstable since the withdrawal of the French in 1954, and a civil war raged there throughout the 1960s. Both the North Vietnamese and the US covertly took a hand in the fighting and Laos found itself inexorably dragged into the war in Southeast Asia.

THE **POSITION** OF **LAOS**

In the Geneva Accords of July 1954 that ended the French presence in Indochina, Laos had been set up as an independent country, a buffer state between Western-orientated Thailand and Communist North Vietnam. A royalist government was set up

under Prince Souvana Phouma in Vientiane, the capital of Laos. From the beginning he faced opposition from his half-brother Prince Souphanouvong, leader of the Communist guerrilla army, the Pathet Lao – 'Land of the Laos' – that controlled the northern provinces along the Chinese border.

With the Cold War at its height, armed conflict between these two factions seemed inevitable. But most Lao opposed this and a strong neutralist faction grew up, with the aim of keeping out foreign influences that might turn fraternal rivalry into full-blown civil war.

In 1957, Souvana Phouma and Souphanouvong tried to work together in a coalition,

Laotian Prince Souphanouvong, chairman of the Central Committee of the Laotian Patriotic Front (Pathet Lao), in Na Pha village, Laos, in January 1970. Although a prince of the royal household, he led the Communist guerrillas against his own half-brother.

but they soon fell out. Souvana Phouma and the Neutralists turned against Souphanouvong and received American backing for their anti-Communist stance. In 1959, the right-wing General Phoumi Nosavan entered the fray. He seized control in 1960, only to be ousted by Captain Kong Le, who was backed by the Neutralists and Souvana Phouma. Fearing that the Neutralists were cooking up a secret deal with the North Vietnam-backed Communists, America shifted its support to General Nosavan.

A new peace conference was convened in

DANIEL ELLSBERG SENT THE PENTAGON PAPERS... TO THE NEWSPAPERS

Geneva in 1961 and the following year a new agreement was drawn up. Under it, Laos was to remain neutral. This was to be ensured by a tripartite government comprising the Neutralists under Souvana Phouma, the rightists and the Pathet Lao. Again the arrangement was not destined to last.

In 1964, the coalition split and civil war broke out. Both the North Vietnamese and the US used this to increase their influence. The Vietnamese Communists had vital interests in Laos, particularly the Ho Chi Minh trail, which for most of its length ran through Laotian territory. On the other hand, it was vital for the US to break this supply route. Consequently Laos was drawn into the larger war. Covertly, America began bombing Laos

to try to stop supplies getting through, further destabilizing the country. The CIA armed anti-Communist guerrillas in Laos and formed the ethnically distinct Meo tribesmen into a guerrilla army to fight the Pathet Lao. The CIA airlines Air America and Continental Airways provided a fleet of some 60 aircraft to supply anti-Communist guerrillas in Laos via a network of 200 grass airstrips, and the CIA also recruited the best officers from the Royal Laotian Army and used them to set up Auxiliary Defense Companies and thirty-man Special Guerrilla Units that were used in action on the Ho Chi Minh trail. The Green Berets and their Civilian Irregular Defense Forces from South Vietnam were also used in cross-border operations into Laos. When America pulled out of Southeast Asia, these men were left to their fate. Many fought on against the Communists and were wiped out.

US Air Force detachments stripped of all identification manned radio beacons in the mountains along the Vietnamese border to direct American bombers against targets in North Vietnam. These were attacked and, in some cases, overrun by the NVA. Forward Air Controllers were also infiltrated into Laos to direct raids on the Ho Chi Minh trail.

In 1971 there was an incursion into Laos, ostensibly by the ARVN, codenamed Lam Son 719 after a historic Vietnamese victory. Although American ground troops were barred from entering Laos by Congress, the operation was conceived by the White House and planned by US commanders in Saigon. It was begun by a US Air Force bombing raid that flattened the Laotian city of Tchepone.

However, the South Vietnamese force that went in was dangerously understrength. The inexperienced ARVN troops were met with a full-scale counter-attack by the battle-hardened North Vietnamese Army. They suffered 50 per cent losses and were forced to withdraw. The US had been confined to a supporting role, but still lost 107 helicopters and 176 aircrew. The debacle left Laos wide open to the North Vietnamese, who used it as a springboard for their Easter Offensive in South Vietnam the following year.

The other result of the incursion into Laos was that it helped convince Pentagon analyst Daniel Ellsberg that the Nixon administration had no intention of ending the war. so he sent copies of the Pentagon Papers detailing the government's deception and incompetence in the conduct of the war to the newspapers.

CAMBODIA

Cambodia was also dragged into the war. Like Vietnam and Laos, Cambodia had been part of French Indochina. When the French departed in 1954, Prince Norodom Sihanouk, hereditary ruler of Cambodia, was recognized as the legitimate authority there. However, he was opposed by both Democrats and Communists. In 1955, Sihanouk quit and formed his own socialist party. He won the backing of former Democrat supporters and, with the help of numerous electoral abuses organized by the police, won every seat in the national assembly. As trouble brewed in Vietnam, Sihanouk tried to keep Cambodia scrupulously neutral. At first he courted the US, then when American troops moved into South Vietnam he shifted towards China. As it became clear that the Vietnamese Communists were going to win the war, he allowed them to use supply routes and bases along the border, believing that the Chinese would prevent them threatening his position.

After the Tet Offensive, General Westmoreland sought approval for attacks on Communist bases in Cambodia. Sensing the danger, Sihanouk began rebuilding bridges with the US. He invited Jacqueline Kennedy to visit the ancient temples at Angkor Wat and gave an interview to the *Washington Post*, inviting President Johnson to send a special envoy to Cambodia. Sihanouk offered Johnson the right of 'hot pursuit' of the Vietcong and NVA into uninhabited areas of Cambodia, provided no Cambodians were hurt in the process. Johnson did not take Sihanouk up on the offer, but it was still on the table when Nixon came to power. He proposed a secret 'short-duration' bombing campaign against Vietnamese strongholds in Cambodia. Sihanouk's military supplied the intelligence for the raids. However, the bombing continued for fourteen months and strayed into inhabited areas. As Cambodian casualties rose, Sihanouk found his country being destabilized.

In March 1970, when Sihanouk was out

of the country, his pro-American prime minister General Lon Nol staged a bloodless, US-backed coup. Lon Nol's ill-trained troops attacked the Vietnamese bases and, for good measure, massacred half a million Vietnamese civilians who had peacefully settled in Cambodia, sending their bodies floating down the Mekong River. The NVA counterattacked, forcing the Cambodians back. Two days later, the US began the illegal bombing and shelling of Vietnamese camps in Cambodia in direct violation of Cambodia's neutrality. Then the ARVN went in. The NVA response was renewed attacks on US positions in Vietnam. Nixon announced the withdrawal of a further 150,000 men by the following spring. At the same time, he sent US troops into Cambodia in support of the ARVN – ostensibly at the 'invitation' of Lon Nol. Nixon promised to 'scrupulously observe the neutrality of the Cambodian people', but the ARVN had no such scruples. After Lon Nol's massacre of the ethnic Vietnamese, they wanted revenge – and not just against the NVA.

The North Vietnamese fled ahead of the American invasion, only turning to make a stand at the small Cambodian market town of Snuol. This brought into the language of the Vietnam War a new verb, 'to snuol', meaning to obliterate completely. Over 90 per cent of the town was reduced to rubble and cinders by a two-day bombardment of rockets, shells and napalm. Nearby, US forces found a huge NVA compound in the jungle. The jungle canopy concealed bunker systems, log huts, cycle paths, bamboo walkways, garages for trucks, street signs, mess halls, a pig farm, chickens, a firing range – even a swimming pool. The grunts nicknamed the two-square-mile complex 'The City'. There were more than 400 thatched huts, sheds and bunkers stuffed with food, clothes and medical supplies. In the area, 182 caches of weapons and ammunition were found, including one containing 480 rifles and another with 120,000 rounds of ammunition.

A few days later a helicopter spotted four trucks on a jungle trail. Ground troops went in and, after a fierce firefight, the NVA scattered, leaving behind the biggest cache taken in the war. It contained over 6.5 million rounds of anti-aircraft ammunition, thousands of rockets, half a million rifle rounds, several General Motors trucks, and even a telephone switchboard. The grunts called it Rock Island East, after the Rock Island Arsenal in Illinois. But Nixon had promised something more. Across the border in Cambodia, he said, lay 'the headquarters for the entire Communist military operation in South Vietnam', the fabled COSVN. MACV had a precise map reference for it, but it wasn't there – so it was claimed that The City was it. However, none of the documents or headquarters infrastructure were found there that would back that claim.

'We're still looking for the guy in the COSVN T-shirt,' said one US intelligence agent.

For Nixon, it was like Christmas. The incursion was an overwhelming success. In just two weeks, the operation had culled 4,793 small arms, 730 mortars, over three million rounds of rifle ammunition, 7,285 rockets, 124 trucks, and two million pounds of rice. Nixon ordered another 31,000 US troops into Cambodia to take out the rest of the sanctuaries along the border. However, he had misjudged the reaction. The Soviet Union and France condemned the extension of the war into Cambodia, and it also led to new demonstrations in the US. Even so, Nixon ordered the renewed bombing of North Vietnam, provoking more protests, which resulted in the killings at Kent State University, Ohio. Nixon was unrepentant. 'When dissent turns to violence it invites tragedy,' he blithely said.

But Congress was not so blasé. It forced Nixon to promise that US troops would penetrate into Cambodia no deeper than 21 miles from the border and withdraw completely within a matter of weeks. Congress also repealed the Gulf of Tonkin Resolution that had given the President the power to go to war in Southeast Asia. Nixon was unconcerned, maintaining that his power to conduct the war rested in his authority as commander-in-chief, not the Gulf of Tonkin Resolution.

As he promised, Nixon withdrew US troops from Cambodia after seven weeks, but continued the illegal bombing of Cambodia. The ARVN continued fighting in Cambodia, with American air support, but made little headway. The NVA now were deployed in Cambodia and in South Vietnam in overwhelming strength. Nixon proposed a 'standstill' ceasefire, leaving troops where they stood on the battlefield. This played well at home, but was rejected by the Communists who were, by then, confident of victory.

On 21 November, the Green Berets staged a daring raid on the prisoner-of-war camp at Son Tay, just 23 miles from Hanoi. Militarily, this attack deep behind enemy lines was a brilliant success. The 60 guards were overwhelmed and the camp taken in a matter of minutes. But the operation was fruitless. Intelligence had been poor and the 70 American pilots held there had been moved shortly before. None were rescued.

That same day, an unarmed US reconnaissance aircraft was shot down. In response, the US unleashed a huge bombing raid against the North. Although Nixon later warned Hanoi

CONGRESS... PROHIBITED THE FURTHER USE OF US FORCES IN CAMBODIA

that more raids would follow if their aggression continued, Congress was slowly tying his hands. It prohibited the further use of US forces in Cambodia, though Nixon determinedly continued his secret bombing, reasoning that by disrupting the NVA build-up in the border regions, he was buying time for Vietnamization and the completion of US troop withdrawals.

Congress also banned the use of US ground troops in Laos. Nixon had indeed been planning a new incursion into Laos, where the Laotian Communist guerrillas, the Pathet Lao, and the NVA had been making advances. Nixon responded with massive illegal B-52 raids, which made refugees out of 700,000 of the population of two million.

North Vietnamese negotiator Le Duc Tho arrives in Paris for peace talks in February 1970. After successfully negotiating the Paris Peace Accords allowing the US to pull out of Vietnam, he was awarded the Nobel Peace Prize jointly with American negotiator Henry Kissinger. Le Duc Tho refused the award; Kissinger did not.

On 8 February 1971 12,000 ARVN troops invaded Laos, supported by American aircraft. Nixon denied that US troops were operating in Laos and refused to curtail the use of US air power. Congress was outraged and Nixon's opponents tried to further limit his power to wage war. It was later admitted that US troops were being sent into Laos on the pretext that they were rescuing downed airmen, prompting a North Vietnamese protest at the Paris Peace Talks. By then, Nixon's popularity had plummeted to the lowest point since he took office and the Weathermen were setting off a bomb in Washington, DC, damaging the Capitol building. The Laos incursion turned into a fiasco. The ARVN were no match for the Communists; they suffered huge losses and were soon forced into a humiliating withdrawal.

On 31 March 1971, Lieutenant Calley received his life sentence for his part in the My Lai Massacre. The sentence provoked storms of protest from those who still supported the war. Nixon went on television to defend his record in Vietnam, restating his hope for an 'honourable' end to the war. But as US losses topped 45,000, he found a powerful new opponent on the streets of Washington: returned Vietnam veterans demonstrating against the war. Nixon found himself in deeper trouble domestically when *The New York Times* began publishing extracts from the Pentagon Papers. His attempts to silence the press made him even more unpopular.

In Paris the peace talks remained dead-locked. However, on 21 February 1970, Kissinger had entered into new secret talks with North Vietnamese negotiator Le Duc Tho in a small house in a Paris suburb. Le Duc Tho, a former commissar for the South, had taken over as head of the Vietnamese delegation when Ho Chi Minh died in September 1969. Born in northern Vietnam in 1912, Le Duc Tho was the son of a civil servant in the old French administration. He was a founder member of the Indochinese Communist Party and played an important part in building up the organization. He was also a founder of the Vietminh and had spent years fleeing arrest or in jail. During the war against the French, he had been commissar in the South. He was still active after the US intervention, hiding in the remote villages or the jungle, supervising the guerrilla war. During the war and after it, he refused to be interviewed and remained unknown in the West. Even to Kissinger, he was a mystery.

Dour and austere, he gave nothing away.

'I don't look back on our meetings with any great joy,' Kissinger said later, 'yet he was a person of substance and discipline who defended the position he represented with determination.'

These backstairs negotiations lasted three years with every detail being communicated back to the new collective leadership in Hanoi. This caused constant delays that left Kissinger exasperated. Nixon's expansion of the war in Southeast Asia had borne no fruit and Kissinger could not understand why a 'fourth-rate power like North Vietnam' did not have a breaking point. What he did not know was that, at the same time as negotiating the peace in Paris, Le Duc Tho was also directing the insurgency in the South. But then Kissinger too was playing a double game: in Paris, he was a dove; at home, he was engineering the clandestine bombing of Cambodia. In 1973, Le Duc Tho and Kissinger were offered a joint Nobel Prize for ostensibly bringing peace to Vietnam. Le Duc Tho had the good grace to decline it; Kissinger, on the other hand, accepted, an act that led satirist Tom Lehrer to comment that political satire was now dead.

As these clandestine talks dragged on, year after year, US troops became so disillusioned with the war that they began to disobey orders. Some refused to go out on patrol, but they were not court-martialled. Politically things were becoming unravelled in South Vietnam too. President Thieu was re-elected, but all the other candidates had boycotted the election, claiming it was rigged.

Vice-President Ky had tried to stand against Thieu, but had been persuaded to return to the air force. Congress further hobbled the ARVN's ability to prosecute the war by freezing military funds. Nixon responded with renewed air strikes on North Vietnam, the heaviest since 1968.

As US casualties mounted and the war became increasingly unpopular at home, Kissinger found his position being undermined. He abandoned Nixon's hope that a sustainable coalition might be established in Saigon and took the position that the best that the US could hope for was a 'decent interval' between US withdrawal and a Communist victory in the South.

Despite the hope that Nixon might still bring peace, the administration was further tarnished by more revelations about the conduct of the war. The government admitted that the CIA was running a 300,000-man army of irregulars in Laos. Reports that the ARVN had committed a number of atrocities against Cambodian civilians provoked the pro-American Cambodian government into demanding their withdrawal. Instead of pulling out, the ARVN went on the offensive as the Khmer Rouge, the Cambodian Communist guerrillas, encircled the capital Phnom Penh.

Throughout 1972, US troop withdrawals continued, but Nixon announced that 35,000 would stay until all US POWs held by the Communists were returned. By this time, even the South Vietnamese had turned against the Americans, who were accused of running out on them. Gangs of youths made life

One of the first F-111As to arrive in Thailand, at Takhli Air Base, in September 1972. F-111s were much sought after by the Soviets, who wanted them shot down with the minimum possible damage so that they could be shipped back to the Soviet Union for analysis.

unpleasant for Vietnamese girls seen with GIs. It was estimated that there were up to a thousand confrontations a month between Vietnamese civilians and US troops, and there were reports of young Vietnamese trying to beat up and even castrate Americans found on their own.

On 25 January, Nixon revealed that Kissinger had been negotiating secretly with the North Vietnamese and unveiled a new eight-point peace plan, which Hanoi promptly rejected. Even so, Thieu regarded it as an American attempt to abandon the South.

Pressure grew as the 1972 presidential election loomed and the NVA made continued gains in the South. But Nixon had an ace up his sleeve: he suddenly revealed that he was planning to visit China, after a 21-year estrangement. In February 1972, he visited Beijing, the first American president to do so. In May of the same year he also became the first US president to visit Moscow. The architect of both these rapprochements was Henry Kissinger. This diplomatic offensive did little to help the situation in South Vietnam, though. Neither Peking nor Moscow had much influence with

Hanoi. In March the NVA began a massive offensive, streaming across the DMZ and taking the ARVN by surprise. A second thrust out of Cambodia attempted to cut the South in two; a third cut Saigon off from the rest of the country.

The NVA were now equipped with the latest Soviet tanks, artillery and anti-aircraft missiles. The US blunted the attack by giving the ARVN heavy air support and sending B-52s against the North. This began a new wave of protests across the US. International protests followed and movie actress Jane Fonda went to Hanoi, where she broadcast an anti-war message on Hanoi Radio.

In protest at the NVA offensive, the US withdrew from the Paris Peace Talks on 8 May 1972 and resumed the full-scale bombing of the North. To halt the supply of new Soviet weapons, bombers mined Haiphong harbour. That and the intense bombing began to cause Hanoi severe economic problems, and gradually the ARVN clawed back the territory seized by the NVA. On 26 September Kissinger and Le Duc Tho, North Vietnam's chief negotiator in Paris, began their nineteenth session of talks, with the North Vietnamese continuing to insist on a complete military and political solution while the US sought an end to the fighting first, the search for a political solution later.

By the time the peace talks resumed in Paris the US had closed down its military headquarters and the last US combat battalion left Vietnam. The only leverage the US had left at the talks was the bombing, which continued until 8 October when Le Duc Tho offered a new peace plan. This broadly accepted the US position decoupling the military and political solutions: a military ceasefire would be put in place first, followed by new talks to establish a political settlement. President Thieu rejected the compromise, but Nixon stopped the bombing and Kissinger announced 'peace is at hand' just in time for the presidential elections. And on 7 November President Nixon was re-elected by a landslide. However, on 30 December, the peace talks broke down again. Nixon resumed the bombing, which wrecked a large part of North Vietnam's infrastructure and devastated its cities. Despite international condemnation, this Christmas bombing brought the North Vietnamese delegation back to the negotiating table. On the battlefield, though, the fighting continued. The NVA attacked Route 1, north of Saigon.

US Defense Secretary Laird declared that the 'Vietnamization' programme was complete, despite the fact that the ARVN was still receiving tactical air support from US bombers. Fearing that the US was abandoning South Vietnam to the Communists, on 13 January 1973 Thieu demanded that the US back an invasion of the North if peace talks broke down again.

On 23 January, the Paris Peace Accords were announced, ending American involvement in the war. Nixon declared it 'peace with honour'. The Paris Peace Accords were signed on 27 January 1973, and a ceasefire began the next day. On 27 January, Lieutenant-Colonel William B. Nolde became the last US serviceman to die on active service in Vietnam.

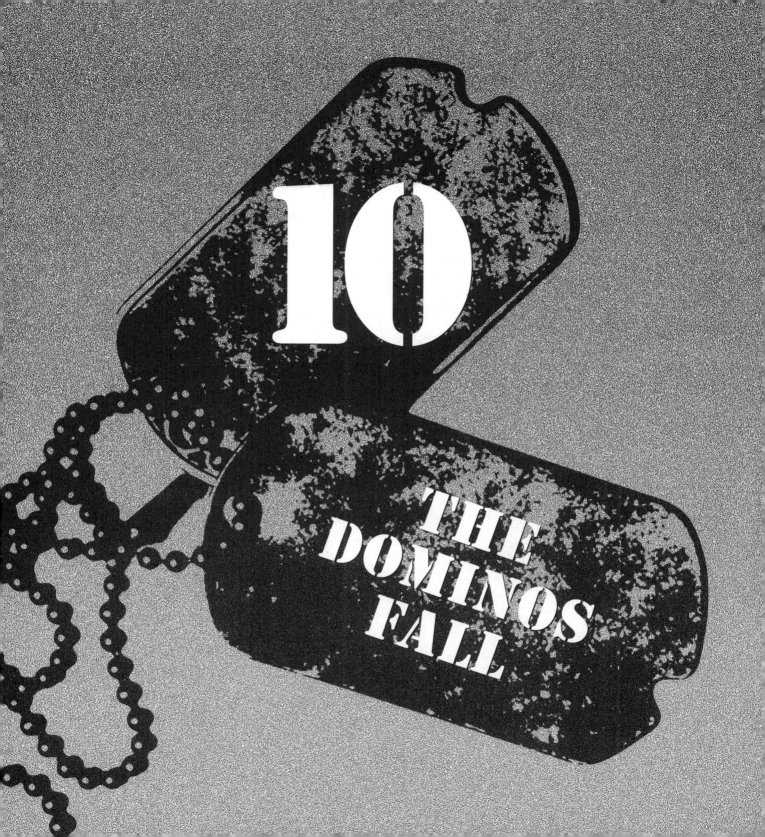

10

THE
DOMINOS
FALL

DESPITE NIXON'S proclamation of 'peace with honour', everybody knew that the Peace Accords were a sham. Kissinger had long realized that the best the US could hope for was a face-saving interval between US withdrawal and a Communist takeover of the South. Le Duc Tho was more frank, and proclaimed the Paris Peace Accords were a 'victory'. Both the Communists and the South Vietnamese began violating the ceasefire almost immediately, while at the same time going through the motions of implementing the Accords. A Joint Military Commission and an International Commission of Control and Supervision were set up to monitor the ceasefire, although they had little power to enforce it. The Saigon government opened new talks in Paris with the NLF, which was now calling itself the Provisional Revolutionary Government (PRG). These were immediately deadlocked, and collapsed the following year.

The foreign ministers of twelve countries, including Britain, France and the Soviet Union, met in Paris to approve the ceasefire agreement. Canada and other Western countries granted the Hanoi government diplomatic recognition. The US withheld recognition until 1974, breaking off diplomatic relations again with the fall of Saigon in 1975. But Washington began talks about the possibility of giving aid to the North straight away. Meanwhile Operation Homecoming – the return of US POWs – got underway. It soon became clear that the exchange of prisoners of war by all sides was not being honoured.

When the Saigon government was accused of holding Communists in its jail, Thieu said they were 'Communist criminals'. However, on 29 March 1973, the last US troops left Vietnam. 'The day we have all worked for and prayed for has finally come,' said Nixon.

The US Navy moved into North Vietnam to clear mines from the ports but, in Cambodia, US bombing continued as the Khmer Rouge threatened Phnom Penh once again. In June 1973, Congress voted to block funds for any further US military action in Southeast Asia. The following month, Congress voted to ban bombing in Cambodia and the Senate Armed Services Committee began hearings on the secret bombings. On 14 August, Nixon stopped bombing Cambodia in accordance with the congressional ban. By this time, Nixon was already being crippled by the Watergate Scandal. During the 1972 presidential election campaign, five men were arrested breaking into the headquarters of the Democratic National Committee at the Watergate building in Washington, DC. Among them were former White House aide E. Howard Hunt Jr and G. Gordon Liddy, general counsel for the Committee for the Re-election of the President. It gradually became clear that the White House was behind numerous 'dirty tricks' during the election and had hampered the investigation of the Watergate break-in. On 25 June 1973, former White House counsel John Dean directly implicated President Nixon himself in the cover-up.

The Paris Peace Accords of 1973 had only ended American ground troops' involvement in Southeast Asia. It permitted the NVA to stay

Opposite: Child soldiers prepare to defend Phnom Penh in 1975. They would be no match for the murderous Khmer Rouge, who aimed to take Cambodia back to 'year zero' by murdering anyone who had any education or might possibly oppose them. Phnom Penh was evacuated and millions died in the 'killing fields'.

in South Vietnam, but they were not to be reinforced. After US troops were gone, North and South Vietnam accused each other of numerous violations of the ceasefire and, inevitably, the NVA went back into action. Despite Hanoi's accusations that the Saigon government and the US were violating the truce, its own forces were making considerable gains in the South. By January 1974, Saigon announced that there had been 57,835 fatalities since the ceasefire. On 9 August Nixon resigned rather than face impeachment over the Watergate scandal and Gerald Ford became the 38th president of the United States. He began his term of office by giving a pardon to Nixon and an amnesty to those who had evaded the draft. In Hanoi the politburo began planning a new offensive for the following spring.

While the NVA and Khmer Rouge made advances in South Vietnam and Cambodia, there was little the US could do but sit and watch. When the US admitted making reconnaissance flights and giving the ARVN technical support, Hanoi complained that these were violations of the Paris Peace Accords. President Ford's request for $522 million in military aid for Cambodia and South Vietnam was blocked in Congress.

'Ultimately Cambodia cannot survive, so why spend hundreds of millions of dollars more?' asked one leading Democrat.

Kissinger, who was now Secretary of State, condemned denying money to South Vietnam,

Destroyed by US bombing and awash with guns, nothing could save Cambodia – until the Vietnamese invaded in 1978.

saying this would 'deliberately destroy an ally by withholding aid in its moment of extremis'. But President Ford ruled out any further intervention in South Vietnam which, in any case, would be out of the question without congressional approval.

Although, at times, the South Vietnamese army discharged itself admirably, the NVA was unstoppable. It had made its sacrifices in blood, and now it was determined to have its victory. Although Giap was accused of making costly tactical errors and was often reckless with the lives of his own men, his strategy had worked. He had forced the US to withdraw and was now within a stone's throw of defeating the South Vietnamese on the battlefield – though it was his protégé Van Tien Dung who was to lead the final assault on Saigon.

Thieu progressively pulled his troops back. By the end of March 1974, amid denials, Saigon abandoned the northern provinces of South Vietnam and the Communist PRG took control. They asked civil servants who had worked for the Saigon government to continue in their posts under the occupying forces; Hanoi had not expected the collapse to come so quickly. The politburo had planned victory in 1976, but now ordered the final push on Saigon.

In Saigon, the US flew out 2,000 orphans for adoption in America, a move that was quickly condemned as propaganda. Thieu tried reshuffling his cabinet, and the ARVN made a last stand at Xuan Loc, just 25 miles north of Saigon, where it found itself outflanked by the NVA. Saigon was now surrounded by 16 Communist divisions, around 140,000 hardened troops facing the 60,000 demoralized men of the ARVN. A last shipment of American artillery arrived without shells and the South Vietnamese Air Force was grounded when it ran out of fuel. President Thieu resigned after making a speech condemning the US and subsequently went to live in England, in the London suburb of Wimbledon. Former vice-president Ky castigated those who fled, but two days later he flew out to the 7th Fleet, and eventually to the USA, where he opened a liquor store in California. Thieu was replaced as president by Tran Van Huong who, a week later, on 28 April, was replaced by Duong Van Minh. Minh attempted to negotiate a ceasefire.

By this time panic had set in. One of the most memorable images of the Vietnam War is people being evacuated by helicopter from the roof of the US Embassy in Saigon as the city was about to fall. This was part of Operation Frequent Wind, a plan to rescue some 200,000 Vietnamese whose close association with the US would put them in danger when the Communists took over. However, the final collapse of the South came more quickly than anyone had imagined, throwing the plans into disarray.

It was not until the third week of April 1975 that Washington ordered the evacuation of all nonessential personnel. It was estimated that there were still around 7,000 Americans in the country. In fact, there were more like 35,000. On 20 April, evacuations began from Saigon's Tan Son Nhut Air Force Base. At first, only Americans were to be taken, but on

the first day between three and four hundred refugees turned up. Soon there were thousands, many of them ARVN troops who would be in danger when the NVA arrived. There were ugly scenes as troops and civilians fought for seats on the departing aircraft. The panic increased as the city came under shellfire. When the airport itself came under sniper fire, the Marine helicopters began picking up people from the roof of the Embassy and other buildings, and carrying refugees out to the carriers waiting in the South China Sea. When the carrier decks were full, helicopters were simply pushed off the side to make room for more. Some pilots ditched in the sea in the hope of being picked up, while a flotilla of small boats made their way out to the US ships.

The crowds outside the US Embassy began to panic. Some climbed over the barbed wire on top of the compound walls. Lines made their way up to the roof where refugees risked being blasted off by the 90mph downdraft from the helicopter rotors. There was no handrail around the roof and one Marine fell off, fracturing his skull. At 4 a.m on 30 April the order was given that only Americans were to be evacuated from then on. The last 865 Marines who secured the Embassy were flown out at 7.53 a.m.

In the last 18 hours of the evacuation 1,373 Americans, 5,595 South Vietnamese, and 85 third-country nationals were flown out – 2,100 from the Embassy roof. In all, 22,294 Vietnamese who had worked for American agencies were evacuated, around a quarter of the 90,000 total, although only 557 of the 1,900 Vietnamese who had worked for the CIA got out. Worse, in the hasty evacuation

At the last moment, the US did what it could to evacuate orphans and those who had aided America. But many were left to their fate. Those who had not supported the Communists found themselves in re-education camps or worse – though some escaped on flimsy craft.

231

of the Embassy, sensitive documents listing the Embassy's Vietnamese employees had been left behind intact, a gift for the incoming Communists bent on tracking down those who had collaborated with the US.

When President Minh's offer of a ceasefire was rejected by the Communists, he announced that he was ready to hand over power 'to avoid the useless shedding of our people's blood'. Less than two hours later, at midday on 30 April 1975, Communist forces entered Saigon. At 12.15, NVA tanks advanced on the Presidential Palace. On one of them was a journalist, Colonel Bui Tin, deputy editor of *Quan Doi Nhan Dan*, the North Vietnamese Army newspaper. NVA soldiers had already hung their flag from the balcony when Bui Tin's tank arrived on the lawn. Although Bui Tin was there to cover the final collapse of Saigon for his paper, when he entered the conference room where President Minh and his aides were waiting, he found himself ranking officer. As such, it was his duty to accept the surrender.

'We have been waiting for you since early this morning so we can turn over power to you,' said Minh.

'There is no question of you turning over power,' said Bui Tin. 'You cannot give up what you do not have. You can surrender unconditionally.'

Suddenly a burst of gunfire erupted outside. Several of Minh's ministers ducked.

'Our men are merely celebrating,' said Bui Tin. 'You have nothing to fear. Between Vietnamese, there are no victors and no vanquished. Only the Americans have been

beaten. If you are patriots, consider this is a moment of joy. The war for our country is over.'

After decades, centuries – indeed, millennia – of fighting, Vietnam was once again a united and independent country. The Vietnam War was over.

THE **KILLING FIELDS** OF **CAMBODIA**

At the same time, Laos fell to the Communists. A month after the signing of the Paris Peace Accords in January 1973, the warring factions in Laos had signed their own Vientiane Agreement, establishing a new coalition government, comprising factions from left and right, under the royalist Souvana Phouma. While fighting broke out again in South Vietnam and Cambodia, peace held in Laos. However, with the Americans gone, the rightists had no backing. When South Vietnam fell, the Pathet Lao took command in a bloodless coup. Prince Souphanouvong became head of state of the Lao People's Democratic Republic and announced the end of Laos's 600-year-old monarchy.

Worse was in store for Cambodia. Lon Nol's ill-trained and corrupt army was no match for the dedicated fanatics of the Khmer

Rouge, but the Communists had been held at bay by US air power, which turned its full force on Cambodia in January 1973 after the Paris Peace Accords ended the bombing of North Vietnam and Laos. However, when the US bombing was halted at the beginning of 1974, the Khmer Rouge were in shelling range of Cambodia's capital Phnom Penh and a prolonged siege of the city began.

Despite US backing and an army which outnumbered the enemy, Lon Nol fled on 1 April 1975, seeking refuge in the US. On 12 April 1975, American personnel were evacuated from Phnom Penh in Operation Eagle Pull. At 9 a.m., 36 Marine helicopters set down close to the Embassy and a 360-man Marine force secured the area. By 10 a.m. 82 Americans, 35 third-country nationals and 159 Cambodians, largely employees of the Embassy and their dependents, were flown out. The US Ambassador John Gunther Dean had offered the Cambodian government and top officials seats on the helicopters. Only one, Acting President Saukham Khoy, accepted the invitation. The rest stayed to meet their deaths.

On 17 April the Khmer Rouge marched down the once smart boulevards of Phnom Penh. It was well known that this army of fanatical Communist guerrillas were extraordinarily well disciplined. They were impervious to argument, bribery, or sentiment. These young troops had not come to loot or rape. They would have no drunken victory celebration. But the expressionless teenagers of this austere fighting force struck a note of terror in the hearts of the inhabitants. The fate that awaited the citizens of Phnom Penh would be much worse than raping and pillaging; 17 April, 1975 was to be Day One, Year Zero.

The Khmer Rouge leader was Pol Pot, the nom de guerre of Saloth Sar, the son of a minor Cambodian official. During the 1940s, he joined the anti-French resistance in colonial Indochina led by Ho Chi Minh. Pol Pot then joined the Communist Party of Kampuchea (CPK) in 1946, and in 1949, he went to France to study radio engineering but

17 APRIL 1975 WAS TO BE DAY ONE, YEAR ZERO

devoted his time there to revolutionary politics, returning to Cambodia in 1953.

During the First Indochina War, the CPK, backed militarily by Vietnamese Communists, infiltrated the nationalist Issarak movement. Rivals were violently suppressed. However, the Communist ascendancy in Cambodia was halted by the signing of the Geneva Accords in 1954, and the movement was then repressed by the Kingdom of Cambodia's hereditary ruler Prince Norodom Sihanouk, who contemptuously dismissed the CPK as the 'Khmer Rouge' – Red Khmers. The Khmer were the aboriginal people of Cambodia. The name stuck.

Meanwhile, dedicated cadres purged the party of those who had lost the faith. In 1962, CPK leader Tou Samoth disappeared on his way back from a secret trip to Hanoi and Pol Pot seized control of the party, but his insistence on pursuing his own revolutionary policies put him increasingly at odds with his Vietnamese sponsors. In March 1970, while Sihanouk was away on holiday in France, Lon Nol seized power, backed by the US who urged him to drive the NVA out of the Cambodian strongholds they used to prosecute the war in South Vietnam. However, the NVA counter-attacked and by the late summer of 1970, they controlled half the country.

Remaining covert, the Khmer Rouge expanded their control behind the Vietnamese lines. They also dominated Sihanouk's united front against Lon Nol's nationalist Khmer Republic in exile in Beijing. By 1973, Pol Pot felt strong enough to strike out on his own with an intensification of the 'class struggle'. Those who opposed the formation of agricultural cooperatives in Khmer Rouge-controlled areas were branded 'feudalists' and 'capitalists' and killed. Cambodian Communists trained in Vietnam were dubbed 'Vietnamese lackeys': they too were arrested. Chinese, Islamic Cham, and other ethnic minorities were excluded; the Khmer peasantry, known as 'base people', were elevated.

The leaders of the Khmer Rouge were Communist zealots, whose Marxism was adapted for the Third World: instead of putting the urban proletariat on a pedestal, as Karl Marx had, they taught that all goodness stemmed from the rural peasantry. Consequently, the city dwellers were going to be turned into peasants, or killed in the attempt. When the Khmer Rouge took over power in Phnom Penh, Pol Pot had promised that only a handful of 'supertraitors' would be killed.

Instead, at least 1.7 million Cambodians were to die in Pol Pot's murderous ideological experiment. The officials of the previous government and army officers were the first to be exterminated. A Khmer Rouge broadcast ordered them to present themselves at the Ministry of Information. Fearing that worse might happen to them if they did not, most turned up as ordered. All were killed.

On the afternoon of 17 April 1975, the whole population of Phnom Penh – swollen by refugees to four times its pre-war number – was ordered to leave for the countryside. There was no transport so they would have to go on foot and were marched out of the city. Even the hospitals were emptied. Those who refused to go or were too ill to walk were killed. The country had been at war for eight years and Phnom Penh had been under siege for 15 months. Many people had been wounded by shellfire or were suffering from disease and malnutrition. For the sick and the aged, this evacuation amounted to a death march. As the great exodus stumbled out of the city into the unknown, under the watchful eyes of the impassive Khmer Rouge, the weak fell by the roadside and were left to die where they lay.

Meanwhile, the teenage soldiers looked for anyone who looked as if they had been well educated or had enjoyed wealthand power. They looked for people with soft hands, or who looked well fed or well dressed. They were pulled out of the human stream and interrogated. Anyone who admitted to being one of the urban elite – a bureaucrat, a businessman, a doctor, a teacher, a lawyer or an engineer – was

Whether on the side of the winners or losers, children never escape the suffering of war.

shot. This was known as 'class vengeance', a favourite slogan of the Khmer Rouge.

By the evening of that day, the tree-lined avenues, the pavement cafés, the chic haute cuisine restaurants, the opium dens and the brothels of Cambodia's capital were empty. The city was silent, deserted. Only a handful of journalists remained behind, huddled in the French embassy. They were evacuated three weeks later.

The evacuation of Phnom Penh was not carried out on a whim; the decision had been made three months earlier. The leadership of the Khmer Rouge realized that they were not strong enough to run the country in a conventional sense. The Communist cadres

'IF THIS MAN LIVES THERE IS NO PROFIT. IF HE DIES THERE IS NO GREAT LOSS'

responsible for building the new society numbered only 1,400. Even their young peasant army was not big enough to control a city whose population numbered over a million. Pol Pot's reasoning was that if you took those city dwellers and dispersed them across the countryside, they would be too disorganized and disorientated to offer any real resistance, leaving the Khmer Rouge with undisputed control.

Manpower was certainly needed in the countryside. The guerrilla war and American bombing had laid waste much of the land. Rice stocks were perilously low, but being

fanatical anti-colonialists, it was an article of faith to the Khmer Rouge that they would not accept any aid from abroad. The economy would be rebuilt by Cambodians themselves. This would be done by turning Cambodia into one huge labour camp.

The evacuation of Phnom Penh was also seen as a great leap forward towards the ideal Communist society. At a stroke, the urban rich lost all their property and became peasants. Those who survived the death march from Phnom Penh had to re-educate themselves through back-breaking peasant labour. Anyone who could not adapt or accept the change was not worthy of the Communist paradise and deserved to die. With urban corruption eradicated, a new utopian society could flourish. Cambodia was to return to Year Zero and be rebuilt from scratch, and it would be modelled on the way of life of the Khmer peasantry.

The seeds of this new society already existed in the 'liberated' areas that had been under Khmer Rouge control during the war. There, they had already abolished money. Private property was outlawed and the peasants had been organized in collective farms. For the meagre rations doled out by the Khmer Rouge leadership, they had worked from dawn to dusk to support the war effort. These collectivized peasants were the Communists' 'old people' and they would instruct the 'new people' from the cities how to be good peasants and good Communists. However, those who survived the forced march from the city arrived at the collectives to find that they did not receive a warm welcome. The peasants resented the easy life the city folk had lived while they were toiling in the paddy fields.

Once they got to work, the city people's incompetence in the fields earned them the contempt of the 'old people'. 'Base people' killed any of the 'new people' who faltered or complained. Those who were completely useless were 'eliminated' for 'economic sabotage'. Most just perished from natural causes. They were not used to the privations the peasants suffered: backbreaking labour, starvation, disease, and lack of medical care. The attitude of the Khmer Rouge was summed up in the slogan 'If this man lives there is no profit. If he dies there is no great loss'.

The identity of the leaders behind their murderous policy remained a mystery for a long time. Alongside the infamous Pol Pot were other Paris-educated intellectuals – Ieng Sar, Ieng Thirith and Khieu Samphan. They had set up headquarters in the ghost city of Phnom Penh and ruled the country with extreme authoritarianism. Cambodia was divided into zones with each zone's party secretary directly answerable to the central authority in Phnom Penh. Below each party secretary was a central committee and, beyond the committee, no one had ever heard of Pol Pot and his merry men. Orders were issued simply in the name of Angka, 'the Organization'.

In March 1976, Cambodia was renamed the Democratic Republic of Kampuchea and Pol Pot and his henchmen pushed forward towards the establishment of their ideal society. Solitary eating was abolished: all food had to be consumed in communal canteens from stocks controlled by the Khmer Rouge. Any private enterprise such as picking wild fruit or vegetables to supplement your meagre diet was punishable by death, and even the consumption of lizards, toads and earth-worms was outlawed.

Family ties were discouraged. Children in the co-operatives slept in dormitories away from their parents and were encouraged to spy on their parents and denounce them if their behaviour fell short of what was demanded by the Angka. Different members of families were assigned to different work parties and sent to opposite ends of the country. With no telephones and no postal system, once contact had been broken family members and friends were unlikely ever to come across each other again.

The teachers and intellectuals – apart from those in the politburo – had already been exterminated. Instead of education, there was a brutal process of indoctrination. Executions were carried out either on the orders of the secret police or of the cooperative ruling committee and they were as discreet and mysterious as the Angka itself. People disappeared in the night: it was not advisable to ask where. Some were killed on pure whim. To possess thick-lensed glasses, for example, meant you had read too much, so you were the target of Pol Pot's butchers.

The favourite method of execution was a blow to the back of the head or neck with the base of an axe-head. Bullets were in short supply. Disembowelling and burying alive were also popular, with victims usually required to dig their own graves first. Whole

In the scramble to evacuate Saigon, helicopters had to be pushed off the sides of aircraft carriers to make room for more coming in.

truckloads of people would suddenly disappear. Curiously, Khmer culture did not feature the struggle between good and evil that is the staple of Western storytelling. It stressed harmony and beauty, and the Cambodians were completely unprepared for the mindless violence that their leaders had brought back with them from France. Many Cambodians would stand in line, awaiting their turn to be struck on the back of the head. A traditionally peaceful people, they had no more intellectual defence against the Khmer Rouge's murderous strategy than they had against bombs falling from American B-52s.

Keeping a firm grip on the reign of terror in the village was easy for the Communists. A few rotting human remains, scattered along the trails into the village, would do the job. Rumours of grotesque tortures were spread. Victims were said to have their throats cut

open by razor-sharp reeds or serrated palm fronds. This had a chilling effect.

After the 'class enemies' – anyone who had an education and anyone who had not been born a worker or a peasant – had been eliminated, the Khmer Rouge started on the ethnic and religious minorities. The Chinese, the Vietnamese and Cham Muslims were 'liquidated'. Pol Pot's aim was ethnic cleansing. He believed in racial purity and minorities were systematically exterminated.

From the beginning of 1977, the Khmer Rouge executioners turned in on themselves. Pol Pot ordered the systematic extermination of CPK members who were thought to have a petty bourgeois or intellectual background. They were accused of deviance. S-21 – a secret security apparatus – tortured fellow party members into confessing that they were CIA agents. Veteran peasant leaders were put to death, after 'confessing' to being agents of the Vietnamese. Those in the party from a 'bourgeois' background were the first to be picked out. Minor party officials were blamed for the continuing failure of the economy, though everyone else saw that the real blame lay with the murderous system itself. They paid with their lives. Pol Pot's aim was to kill almost all surviving CPK veterans, believing that the whole party apparatus must be replaced for his policies to succeed.

Food shortages continued, because agriculture was now in the hands of people who knew nothing about it. Irrigation projects and dams were build by hand without engineers and experts to supervise the work: they were all dead. When the first rain came, these massive civil-engineering projects that had cost thousands of lives in their construction were simply swept away. As far as the party was concerned, these failures could not be the fault of the system; they must be sabotage by enemies of the state. The Khmer Rouge became consumed by paranoia and dozens of torture centres were set up around the country, the most notorious of which was Tuol Sleng in Phnom Penh, where expert Khmer Rouge torturers 'uncovered' conspiracies that usually implicated more people who would suffer their tender mercies. Tens of thousands died horribly.

The killings became so indiscriminate and widespread that, by mid-1977, Pol Pot himself tried to call a halt. In September 1977, he went public for the first time, making clear his own dominant role in the Communist Party that was now running Kampuchea. In an

address to the people, he claimed to have liberated them from 2,000 years of 'despair and hopelessness'. But most of his speech was devoted to the need to defend Kampuchea against foreign aggression.

The Khmer Rouge had always distrusted the Vietnamese who, in pre-colonial times, had dominated the region. There had been border clashes immediately after the fall of Phnom Penh back in 1975. In the autumn of 1977, the border conflicts flared up yet again. The Khmer Rouge central committee sent out a new instruction: purge all those who had contact with Hanoi. More party members died.

At the same time, Pol Pot had ordered incursions into Vietnam, in an attempt to redraw the Kampuchean–Vietnamese border. The Eastern Zone committee came under suspicion as their region actually butted up against Vietnamese territory. Pol Pot maintained they were not doing enough to resist the highly efficient Vietnamese Army, who had, after all, ousted the US.

The Eastern Zone was one of the seven major administrative areas where the conditions were better than in the rest of the country. Pol Pot had long feared that opposition might coalesce around the zone chief there, Sao Pheum. Fearing that resistance would plunge Kampuchea into a fully fledged civil war, Pheum committed suicide. At the beginning of 1978, the Eastern Zone leadership was purged, but some escaped the Khmer Rouge executioners by fleeing across the border into Vietnam. In order to maintain control, Pol Pot set the other zone chiefs at

each other's throats, favouring Ta Mok, leader of the Southwest Zone and the country's most efficient killer. Nevertheless, by late 1978, Ta Mok's cadres were also marked for extermination. No one was safe.

One of those who fled the Eastern Zone was Heng Samrin. A former CPK commissar, he organized the Kampuchean National United Front for National Salvation in exile. With credible Cambodian leadership in their territory, the Vietnamese took a hand. They feared that the excesses of Pol Pot and the Khmer Rouge were undermining their victory in Vietnam and inviting renewed foreign intervention. On 21 December 1978, Kampuchea was 'liberated' once more – this time with a full-scale Vietnamese invasion. One hundred thousand Vietnamese supported 20,000 United Front troops.

On 7 January 1979, Samrin declared the People's Republic of Kampuchea, supplanting the CPK's Democratic Kampuchea. In response, 85,000 Chinese troops – later reinforced to 200,000 – invaded Vietnam from the north. Even though Vietnam's main force was in Kampuchea, a 60,000-man defensive force, comprising largely border guards and regional forces, held off the People's Liberation Army, which had not seen active service since the end of the Korean War in 1953. After overrunning Lang Son on 5 March, the Chinese decided that Vietnam had been punished enough for the invasion of Cambodia and withdrew.

Pol Pot's first wife, the ideologue whose crazy ideas had underpinned Year Zero, went mad. Pol Pot himself abandoned Phnom Penh and took to the jungles where, with the backing of the US, Chinese and British governments, he and his cohorts continued to exercise considerable political influence. The Vietnamese intervention in Cambodia was not the end of Pol Pot's atrocities. For arcane political reasons, the world embargoed Vietnam until it withdrew its troops. The Khmer Rouge fought on, killing and maiming with the indiscriminate use of land mines. It was only in 1998 that Pol Pot was captured. He was tried, but he died of natural causes before he could be punished for the atrocities he had committed.

No one knows how many people died in the killing fields of Pol Pot's Kampuchea, or what proportion of deaths were due to malnutrition and disease – much of which was caused by ideology-led dislocation – as against deliberate execution. But available figures suggest that around 21 per cent of the population of Cambodia died under Pol Pot's regime. Some 50 per cent of the country's Chinese population were slaughtered, along with 30 per cent of the Islamic Cham. A quarter of the Khmer forcibly evacuated from the urban areas perished. Khmer peasant 'base people' lost probably 15 per cent. Of the Khmer Republic elite and the original CPK cadre, 75 per cent or more were exterminated. Perhaps as many as two million people died at the hands of their own countrymen, making Cambodia's Year Zero a greater human catastrophe, per capita, than Hitler's Germany. Unexploded ordinance and the indiscriminate use of land mines has ensured that the Khmer Rouge's toll of death and maiming will also continue to rise for a long time to come.

Opposite: For the people left behind there would be no escaping the Khmer Rouge. No one knows exactly how many died, but it seems as many as two million were killed by their own countrymen.

241

EPILOGUE

DURING THE Vietnam War 46,370 US servicemen died in battle. More than 10,000 died from noncombat-related causes, while a further 300,000 were wounded. Australian casualties ran at 496 killed and 2,398 wounded, and the ARVN lost 2.5 per cent of its manpower each year, amounting to 185,000 soldiers killed between 1961 and the January 1973 ceasefire.

Accurate figures for NVA losses have never been established but estimates have put the figure as high as 900,000 – that is over 15 times US losses and nearly five times the South Vietnamese army's losses. That did not prevent them from invading Cambodia to put an end to the murderous regime of Pol Pot in 1978 and stoutly defending Vietnam's northern border against a Chinese attack in 1979.

Senator Edward Kennedy's committee on refugees estimated that around 430,000 South Vietnamese civilians were killed between 1965 and 1974, and over a million injured or wounded. Later estimates reduced this to 250,000 killed and 900,000 wounded. Even this lower estimate means that five civilians lost their lives for each American killed in

A segment of the Vietnam Veterans Memorial Wall in Constitution Gardens, Washington DC. The memorial was dedicated in November 1982 to the 2.7 million men and women of the US military who served in the Vietnam war zone.

The Vietnamese photographer Nick Ut took this photograph of children fleeing after a napalm attack on their village in 1972. It shocked the world and won him a Pulitzer prize.

South Vietnam alone. Estimates for the number of civilians killed in Southeast Asia during the American involvement there stand at over a million.

In June 1974, the US Department of Defense estimated that the total cost of the war had been $145 billion at 1974 prices. However, there were other hidden costs – the inflation that the war economy brought, lost production, interest on loans and continuing benefits for Vietnam veterans. The true cost of the war, it has been estimated, was something like $300 billion – around $1,100 for every American citizen. Aircraft losses were particularly expensive: the US lost 4,865 helicopters, costing a quarter of a million dollars each.

Shells cost only around $100 each, but at the height of the fighting 10,000 – a million dollars' worth – were being loosed off each day. Two millions tons of shells were expended in all. Eight million tons of bombs were dropped on Vietnam, Laos and Cambodia, four times the amount dropped during the whole of World War II. A B-52 dropped $800,000-worth of bombs out of its bomb-bay doors on each mission. During 1966 alone, 148,000 missions were flown over North Vietnam, costing $1.25 billion, even leaving aside the cost of the 818 aircraft lost. A further 3,720 fixed wing aircraft were lost. That year, American bombing was estimated to have caused $130 million of damage. In other words, for every dollar's-worth of damage it caused the US had to spend $9.6.

Between 1965 and 1971, North Vietnam's

Surprisingly, Vietnam quickly got over the war. A new generation grew up who knew nothing of the fighting. The Communist government eventually allowed economic reform, and by the 1990s people could visit this theme park in Ho Chi Minh City, as Saigon had been renamed.

defence budget ran to $3.56 billion. The Soviet Union contributed a further $1.66 billion and the Chinese $670 million, which gave the Communists a total amount of $5.89 billion. They won. South Vietnam, which lost, spent 17 times that amount, while the US squandered 50 times the Communists' outlay. By comparison the Australian government got off lightly, spending something in the order of $A500 million.

There were other costs for the Vietnamese. Around 18 million of them lost their homes because of the war. Some 3 per cent of the area of the South was totally devastated, while 32 per cent was severely damaged by

THE USE OF DEFOLIANTS... HAS LEFT A LEGACY OF SEVERELY HANDICAPPED BABIES

explosives and defoliants. One fifth of all the timberland was destroyed and, by 1975, there were more than 20 million bomb and shell craters covering some 350,000 acres in all. At the end of the war an estimated 27,000 tons of unexploded bombs and shells were littered throughout the country, which remain an ever-present danger to farmers tilling their fields, people walking in the jungle and children out playing. There were 17 million pieces of live ordinance cleared from the area along the DMZ and the McNamara line. They were removed in the cheapest way possible, using human mine detectors, mostly former AVRN soldiers. It is said more than 1,700 men were

killed or maimed in this operation. And the widespread use of defoliants – 18 million gallons in all – has left a legacy of severely handicapped and malformed babies.

The imposition of a strict Communist regime in the South meant that former soldiers, government officials and businessmen, along with bar girls and prostitutes, were sent to re-education camps. It has been estimated that as many as 50,000 were still being detained as political prisoners in 1986. To transform Saigon, now renamed Ho Chi Minh City, to a socialist haven 700,000 were forced to move out into the 'New Economic Zones'. It is estimated that, in all, 1.3 million people were relocated from urban areas to make a life for themselves in the countryside, with all its attendant hardships, while the last remnants of Western culture were rooted out. Religion was suppressed and there was inevitable friction as Southerners resented being ordered around by Northerners.

In 1977, the US vetoed Vietnam's application to join the United Nations. After the invasion of Cambodia, the rest of the world shunned Vietnam as an aggressor. America imposed a trade embargo and the US and Japan blocked loans to Vietnam from the IMF and the World Bank. The Vietnamese economy became a basket case and, by August 1979, an estimated 865,000 people had fled the country. Some 250,000 of these were ethnic Chinese who found themselves persecuted by the Hanoi government and made the long trek north into China. The rest took to the open sea in open craft in the hope of washing up on friendly shores. Many of these 'boat people' did not make it, falling victim to storms, matchwood boats and pirates, but by 1979, over 120,000 had reached Malaysia and 60,000 were in Hong Kong, then still a British colony. There were 40,000 in Indonesia, 30,000 in Thailand and 11,000 in the Philippines. Simply providing them with food and shelter put enormous strains on their hosts. In July 1979, a conference was convened in Geneva to try to persuade the Vietnamese to stem the flow of refugees. But in 1984, a fresh round of repression unleashed a new wave of boat people on the high seas. Some were forcibly returned, but most were found permanent homes in non-Communist countries.

While much of Southeast Asia had been devastated by the war, America had benefited economically – government bonds floated to support the war effort fuelled the boom of the 1980s and 1990s. However, politically and psychologically the US had been damaged. It had been split in two by the anti-war movement and, in the end, a superpower had been humiliated by what America itself had dismissed as an army of peasants. In the process, the high ideals that were enshrined in the Declaration of Independence and the Constitution had been tarnished. By the time the war was over, the politicians who had prosecuted it were out of office. Lyndon Johnson himself died on 22 January 1973, just as the Paris Peace Accords were being finalized. Those who bore the guilt for the war were the veterans, many of whom found themselves shunned for years after.

America's trauma was reflected most vividly in the attitude of Hollywood, which

A Vietnamese postage stamp depicting a captured US airman. Taken from a famous propaganda photograph of 1967, it celebrates the contribution of diminutive Vietnamese women in toppling the American giant.

had avoided the awkward topic of Vietnam since the shameless propaganda of *The Green Berets* in 1968. Although *In the Year of the Pig*, putting the anti-war case, won an Oscar the following year, this was hardly mass-market entertainment. Even though a younger generation of movie makers began producing movies with a distinctly hippy vision of the world, such as *Easy Rider* and *Alice's Restaurant* in 1969, Vietnam was conspicuous by its absence. Instead directors made their comments through black comedies such as *Catch 22* and *M*A*S*H*, both made in 1970 and set in World War II and Korea respectively. Westerns such as *The Wild Bunch* (1969), *Soldier Blue* (1970) and *Ulzana's Raid* (1972) also betray anti-war sympathies.

US airman Major Wesley D. Schierman is greeted by his family at Travis Air Force Base after his return from captivity in February 1973. The question remains: were all his fellow prisoners returned?

the way, they earned their keep by helping out people in trouble, even though they rarely accepted money for their services. This was Robin Hood updated, with incompetent generals, self-serving politicians, and fat cats on the make back home taking the roles of King John, the Sheriff of Nottingham and the evil Guy of Gisborne.

In 1977, Hollywood tackled the war directly with *The Boys in Company C*, which took a low-budget World War II-style movie and infused it with the Vietnam War cynicism – an exploitation movie, 'like dirty TV', said *The New York Times*. Then in 1978, Jane Fonda got to parade her anti-war credentials once more with John Voight in *Coming Home*, a story about an embittered, disabled veteran who falls for the wife of a serving Marine, winning Oscars for Best Actress and Best Actor. The movie also won Best Screenplay.

The same year, old-time movie star Burt Lancaster discovered for himself that the American effort in Vietnam was doomed in *Go Tell the Spartans* and the corruption caused by the war was revealed in *Who'll Stop the Rain* (released as *Dog Soldiers* in the UK) about a Vietnam veteran smuggling heroin back to the US. Another 1978 movie, Michael Cimino's *The Deer Hunter*, again starring Robert DeNiro, won three Oscars. It told the story of three buddies from a steel town in western Pennsylvania who went to fight in Vietnam. Although it was criticized for portraying the Vietcong as blood-thirsty killers while the Americans were innocents, it is really a story about how second-generation blue-collar immigrants fit into American

After the war, the Vietnam veteran became a shorthand for madman as in the vengeful psychopath of *Taxi Driver* (1976), played by Robert DeNiro, or the crazed visionary of *Birdy* (1984), though in *Tracks* in 1976 Hollywood began to take a sideways look at the Vietnam War through the eyes of a veteran travelling across the US with the remains of his dead buddy. The crazed Vietnam veteran became a stock character in cop operas such as *Kojak*, though the eponymous protagonist of the Hawaii-based detective show *Magnum P.I.* was relatively sane. And then there was *The A-Team*, a show about a Special Forces A-Team who had served honourably in Vietnam, but had had to go on the run to prove their innocence after heinous accusations. Along society with Vietnam as part of the backdrop.

The following year, Francis Ford Coppola spent $31 million on *Apocalypse Now*. But instead of taking a straightforward look at Vietnam he transposed Joseph Conrad's short novel *Heart of Darkness* from Africa to Southeast Asia. The movie fancied itself as high art and took so long to make that it was known in Hollywood as Apocalypse Later. In 1984, a British production company squared up to the horrors of the Cambodian holocaust in *The Killing Fields*. Then in 1986, Vietnam veteran Oliver Stone made *Platoon* for just $7 million in eleven weeks in the Philippines. Filmed from the point of view of the grunt, it did not shy away from the shocking realism of gang rape, village-burning and fragging. It was quickly followed in 1987 by Stanley Kubrick's *Full Metal Jacket*, which followed a group of Marines from boot camp through the battle of Hué; Coppola's *Gardens of Stone*, set in the Arlington National Cemetery; *Hanoi Hilton*, a POW drama set in North Vietnam's Hoa Lo prison; and *Hamburger Hill*, a portrayal of one of the war's bloodiest battles. Hollywood and America were coming to terms with the war.

The Vietnam genre also threw up the phenomenon of the Rambo movies. In 1982's *First Blood*, the muscle-bound, inarticulate Sylvester Stallone plays John Rambo, a former Green Beret who discovers that his status as a Vietnam combat veteran excites only contempt on the part of the sheriff's office of a small town in California, and on which office he wreaks a terrible vengeance.

Then in *Rambo: First Blood, Part II* in 1985, Stallone takes on the entire US political and military establishment – not to mention the whole Vietnamese army – to rescue some American POWs left behind in Vietnam. According to the movie, they had been held in captivity in appalling conditions for more than ten years after the American withdrawal. It was a box office smash and one of the most pirated videos of all time.

Other films, such as *Uncommon Valor* in 1983 with Gene Hackman, had already covered the same ground: that the Vietnamese were holding American POWs and lying about it, that there were American heroes still languishing in jail in Southeast Asia, waiting to be rescued, and that the lily-livered sons-of-bitches in the White House, the Pentagon and up on Capitol Hill were conniving in a cover-up. What you needed was a muscle-bound celluloid action man – such as Chuck Norris in *Missing in Action* in 1984 – to go in and get the boys home.

Seemingly, American audiences could not get enough of this macho myth. In fact, Sylvester Stallone was working at a girls' finishing school in Switzerland during the Vietnam War. When he filmed *Rambo*, he went no closer to Vietnam than the Philippines. Muscle-bound he may be, brave less so. But there are some real-life Rambos, men who have dedicated themselves to getting any POWs left behind out – by any means necessary. Some of them were backed by real-life movie stars, such as Charlton Heston, Clint Eastwood, William Shatner, and even Ronald Reagan – though notably not Mr Stallone.

MISSING in ACTION

The fate of those listed 'missing in action' (the MIAS) became a focus for the American people's feelings about the Vietnam debacle after the end of the war. In the 1980s, it was not uncommon to see the black MIA/POW flag – showing a bowed head in silhouette under a watchtower and bearing the legend 'You will not be forgotten' – fluttering alongside the Stars and Stripes and people wearing MIA/POW bracelets bearing the names of men still unaccounted for.

Although the fate of those listed MIA did not become an issue until after America's withdrawal from Vietnam, there were grave concerns throughout the war over what the Vietnamese planned to do with the Americans they had captured. As the North Vietnamese claimed that the Geneva Conventions did not apply, they did not return lists of the American prisoners they held. Representatives of the International Red Cross or neutral nations were not allowed access to the prisoners of war in North Vietnamese hands, so men who were actually POWs had to be listed simply 'missing', along with those who had been blown to bits, got lost in jungle, deserted or crashed into the sea.

Fearing that the fate of the POWs might be overlooked by Washington, the National League of Families of the Prisoners and Missing in South-East Asia was set up in San Diego in 1966 by Sybil Stockdale, wife of the ranking POW, Commander James B. Stockdale. After the war, the National League of Families fought to keep the fate of the MIAS in front of the American public.

Throughout the war, American intelligence combed through Communist newspapers and propaganda films and the work of foreign journalists and TV crews who visited North Vietnam in an effort to compile a list of Americans the Vietnamese Communists held. The National Security Agency attempted to follow the fate of downed American pilots by eavesdropping on Vietnamese military communications. They believed that pilots who had special skills – back-seat electronic warfare officers, the crews of the brand new F-111, those who had been on the space programme, or men with other special qualifications – were flown into the Soviet Union. No airman shot down over Southeast Asia was ever returned from the USSR though, in 1992, President Boris Yeltsin admitted that Americans had been taken there.

The NSA believed that some badly injured pilots were sent to the medical facilities at Shanghai in China. They did not return, but may have died. Others were thought to have been used as slave labour on installations of strategic importance along the Ho Chi Minh trail. As the war between North and South Vietnam continued after America withdrew, these men could not be handed back.

The US Government also knew that after the French had been defeated at Dien Bien

Phu in 1954 they had spent many years nego- tiating for the return of their prisoners in return for aid and reparations. Indeed, there was evidence that the trade was still going on. The last French POW was returned in the mid-1970s. Throughout the Vietnam War, the North Vietnamese people were told that prisoners of war were valuable. Leaflets explained that downed American pilots could be exchanged for factories, hospitals, schools and money. When the Paris Peace Talks began in 1968, the first thing the North Vietnamese delegation asked for was reparations.

Even when the Peace Accords were con- cluded in 1973, the US delegation had little idea of how many Americans the North Viet- namese held. When the North Vietnamese produced a list, it contained less than half the number the US had been expecting. Indeed, men whose names and pictures had appeared in Communist newspapers and propaganda films were not on the list. Little could be done. The war was deeply unpopular at home, so the American delegation in Paris had no leverage.

None of more than 600 men the US thought had been captured in Laos appeared on the lists. When the US delegation com- plained, the North Vietnamese told them to speak to the Pathet Lao. In protest America even halted troop withdrawals from Vietnam. The North Vietnamese quickly found nine men who had been captured in Laos by the North Vietnamese Army, not the Pathet Lao, the guerrilla army there. No US prisoners of war held by the Pathet Lao were ever returned. Nor did any who had fallen into the murderous hands of the Khmer Rouge in

Cambodia. Some men held by the Vietcong were handed over. Others were moved to forward ready to be handed over, only to be returned to their jungle compounds when the VC discovered that the US had handed its prisoners over to the South Vietnamese, and they were not about to hand them back in exchange.

Among the men returned in Operation Homecoming there were none of the burn cases or amputees that might be expected among downed airmen. Hanoi feared that disfigured men shown on TV might stiffen US resolve to back their South Vietnamese allies. An analysis also showed that highly trained back-seaters were also missing.

PRESIDENT CARTER WANTED TO HEAL THE WOUNDS LEFT BY THE VIETNAM WAR AND HAD ALL THE REMAINING MIAS DECLARED DEAD

The Nixon administration promised the North Vietnamese $3.25 billion in reparations. However, immediately after the Paris Peace Accords were signed, President Nixon was embroiled in the Watergate scandal and could not get Congressional approval for the funds. When President Carter came to power he wanted to heal the wounds left by the divisive Vietnam War and had all the remaining MIAS declared dead.

In 1979, six years after America had with- drawn from Vietnam, a US Marine named Bobby Garwood returned. He had been taken

Reviewing an old enemy: President Bill Clinton is greeted by a guard of honour on his arrival in Hanoi on 17 November 2000, after he had finally recognized the government in 1995. A US Senate Select Committee in 1992 that was designed to resolve the question of the missing MIAs and POWs failed to achieve that objective and a significant lobby are still asking where the misssing men are.

prisoner in 1965 and declared missing. Although he had been held in a number of POW camps in North Vietnam, the Communists repeatedly denied all knowledge of him. Garwood claimed that he was an uncooperative prisoner until 1968. Then he was being moved between camps when the truck carrying him stopped so the driver could have a rest. Garwood saw tall white men working in a field and approached them. They spoke French. Garwood knew that the French war in Indochina had ended in 1954. The Vietnamese had told him, 'We can keep you forever.' He now realized that they were very serious.

Garwood then began to cooperate. He fixed jeeps and did other odd jobs, and in 1973 he was not returned. Between 1973 and 1979, he said he often saw other Americans still being held prisoner. In 1979, Garwood persuaded his jailers to take him to Hanoi where, as a foreigner, he would be able to buy cigarettes that they would sell on the black market. On one of these trips he managed to slip a note to a Finnish official of the World Bank named Ossi Rakkonen. Rakkonen passed the note to the State Department. But, despite this evidence to the contrary, Garwood was declared dead.

However, Rakkonen also informed the BBC, who broadcast the story. The US government then asked for Garwood back. The Vietnamese denied having him, then handed him over. He was immediately arrested for desertion and collaboration. He was found guilty of collaborating with the enemy, fined the exact amount of his back pay, and dishonourably discharged from the service.

When Ronald Reagan entered the White House in 1981, he received a telegram from the Hanoi government via Canadian Intelligence asking for $4 billion for the return of an unspecified number of American prisoners of war from Southeast Asia. He had just ridden into office on the back of one hostage crisis –

the 52 Americans detained in the US Embassy in Tehran – and was not eager to plunge himself into another. After discussions with his vice-president George Bush and others, he decided to authorize a clandestine Rambo-style rescue mission. When this failed, he had to back away from the issue. But a number of unofficial rescue missions were mounted by the real-life Rambo, former Green Beret Lieutenant-Colonel James 'Bo' Gritz. He also came up empty-handed and it was generally assumed among the MIA/POW lobby that he had been thwarted by the elements within the government responsible for leaving the men behind in the first place.

Throughout the 1980s, the Vietnamese played a diplomatic game over the fate of the MIAS, periodically allowing in family members and US missions to excavate crash sites and dig up bones. When the diplomatic chill thawed, the Vietnamese would return coffins containing remains they claimed to have just found, though Garwood maintained that the Viet-namese kept pre-packed remains in a charnel house in Hanoi.

The matter was finally laid to rest by a Senate Select Committee in 1992. In its thousand-page report, it found that American prisoners of war had indeed been left behind in Communist hands. However, it concluded that they had all perished since, though it does not specify where or when they died. This left the way open for the Clinton administration to drop the trade embargo in 1994 and formally recognize the Hanoi government in 1995. A US Embassy was opened in Hanoi that year and President Clinton, chided as a draft dodger during the 1992 election campaign, finally visited Vietnam in November 2000. This finally healed the rift that the Vietnam War had caused in the US.

In the meantime, the Berlin Wall had been torn down. The Soviet Union had imploded and Communism was in decline. The policy of containment had worked. The dominos that had fallen after World War II and the Vietnam War had been stood up again. True, North Korea maintains a hard-line Stalinist stance, while its people starve. But the People's Republic of China has liberalized its markets and opened its ports, and Fidel Castro's Cuba runs a dollar economy and panders to tourists. Vietnam itself is home to a Coca-Cola plant and there is a theme park in Ho Chi Minh City. Nike have a factory there, as do many other Western corporations, including McDonald's and Disney; many of these factories pay less than the minimum wage and have appalling working conditions. The country that so stoutly opposed America for eight long years is now practically a colony, enslaved by the US dollar. It can be argued that the war in the Vietnam prolonged the Cold War. While the US was pouring billions of dollars into its war effort, for a relatively small commitment to Hanoi the Soviet Union was able to maintain parity in investment in its strategic systems. But, in the end, the West did win the Cold War – without it ever turning hot or the nuclear weapons developed for its pros-ecution being used.

America might have lost on the ground in one small corner of Southeast Asia, but in global and in historical terms, it won.

BIBLIOGRAPHY

Albright, John, *Seven Firefights in Vietnam*, US Government Printing Office, Washington, DC, 1970

Anderson, William, *Bat-21*, Bantam Books, New York, 1983

Baker, Mark, *Nam: The Vietnam War in the Words of the Men and Women Who Fought There*, William Morrow, New York, 1981

Burchett, Wilfred, *Grasshoppers and Elephants: Why Vietnam Fell*, Urizen Books, New York, 1977

Butler, David, *The Fall of Saigon*, Simon and Schuster, New York, 1985

Carhart, Tom, *Battles and Campaigns in Vietnam*, Bison Books, Greenwich, Connecticut, 1984

Cawthorne, Nigel, *The Bamboo Cage*, Leo Cooper, London, 1991

Chinnery, Phillip, *Vietnam Air Wars*, Bison Books, Hamlyn, London, 1987

Croizat, Victor, *Vietnam River Warfare 1945–75*, Blandford Press, London, 1986

Donovan, David, *Once a Warrior King*, Weidenfeld and Nicholson, London, 1986

Frost, Frank, *Australia's War in Vietnam*, Allen and Unwin, Sydney, 1987

Gershen, Martin, *Destroy or Die: The True Story of My Lai*, Arlington House, New Rochelle, 1971

Giap, Vo Nguyen, *Unforgettable Days*, Foreign Language Press, Hanoi, 1978

Grant, Zalin, *Survivors*, W.W. Norton, New York, 1975

Herr, Michael, *Dispatches*, Knopf, New York, 1978

Karnow, Stanley, *Vietnam: A History*, Viking, New York, 1983

Mason, Robert, *Chickenhawk*, Viking, New York, 1983

McKay, Gary, *In Good Company*, Allen and Unwin, Sydney, 1987

O'Brian, Tim, *If I Die in a Combat Zone*, Calder and Boyars, London, 1973

Padden, Ian, *The Fighting Elite*, Bantam Books, New York, 1985

Page, Tim, *Page After Page*, Paladin, London, 1990

Pimlott, John and Page, Tim (consultant editors), *Nam – The Vietnam Experience 1965–75*, Hamlyn, London, 1988

Santoli, Al, *To Bear Any Burden*, Sphere, London, 1988

Shawcross, William, *Kissinger, Nixon, and the Destruction of Cambodia*, Simon and Schuster, New York, 1979

Simpson, Charles, *Inside the Green Berets*, Arms and Armour Press, London, 1983

Snepp, Frank, *Decent Interval*, Random House, New York, 1977

Terry, Wallace, *Bloods: An Oral History of the Vietnam War by Black Veterans*, Ballantine Books, New York, 1985

Uhlig, Frank, *Vietnam: The Naval Story, Naval Institute Press*, Annapolis, Maryland, 1986

Wilcox, Fred, *Waiting for an Army to Die: The Tragedy of Agent Orange*, Random House, New York, 1983

Zaroulis, Nancy, and Sullivan, Gerald, *Who Spoke Up? American Protest Against the War in Vietnam 1963–1975*, Doubleday, New York, 1984

INDEX

PICTURE CREDITS

Corbis: pages 16, 23, 25, 35, 95, 100, 103, 104, 108, 117, 118, 162, 215, 224, 229, 231, 235, 238, 240, 242-45, 248, 252
Getty Images: page 162
Robert Hunt Library: pages 22, 32, 44, 46, 48-9, 52, 56, 59, 72, 80, 98, 113, 122, 143, 156, 160, 165, 172-3, 179, 182, 196, 206, 220, 226
Mirco de Cet: pages 12, 15, 28, 29, 31, 36, 38, 41, 43, 47, 51, 63-4, 67-8, 74, 76-7, 79, 82, 84-5, 88, 91-2, 1-5-6, 110, 114, 116, 124-6, 128, 130-2, 134-5, 137, 140, 147-8, 150, 152-4, 158-9, 174, 176-7, 180. 183, 191-2, 200, 204, 209, 211, 222, 247
United States Army Military History Institute: pages 10, 70, 97.

All maps copyright © Arcturus Publishing Limited